Argentina's Radical Party
and Popular Mobilization, 1916-1930

Argentina's Radical Party and Popular Mobilization, 1916-1930

Joel Horowitz

The Pennsylvania State University Press
University Park, Pennsylvania

Library of Congress Cataloging-in-Publication Data

Horowitz, Joel, 1949–
  Argentina's Radical Party and popular mobilization, 1916–1930 / Joel Horowitz.
    p.   cm.
Summary: "Examines how Argentina's Radical Party rallied popular support in Buenos Aires from 1916 to 1930. Argues that the methods used for popular mobilization helped to undermine democracy. The popularity of President Hipolito Yrigoyen is explored, as well as the government's relationship with unions"—Provided by publisher.
Includes bibliographical references and index.
ISBN 978-0-271-03405-8 (pbk : alk. paper)
1. Argentina—Politics and government—1910–1943.
2. Democracy—Argentina—History—20th century.
3. Unión Cívica Radical.
I. Title.

F2848.H675 2008
324.282'07409042—dc22
2008019184

Copyright © 2008 The Pennsylvania State University
All rights reserved
Printed in the United States of America
Published by The Pennsylvania State University Press,
University Park, PA 16802-1003

The Pennsylvania State University Press is a member
of the Association of American University Presses.

It is the policy of The Pennsylvania State University Press to use acid-free paper.
This book is printed on stock that
meets the requirements of American National Standard for Information
Sciences—Permanence of Paper for Printed Library Material,
ANSI Z39.48–1992.

TO CAROL, RACHEL, AND SARAH
with love and gratitude

Contents

ACKNOWLEDGMENTS		ix
LIST OF ABBREVIATIONS		xi
	Introduction	1
1	The Economic and Political Setting	12
2	Creating the Image: Construction of the Images of Yrigoyen and Alvear	35
3	The Limits of Patronage	65
4	When Bosses and Workers Agreed: The Failure of Social Welfare Legislation	95
5	Yrigoyen and the Limitations of *Obrerismo*, 1916–1922	115
6	Alvear and the Attempted Establishment of an Institutionalized Relationship with Labor, 1922–1928	149
7	Yrigoyen and the Failure to Reestablish *Obrerismo*, 1928–1930	177
	Conclusion	201
	BIBLIOGRAPHY	211
	INDEX	231

Acknowledgments

Over the approximately fifteen years that I took to write this book I have accrued a great number of debts, large and small, to people and institutions. If I have forgotten to mention any of them it is not because I am ungrateful but rather because I have so many to thank.

Funding for research was provided by a Fulbright Research Grant and by various grants from St. Bonaventure University. I would in particular like to thank two of the administrators at St. Bonaventure, Edward Eckert and Stephen Stahl, for their interest in my work. Being a faculty affiliate of the David Rockefeller Center for Latin American Studies at Harvard University allowed me to use the wonderful facilities at Widener Library. I would like to thank John Coatsworth for his help arranging this.

The staffs of numerous libraries and archives have proved wonderfully helpful: Archivo General de la Nación; Biblioteca Juan B. Justo; Biblioteca Nacional; Instituto Ravignani; the Confederación General del Trabajo; the Fundación Simón Rodríguez; Universidad Di Tella; Widener Library of Harvard University; and the Nettie Lee Benson Library at University of Texas, Austin. Theresa Shaffer, the interlibrary loan librarian at St. Bonaventure, regularly performed minor miracles and did it with grace and speed.

Research and writing tends to be a solitary affair, but it cannot be done without support. Friends and colleagues provided critical aid and information and made the process much more enjoyable: Samuel Amaral, Torcuato Di Tella, Mario Gasparini, Donna Guy, Ruth Horowitz, Nils Jacobsen, Juan Carlos Korol, Mirta Lobato, Silvana Palermo, Hilda Sabato, Juan Suriano, Horacio Tarcus, Juan Carlos Torre, and Gardenia Vidal.

Estela Domínguez, Juan Carlos Korol, Elsa Pintow, and Mauricio Schaikevich shared their city of Buenos Aires with me; they offered friendship and help in many ways. Mariano Plotkin and Piroska Csurí gave me the hospitality of their beautiful apartment in Buenos Aires and made me feel truly welcome.

Mariano Plotkin, who as always had intelligent things to say, read portions of the manuscript and, as importantly, urged me to go ahead and publish it. Tulio Halperín Donghi read a portion and as usual offered sage advice. He continues to inspire me. The two readers for the Press, James Brennan and an anonymous reader, made helpful suggestions. I, of course, am responsible for the opinions and any errors in the text.

I would also like to thank Sanford Thatcher at Penn State University Press. Nicholas Taylor has proven to be a skillful and insightful copyeditor.

The late Jean Horowitz and the late Morris Horowitz gave me love and offered help in ways they will never know. Sarah and Rachel literally grew up with this book. I hope it turned out as well as they did. Finally, I would like to thank Carol Hirschfeld Horowitz. She read and commented on the whole manuscript; she offered advice; but, most important, she believed in me. She has made the journey a joy.

Abbreviations

AT	Asociación del Trabajo
ATC	Asociación Trabajadores de la Comuna
COA	Confederación Obrera Argentina
DNT	Departamento Nacional del Trabajo
FOET	Federación Obreros y Empleados Telefónicos
FOF	Federación de Obreros Ferroviarios
FOM	Federación Obrera Marítima
FORA	Federación Obrera Regional Argentina
PAN	Partido Autonomista Nacional
UCR	Unión Cívica Radical
UF	Unión Ferroviaria
UIA	Unión Industrial Argentina
UOL	Unión Obrera Local
UOM	Unión Obrera Municipal
UOMAR	Unión Obrera Marítima
USA	Unión Sindical Argentina

Introduction

In recent decades the establishment of democracy has become a panacea for political, social, and economic problems.[1] Often forgotten in the desire to create democracies and the difficulties in establishing them is the problem of sustaining them. Democracy is an extremely volatile form of government, particularly in societies in which it is not deeply rooted enough to overcome crisis.

Argentina's difficulty in sustaining a democracy has always been puzzling. It certainly met many of the criteria that theorists in the 1950s and 1960s posited that nations needed for a functioning democracy: a sizeable middle class, urbanization, relatively high literacy rates, and so on.[2] Yet after a relatively brief experiment with democracy between 1916 and 1930, Argentina descended into an ever-worsening cycle of political failure, which hopefully has recently been overcome.[3]

The nature of that initial experiment with full democracy is vital to understanding Argentina's subsequent political history. As Peter Smith has stated in his recent study of democracy in Latin America:

> History matters. One of the most conspicuous weaknesses of the current literature on democratization in Latin America tends to

---

1. See, for example, the remarks of George W. Bush, "President Bush Discusses Freedom in Iraq and Middle East: Remarks by the President at the 20th Anniversary of the National Endowment of Democracy," November 6, 2003, http://www.whitehouse.gov/news/releases/2003/11/20031106-2.html, 12/29/2005.

2. See, for example, Seymour Martin Lipset, "Some Social Requisites of Democracy: Economic Development and Political Legitimacy," *American Political Science Review* 53, no. 1 (March 1959): 69–105. Also see comment by Peter H. Smith in a much more complex argument, "The Breakdown of Democracy in Argentina, 1916–1930," in *The Breakdown of Democratic Regimes: Latin America*, ed. Juan J. Linz and Alfred Stepan (Baltimore: Johns Hopkins University Press, 1978), 4.

3. The overthrow of democracy has recently received renewed attention. See, for example, Nancy Bermeo, *Ordinary People in Extraordinary Times: The Citizenry and the Breakdown of Democracy* (Princeton, N.J.: Princeton University Press, 2003). This study, while interesting and including Argentina, does seem to a historian oddly truncated. It discusses the period 1973–76 as if the military coup of March 1976 was not part of an interconnected cycle of coups that began in 1930. In her general argument, Bermeo states that the fragmentation of

be shortsightedness. Analyses concentrate on trends and events of the past quarter century, with only a passing nod, at most, to earlier political experience. Yet awareness of the past is vital. As the historical record indicates, democratization is by no means an inexorable process: democracies can rise, fall, and return. History also shapes the collective imagination. In nations with long-standing and continuous democracies . . . citizens find it hard to imagine plausible alternatives. In new democracies, however, people have no reason to share this assumption.[4]

We have known very little about how that initial Argentine democratic political system functioned, but its legacy persists and it set the style of politics for generations. The Radical Party, which dominated the initial opening to democracy, remains a key factor in politics, and the Peronists, its principal rivals, see themselves as the true inheritors of Radical traditions. For example, the logo of the 2002 presidential campaign of Peronist Adolfo Rodríguez Saá contained a photograph of Hipólito Yrigoyen, the dominant Radical figure during the period we are considering, along with images of the national hero, José de San Martín, and Juan and Eva Perón.[5] The Peronists' historical tie to the Radicals is more than just rhetorical. It is clear that Perón borrowed a great deal of his approaches to the popular classes from the Radicals, though he took their ideas much further.

Despite its fundamental importance, studies of the Radical Party have until recently largely been avoided by scholars, except those closely associated with the party. This has begun to change, but to a surprising extent our vision of the Radical Party has been shaped by the excellent and pioneering work of David Rock, written more than thirty years ago.[6]

---

society was generally not on a left/right basis. In Argentina in 1930 that was obviously true, but it was much less clear in the 1970s.

4. Peter H. Smith, *Democracy in Latin America: Political Change in Comparative Perspective* (New York: Oxford University Press, 2005), 12.

5. LANACION.com. August 18, 2002, http://www./anacion.com.ar/archivo/nota.asp?notaid = 423490&origen = acumulado&acumuladoid =, 4/04/08.

6. David Rock, *Politics in Argentina, 1890–1930: The Rise and Fall of Radicalism* (Cambridge: Cambridge University Press, 1975). For examples of recent monographs, see Tulio Halperín Donghi, *Vida y muerte de la República verdadera (1910–1930)* (Buenos Aires: Ariel, 2000); Mathew B. Karush, *Workers or Citizens: Democracy and Identity in Rosario, Argentina (1912–1930)* (Albuquerque: University of New Mexico Press, 2002); Ana Virginia Persello, *El partido radical: Gobierno y oposición, 1916–1943* (Buenos Aires: Siglo XXI Editores Argentina, 2004); Luciano de Privitellio, *Vecinos y ciudadanos: Política y sociedad en la Buenos Aires de entreguerras* (Buenos Aires: Siglo XXI Editores Argentina, 2003); Gardenia Vidal, *Radicalismo de Córdoba, 1912–1930* (Córdoba: Universidad Nacional de Córdoba, Dirección General de Publicaciones, 1995).

This work differs from Rock's in several ways. It argues that by opening up the political system to all male citizens, the Radicals profoundly changed the nature of Argentina. This was less a result of programmatic beliefs than of the Radicals' restless search for votes and their uncanny ability to attract popular support. It stresses that Yrigoyen's search for votes through his support of strikes ended in 1921 rather than 1919. Moreover, Yrigoyen continued to try to build a different kind of relationship with the labor movement after 1921. In addition, contrary to Rock's argument, patronage and clientelism cannot explain the popularity of Yrigoyen and the Radicals. Popularity grew out of the Radical Party's strategy toward the popular classes, called *obrerismo,* and out of Yrigoyen's image. The popular devotion centered on Yrigoyen cannot be underestimated. In addition, this work takes seriously the Alvear administration, which almost all studies have tended to slight. This allows us to contrast the two administrations and shows that there was much less difference than is usually seen.

This book focuses on how the Radical Party attempted to rally support and widen its base, especially within the city of Buenos Aires. This emphasis is based on several premises. More than an organization driven by ideas, the Radicals were motivated by the hope of electoral success. Most of their policies were based on a desire to win an increasing number of votes. The manner in which they went after votes helped to create important fissures in the society. The concentration on Buenos Aires is based on practicality. Argentina is a large country with a federal tradition. The Radical Party differed greatly from province to province, although certain characteristics remained constant. The city of Buenos Aires was and is the center of power and what happens there has an exaggerated impact on the rest of the country. For example, in 1930 the Radical defeat in the congressional elections in Buenos Aires clearly outweighed its respectable showing in the rest of the country; this development helped lead to the coup that ended the experiment in democracy.

The Radical era began after the first fair presidential election in Argentine history with Yrigoyen's assumption of the presidency in October 1916 and continued until his overthrow by the military in September 1930. The Radical era is not a united whole. The two presidents, Hipólito Yrigoyen (1916–22, 1928–30) and Marcelo T. de Alvear (1922–28), were very different. The period under examination could just as easily be labeled the age of Yrigoyen; he was dominant regardless of whether he sat in the presidential palace. He became a larger-than-life figure with a widespread popular appeal that is, to some extent, difficult to understand three-quarters of a century later. Alvear, although he became president because he was the choice of Yrigoyen, tried to a limited extent to break free of Yrigoyen's influence. Alvear, however, failed to establish widespread popularity or a clear set of policies.

The traditional writing on Yrigoyen fails to explain how he built overwhelming support from large sectors of the population. Skillful use of patronage is simply insufficient to produce the popular fervor that surrounded him. This can only be explained by an in-depth examination of why he had such a popular appeal and how he constructed it. Because historians have largely ignored Alvear, his presidency can almost be seen as a blank slate. Yet Alvear did attempt to mobilize popular support in ways that do not always fit his traditional image.

As this work was originally conceived, it was going to focus on the Alvear presidency. Alvear and those who broke with Yrigoyen have tended to be pictured as the elite, more conservative wing of the Radical Party. Although not without some truth, this vision is also misleading. Alvear's support came from different elements within the party, some of whom cannot fairly be labeled conservative. In addition, at times it is difficult to call the Alvear administration's policies conservative. It became rapidly apparent that Alvear needed to be looked at in the context of Yrigoyen. Yrigoyen had a large hand in shaping the political world in which Alvear operated and was judged. Those who supported Alvear did so mostly because of their opposition to the tactics and personality of Yrigoyen. This work therefore examines both leaders and does so in a topical rather than purely chronological fashion.

The focus is primarily on the Radical Party's search for votes. With the passage of the Ley Sáenz Peña in 1912, which limited the use of voting fraud, voting became the key legitimizing act for politicians. Even the Conservatives argued for the importance of voting. In the debate on the electoral reform measure, Ramón J. Cárcano argued, "The proof . . . is there in Santa Fe which offers the most grand and noble spectacle of democracy. No one fails the appointment at the ballot box. All are fighting in a manly manner for their ideals, even the revolutionary party advances to the election not with arms but with their vote with the ordinary encouragement of faith and of hope." In a message to congress in 1912 President Roque Sáenz Peña quoted Carlos Pellegrini as having said, "The generation that succeeds in taking the country out of its lethargy and guides it to the voting box will have given such transcendent service as that of independence." At least through the early years of the Radical period, almost all major political actors believed in the legitimacy conferred by the vote. As Ana María Mustapic has argued, Yrigoyen saw himself as executing the mandate given to him by the people. The Buenos Aires of the 1860s and 1870s so brilliantly described by Hilda Sabato, where legitimacy was in large part bestowed by civil society and its public demonstrations of support, had been changed. By 1916 the percentage of foreign adult males had declined (and they were excluded from voting) and the percentage of Argentine males who did vote went up considerably. Elections had become meaningful exercises that could bestow legitimacy by demonstrating popularity.[7]

The Radicals continued to organize demonstrations, many of them leading up to elections, but they were in large part geared to raise the enthusiasm of potential voters and to dishearten the opposition. They did so during a time of a burgeoning civil society, as organizations of all types were being formed, from unions to neighborhood associations and soccer clubs. Despite economic downturns, it was a relatively prosperous country and one that, with the exception of the era of World War I, attracted immigrants.

To begin to understand why subsequent experiments in democracy in Argentina failed, one needs to understand better why the first one collapsed. Although it is clearly impossible to give a full and definitive set of reasons, it is possible to examine some of them. Certainly a key reason was the unwillingness, or at least the failure, to set out clear rules of the game and play according to them. Some of the elites objected to being ruled by the middle class. The inability of the Radicals to accept other political parties as legitimate is also very important, as was the Radicals' consistent attachment to the leadership of one person, Hipólito Yrigoyen. This dependence on one person helped limit the potential outcomes, but, as important, the personalism led to a dependence on individuals rather than laws and institutions. For example, the Radicals never made a major effort to bureaucratize their relationships with the labor movement; they preferred to depend on personal relationships. They also neglected the

---

7. Halperín Donghi, *Vida y muerte*, 288; Roque Sáenz Peña, *La reforma electoral y temas de política internacional americana* (Buenos Aires: Editorial Raigal, 1952), 118–19; Ana María Mustapic, "Conflictos institucionales durante el primer gobierno radical: 1916–1922," *Desarrollo Económico* 93 (April–June 1984): 106; Hilda Sabato, *La política en las calles: Entre el voto y la movilización, Buenos Aires, 1862–1880* (Buenos Aires: Editorial Sudamericana, 1998); Oscar Cornblit, "Inmigrantes y empresarios en la política argentina," in *Los fragmentos del poder*, ed. Torcuato S. Di Tella and Tulio Halperín Donghi (Buenos Aires: Editorial Jorge Alvarez, 1969), 401.

building of efficient bureaucracies.⁸ Conjunctional issues also played a key role: the Depression, the failing health of Yrigoyen, the fracturing of party unity, and the inability of Yrigoyen's opponents to mount serious electoral challenges.

In cataloging the Radicals' shortcomings, it is necessary to remember that luck counts. If it were not for the Depression and its immense economic and social consequences, it is quite possible that the party would have managed to overcome the series of crises that helped lead to its overthrow in September 1930.

We need to be careful not to exaggerate the Radicals' failings in carrying out democracy. As Alan Knight has noted recently, even the paradigm of liberal democracies in this epoch, the United States, had severe lapses. The Red scare and labor violence marked the era. The labor-related violence in Argentina, although clearly a major flaw, is a product of similar historical forces.⁹ This does not mean that it had no impact, but we need to keep the context in mind when we look at the problems of democracy in the era. Similarly, the large amounts of patronage dispersed by the Radicals should not necessarily be seen as abnormal for democracies of the time.

What this study will make clear is how, despite several massacres that killed hundreds (the Tragic Week in Buenos Aires in 1919 and the slaughter of ranch hands in Patagonia in 1921–22, both discussed in Chapter 5), the Radical governments garnered significant popular support, which was frequently extremely fervent. The Radicals had a special opportunity to shape the norms for mobilizing popular support: only with the passage of electoral reforms in 1912 (the Ley Sáenz Peña) did fair voting became the norm. Before 1912, the pursuit of popular support was not a vital part of the electoral process. The psychological importance of the establishment of fair voting should not be underestimated. Pierre Rosanvallon has argued that in France universal suffrage transformed the society.¹⁰ The man-

---

8. Government records of both the periods before and after the Radicals are more accessible and more complete. Archives, published statistics, and other documents are not usually produced for the historian but for the bureaucrat, and the bureaucrats had little to look back at for precedent.

9. Alan Knight, "Is Political Culture Good to Think?" in *Political Cultures in the Andes, 1750–1950*, ed. Nils Jacobsen and Cristóbal Aljovín de Losada (Durham, N.C.: Duke University Press, 2005), 48–49. For some of the problems facing democracies of the epoch, see Charles S. Maier, *Recasting Bourgeois Europe* (Princeton, N.J.: Princeton University Press, 1975).

10. Recent research has made obvious that the electoral reform produced a less sharp break than had previously been thought. Public opinion counted previously. See Sabato, *La política en las calles;* Paula Alonso, *Revolution and the Ballot Box: The Origins of the Argentine Radical Party in the 1890s* (Cambridge: Cambridge University Press, 2000). The beginning

ner in which popular support was mobilized served as a model for later politicians.

A key focus will be the government's relations with unions. Unions became an important mechanism through which the Radicals attempted to mobilize support. In addition, this will enable the reader to see more clearly the nature of the government and how it operated concerning an important social question. Although relationships with unions were never defined by law and remained highly vague, they existed and were more complex than previous authors have stated. Ideology did not characterize the Radical interest in labor. They never articulated any clear goals beyond the vague doctrine of *obrerismo*, a stated concern for the betterment of the working class, which had paternalistic overtones. The concept will be discussed in much more detail in the following chapters. A clear, if usually unstated, goal was the attraction of popular support that would be then transferred to the electoral arena. Juan D. Perón pursued similar strategies during the 1940s. Perón built on an existing model in a more industrialized country, however, and pursued his goals with more intensity and success.

The Radicals called on nationalism and identified their party with the nation itself. They became the sole embodiment of good. The Radicals developed around Yrigoyen what almost could be called a cult of personality. Despite their nationalism, they also appealed to immigrant communities.

Although creating a new political style, the Radicals also depended on traditional methods of attracting popular support. Clientelism, a practice of long standing, was further developed. The Radicals dispensed jobs as political rewards. The party and its bosses also helped secure cheap food (the so-called *pan radical*), toys for children, and free or inexpensive medical care. Through the use of patronage, the Radicals created well-oiled machines in different regions of the country, especially in Buenos Aires. Although such activities engendered gratitude and loyalty, it is doubtful that they could do more than that. This was a reciprocal arrangement—political support in return for favors—but the popular classes had too many alternatives to ensure passionate loyalty. Rival political forces also used similar tactics with much less success.

Clientelism was not the only traditional mechanism that was deployed.

---

of fair elections in most districts, however, meant that the pursuit of popular support had to be strongly intensified. Pierre Rosanvallon, *Le sacre du citoyen: Histoire du suffrage universel en France* (Paris: Editions Gallimard, 1992).

The police continued to play a crucial role in the political world. This paralleled traditional practices in the countryside, where police powers and political activity always had been combined. Police chiefs became the principal contacts with labor unions. This reflected the Radicals' tendency to keep things at a personal level. This was much more common under Yrigoyen than Alvear, but it remained a consistent feature.

The political machinery of the Radicals enabled them to stage large, centralized rallies and parades but also to conduct political activities in each of Buenos Aires's neighborhoods. Elections became popular spectacles. The rhetoric of the Radicals helped rally support for the party. They represented the nation; they stood for fair elections and nationalism. Although operating within a democratic system, the Radicals viewed all opposition as unpatriotic. Only they understood the nation and strived for its betterment. They constructed a vision of the political system in which they portrayed themselves as the true representatives of the people; opposition forces were portrayed as the other. This vision of the political world, while not without precedent in Argentina, made the continuation of democracy difficult, especially when the Radicals came close to dominating all branches of government, as they did by 1930.

The Structure of the Book

The first chapter presents the political and economic background to the 1916–30 period. It sketches the political culture from which the Radicals emerged. It also examines briefly the nature of Buenos Aires and its citizens. In addition, it draws in broad strokes the characteristics of the Radical governments and of the economy from 1916 to 1930.

The second chapter will examine how the two presidents and the Radical Party attempted to construct their images and, in general, how they constructed popular support. For Yrigoyen, this became a central task as he created an image, at least among many, as almost a secular saint who cared deeply for those who were less fortunate. Not only did he come to represent the nation, but for many he also came to be the party. This presented a serious problem for some party members who desired a more independent role for themselves. Alvear projected a much more standoffish image and never succeeded in creating a clear impression of himself, though he used some of Yrigoyen's tactics.

The next chapter examines the role of patronage in building Radical support. Yrigoyen's popularity is often seen as coming directly from his use of patronage.[11] Contemporaries and later commentators have seen the widespread use of clientelism as a deformation of the political system that prevented the full development of democracy. Both Yrigoyen and Alvear used patronage as a critical aspect of their political efforts, but so did most other political factions. As we shall see, however, it cannot explain Yrigoyen's popularity, nor does the use of patronage necessarily indicate a deformation of politics. Much of the expansion of the government workforce during these years represents an increase in the scope of government. Given the nature of the record keeping of the Radicals, it is not possible to give an accurate account of the number of government employees. Their numbers did increase significantly at both the municipal and national level, and politics played a crucial role. As in numerous other countries, patronage helped created a system of bosses who mobilized those who received jobs for political work. This helps explain the large number of Radical Party members, but it cannot explain popularity. Although both Yrigoyen and Alvear used patronage, the former became immensely popular, but the latter failed to become so.

Next, the book looks at the effort begun by the Yrigoyen administration and carried to completion by that of Alvear to establish a large-scale social welfare system. The proponents hoped to provide pension funds for a large sector of the working population. They also intended to tie workers to the political system. The legislation was poorly drafted, which helped create opposition to the plan after it had already been sanctioned. As important as any problems with the specifics of the law, however, was ideological opposition from both labor and management. This produced a rare alliance that led to a strike/lockout and the repeal of the legislation. Much more important, it destroyed the idea of using large-scale social welfare legislation to widen political support and was the last such attempt for generations.

The next three chapters examine in chronological order, divided by presidential term, the government's rapidly shifting relationships with unions and how this had an impact on the administrations' political support. Both presidents consistently used organized labor as a bridge to the working class. This was a critical element in their *obrerista* tactics. There are clear differences, however, in the nature of the relationships that developed during the administrations. This is not terribly surprising, but the

---

11. Rock, *Politics in Argentina*.

way that they differed is. In certain aspects of his labor policy Alvear, who has always been portrayed as being conservative, can be seen as arguably more supportive than Yrigoyen. Alvear's relationship with the largest railroad union, the Unión Ferroviaria, set the model for future governments. Yrigoyen's approach tended to be extremely personalistic but shifted according to his political needs. These relationships heightened disagreements with certain sectors of the elites and middle classes, which contributed to political tensions; these tensions worsened the problems created by the fissures in the political structure and the Depression, all of which helped lead to the September 1930 coup.

1

THE ECONOMIC AND POLITICAL SETTING

The Radical Party did not flourish in a vacuum. It grew in response not only to the tactics and practices of Hipólito Yrigoyen and other Radicals, but also in response to the political and economic world of Argentina, which was dominated by Buenos Aires.

The Socioeconomic Setting Prior to 1916

In 1914, on the eve of World War I, Argentina was a wealthy nation by almost any standard. In 1940 the Australian economist Colin Clark argued that in the period from 1925 to 1934 Argentina's real income per worker made it one of the seven wealthiest countries in the world. It shared this ranking with the United States, Canada, Australia, New Zealand, Great Britain, and Switzerland. Although Clark's calculations probably overstate Argentina's wealth, they are not implausible.[1]

Argentina depended on the relatively free movement of people, goods, and services that marked the era prior to the Great Depression. Traditionally, it had been a labor-short economy and therefore wages were relatively high. As Roberto Cortés Conde has shown, real salaries were higher in Argentina than in Italy in the two decades before 1900.[2] Immigrants poured into the country from Europe, primarily from the south and the east, looking for a better life and providing much of the growing demand

---

1. Colin Clark, *The Conditions of Economic Progress* (London: Macmillan, 1940), 2.
2. Roberto Cortés Conde, *El progreso argentino, 1880–1914* (Buenos Aires: Editorial Sudamericana, 1979), 265.

for labor. The rural economy of the pampas region, the flat, fertile plain that surrounds Buenos Aires, provided the basis of Argentina's wealth. Argentina had by 1914 become a leading exporter of wheat, corn, meat, and wool. The great prosperity in the pampas permitted growth in other regions but did not eliminate the more traditional economies or their greater poverty.[3] The overall wealth of the society allowed a fairly large state sector, especially schools, to exist in all parts of the country.

In 1916, when the Radicals came to power, the city of Buenos Aires largely still remained what James Scobie called a commercial-bureaucratic city.[4] It was the site of the national government and of the most important university. It held the nation's principal port, and much of the extensive railroad network fanned out from the city. Although industry in 1914 employed some one-third of the city's labor force, many worked in the small shops that supported the city's role as the hub of transportation and the key center of exports. As Fernando Rocchi has pointed out, a significant number of large factories also existed. At least until 1914, workers frequently left the city to work in the high-paying harvests on the pampas and then returned to the city. As industrialization intensified in the twenties and farmers turned to increased mechanization, this phenomenon lessened. Still, factory work often remained temporary. Many immigrants went back to Europe. Workers moved from job to job. Sometimes they did this voluntarily; other times it occurred because of the wishes of employers.[5]

---

3. For example, see Cortés Conde, *El progreso argentino*, and *La economía argentina en el largo plazo* (Buenos Aires: Editorial Sudamericana/Universidad San Andrés, 1997); Gerardo Della Paolera and Alan M. Taylor, eds., *A New Economic History of Argentina* (Cambridge: Cambridge University Press, 2003); Carlos F. Díaz Alejandro, *Essays on the Economic History of the Argentine Republic* (New Haven, Conn.: Yale University Press, 1970), 1–66; Guido Di Tella and Manuel Zymelman, *Las etapas del desarrollo económico argentino* (Buenos Aires: EUDEBA, 1967), 37–102, 277–420; H. S. Ferns, *The Argentine Republic, 1516–1971* (New York: Barnes and Noble, 1973), 87–115.

4. "Buenos Aires as a Commercial-Bureaucratic City, 1880–1910: The Characteristics of a City's Orientation," *The American Historical Review* 77, no. 4 (October 1972): 1035–73.

5. Fernando Rocchi, *Chimneys in the Desert: Industrialization in Argentina During the Export Boom Years, 1870–1930* (Stanford, Calif.: Stanford University Press, 2005); Michael Johns and Fernando Rocchi, "The Industrial Capital and Urban Geography of a Primate City: Buenos Aires at the Turn of the Century" (paper delivered at the American Historical Association Convention, 1991), 3, 5–7; Roberto Cortés Conde, *El progreso argentino*, 191–274; Fernando Rocchi, "La armonía de los opuestos: Industria, importaciones y la construcción urbana de Buenos Aires," *Entrepasados* 4, no. 7 (fines de 1994): 43; Mirta Zaida Lobato, "La ingeniería, la industria y la organización en la Argentina de las primeras décadas del siglo XX" (paper delivered at the Latin American Studies Association Congress, 1995); Joel Horowitz, "Occupational Community and the Creation of a Self-Styled Elite: Railroad Workers in Argentina," *The Americas* 42, no. 1 (July 1985): 67; Carl E. Solberg, *The Prairies and the Pampas:*

Buenos Aires grew quickly during the first half of the twentieth century; its population almost doubled in twenty-seven years. In 1909 it had a population of 1,231,797, expanding to 1,576,545 in 1914 and 2,413,839 in 1936.[6] The rapid growth reflected the available opportunities. The speed of the increase, however, created problems in providing housing and other necessities.

Crucial to understanding the nature of politics was the large presence of foreigners. In 1914 in the capital, the number of foreigners stood at 777,845, or 49 percent of the population. For males, the percentage of foreigners was higher, 54 percent. For the entire country, foreigners composed 29.4 percent of the population. If one looks in the capital at adult males age twenty and older (potential voters; male citizens could vote at eighteen), three times more foreigners than native-born Argentines lived there. Nationwide there were slightly more foreign adult males than there were native-born ones. Especially in the capital, immigrants owned a disproportionate amount of industry and commerce. They also held a disproportionate share of skilled jobs.

Unlike most other countries that received large-scale immigration, not many immigrants adopted local citizenship, thus excluding them from direct political participation. In the capital in 1914, just 18,450 people, representing 2.4 percent of the foreign population, were naturalized. Nationwide just 1.4 percent had been naturalized.[7] A very significant portion of the adult male population remained excluded from voting. The full implications of the delay in political incorporation for an entire generation have not been explored; especially in the capital, however, it limited the effectiveness of appeals to working-class constituencies because a high percentage were immigrants. It is important to note, however, that employers were also heavily foreign, making appeals to their workers less

---

Agrarian Policy in Canada and Argentina, 1880–1930 (Stanford, Calif.: Stanford University Press, 1987), 96, 107–8; María Inés Barbero and Susana Felder, "Los obreros italianos de la Pirelli Argentina (1920–1930)," in *Asociacionismo, trabajo e identidad étnica: Los italianos en América Latina en una perspectiva comparada*, ed. Fernando J. Devoto and Eduardo J. Míguez (Buenos Aires: CEMLA-CSER-IEHS, 1992), 193; Mirta Zaida Lobato, "Una visión del mundo del trabajo: Obreros inmigrantes en la industria frigorífica 1900–1930," in ibid., 218–19.

6. Richard J. Walter, *Politics and Urban Growth in Buenos Aires: 1910–1942* (Cambridge: Cambridge University Press, 1993), appendix A1.

7. Comisión Nacional del Censo, *Tercer censo nacional, levantado el 1º de junio de 1914* (Buenos Aires: Talleres Gráfico de L. J. Rosso, 1916), 2:109; Cornblit, "Inmigrantes y empresarios," 389–437, esp. 416; Alejandro Bunge, *Una nueva Argentina* (Buenos Aires: Editorial Guillermo Kraft, 1940), 115; Gino Germani, *Política y sociedad en una época de transición*, 5th ed. (Buenos Aires: Editorial Paidós, 1974), 274.

politically costly. It also lowered the political importance of the foreign communities, though their role may have been larger than has frequently been thought. The sons of immigrants did vote and even nonvoters could provide money or labor for political campaigns. As we shall see, the Radicals did make appeals to the various immigrant communities. Women also lacked the ability to vote, but they received patronage and at least sometimes their interests were taken into account. Like immigrants, their relatives voted and they participated in other forms of political activity.

In 1914 by far the largest groups of immigrants had come from Italy and Spain, almost three-quarters of the total; in terms of religion, language, and customs, the newcomers were reasonably close to the local culture. This did not mean that immigrants were not resented and at times feared. Frequently they received blame for whatever problems the nation had. Nor should superficial resemblances to the host culture suggest that immigrants did not face major problems adjusting to their new world. The percentage of immigrants coming from Italy and Spain declined after World War I. A growing number came from central and eastern Europe, many of whom were Jews, and from what had been the Ottoman Empire (the largest number of whom were Syrio-Lebanese). Culturally and religiously more distinct, these groups faced greater discrimination than had earlier waves of immigrants.[8]

Political Background

In the half century after breaking with Spain, Argentina saw violence, civil wars, and a tendency toward regionalism. Only with the defeat of Juan Manuel de Rosas in 1852 did Argentina begin to create a true national state. The rivalry between the Province of Buenos Aires and the rest of the provinces for political dominance and for control of the city of Buenos Aires only ended in 1880 with the military victory of General Julio Roca and the provinces over Buenos Aires, which permitted the nationalization of the capital.[9]

---

8. Comisión Nacional del Censo, *Tercer censo nacional*, 2:399. The writing on immigration in the last two decades has been extensive. For an excellent recent overview, see Fernando Devoto, *Historia de la inmigración en la Argentina* (Buenos Aires: Editorial Sudamericana, 2003).

9. For a good brief overview of Argentine history, see Jonathan C. Brown, *A Brief History of Argentina* (New York: Checkmark, 2004). See also, for recent work, David Rock, *State Building and Political Movements in Argentina, 1860–1916* (Stanford, Calif.: Stanford University Press, 2002); Sabato, *La política en las calles*.

In the last few years, historians have been revising their visions of the nature of the political regime that oversaw the rapid economic growth that characterized Argentina from 1880 to 1916. Roca dominated politics for a generation through a political party, the Partido Autonomista Nacional (PAN), but only as the first among equals in an elite-dominated political process. As has become increasingly clear, Roca's hold on the political process depended on his vast skills as a politician. The important players were a political elite, who, as Roy Hora has recently proved, at least for the Province of Buenos Aires, did not directly or necessarily represent the rural interests. Constitutional norms were followed, at least on paper. Presidents and congresses were duly elected and the press was largely free. Although elements of popular mobilization existed, especially in the city of Buenos Aires, as did universal suffrage for adult males born in Argentina, the electoral process was badly flawed: Voting was public. Violence, fraud, and vote buying determined most elections, and few voted. Political bosses mobilized voters and brought them to the polls. Coalitions of electoral elites dominated a political situation until coalitions shifted or broke. The central government used its powers to rearrange politics at the local level, usually through interventions (the legal takeover of provincial governments). The constitution permitted the central government to temporarily install leaders in provinces if there was significant political misbehavior or violence. If congress was in session, the government needed its approval; otherwise, the president could act alone. When new elections were held, results tended to favor candidates backed by the new authorities.

The major challenge to this system developed out of a failed revolt in 1890. The target was the president, Miguel Juárez Celman, the brother-in-law of Roca, from whom Roca had separated politically. Corruption, economic depression, and a growing group of elites who felt excluded from power combined to produce a rebellion. It failed, but it did succeed in forcing Juárez Celman to resign in favor of his vice president. The system, however, regained its footing. After considerable political maneuvering and the passage of time, Roca and his allies restored the system to a good semblance of the way it had been before. The principal claimant to the legacy of the revolutionary forces was the Unión Cívica Radical (UCR), or the Radical Party. This party, the focus of this book, played a crucial role in creating the opening toward a full democracy and producing the first truly democratic governments.

From the Radical Party's founding in 1891 by key elements from the revolt of 1890, until Hipólito Yrigoyen's victory in the presidential election of 1916, the party went through three basic stages. The first, from 1891 to 1896, has been well described recently by Paula Alonso. She examined a party whose leadership did not differ in any socioeconomic sense from that of PAN and had no particular interest in the social question. The party took part in elections but also sponsored rebellions, hearkening back to political traditions established before the hegemony of the PAN. In Santa Fe province, Radical revolts received significant popular support from agricultural colonists, almost all of whom were foreigners or their Argentine-born children. Colonists wanted a greater say in local government and a change in the taxation system. Popular mobilization reached sizeable proportions in parts of Santa Fe. After the suicide in 1896 of the Radical Party's first leader, Leandro Alem, the party went into rapid decline and for all intents and purposes disappeared.[10]

In 1903 it reemerged under the leadership of Alem's nephew, Yrigoyen. Yrigoyen, who will be discussed at great length in later chapters, was a brilliant political organizer. He built the sinews of a modern political party by creating an elaborate organizational structure. He also de-emphasized the idea of armed revolution—the party's last attempt was in 1905—and focused attention on political morality. The Radicals refused to participate in what they considered a corrupt political system. The Radical Party rejected it as evil and called for moral rejuvenation and a new system. Yrigoyen stressed the importance of a fair voting process:

> It is essential to reconquer that constitutional character, based on the legitimacy of all the powers that have been denaturalized to

---

10. Natalio R. Botana, *El orden conservador: La política argentina entre 1880 y 1916* (Buenos Aires: Editorial Sudamericana, 1977); Natalio R. Botana and Ezequiel Gallo, *De la República posible a la República verdadera (1880–1916)* (Buenos Aires: Ariel, 1997); Rock, *State Building*; Ezequiel Gallo, "Argentina: Society and Politics, 1880–1916," in *The Cambridge History of Latin America*, ed. Leslie Bethell (Cambridge: Cambridge University Press, 1986), 5:359–91; Roy Hora, *The Landowners of the Argentine Pampas: A Social and Political History, 1860–1945* (Oxford: Oxford University Press, 2001), 35–131; Eduardo A. Zimmermann, *Los liberales reformistas: La cuestión social en la Argentina, 1890–1916* (Buenos Aires: Sudamericana/San Andrés, 1995); Lilia Ana Bertoni, *Patriotas, cosmopolitas y nacionalistas: La construcción de la nacionalidad argentina a fines del siglo XIX* (Buenos Aires: Fondo de Cultura Económico, 2001); Alonso, *Revolution and the Ballot Box*; and "La Unión Cívica Radical: Fundación, oposición y triunfo (1890–1916)," in *El progreso, la modernización y su límites (1880–1916)*, vol. 5 of *Nueva Historia Argentina*, ed. Mirta Zaida Lobato (Buenos Aires: Editorial Sudamericana, 2000), 209–59; Ezequiel Gallo, *La pampa gringa: La colonización agrícola en Santa Fe (1870–1895)* (Buenos Aires: Editorial Sudamericana, 1983), esp. 379–427; Mirta Bonaudo, "Society and Politics: From Social Mobilization to Civic Participation (Santa Fe, 1890–1909)," in *Region and Nation: Politics, Economy, and Society in Twentieth-Century Argentina*, ed. James P. Brennan and Ofelia Pianetto (New York: St. Martin's Press, 2000), 1–47. See also the articles on

such a point that the leaders proceed only on their own exclusive account and their own interest.

It is thus indispensable to recover the electoral process, legally exercised, under democratic principles with which peace and public order will be everlasting, after which the current vices will be extinguished.

The Republic will cease to be the government of a man, of groups or of factions . . . that make illusionary all liberties and rights. It will be a government of popular will through the means of parties or corporations with the soothing and enlivening sense of bringing to its breast all types of opinions.[11]

In the minds of many, the Radical Party came to stand for a demand for a fair system of politics and honesty in choosing governments. It also became an organization of real size, acquiring the trappings of a "modern" political party. What it lacked was an opportunity. The growth of urban areas and the concurrent emergence of the "social problem" helped create pressure to change the political system.[12]

Not surprisingly, given Argentina's openness to the outside world, a labor movement developed early in relation to the state of industrialization and economic modernization. Many of the ideologies and personnel of the early union movement came from abroad. Unions first emerged in the 1880s, although most tended to be ephemeral. An intense rivalry existed between Socialists and Anarchists, but the latter clearly had more influence. The labor movement did not attract a great deal of attention from the government until approximately 1900, when the assassinations of King Humbert I of Italy and President William McKinley of the United States (among others) raised fears that something similar would happen in Argentina.[13] Increased government interest coincided with an intensification

---

the crisis of 1890 in "Dossier: La Crisis de 1890. Política sociedad y literatura," *Entrepasados* 12, no. 24–25 (2003): 19–147.

11. Yrigoyen to Pedro C. Molina, September 1909, *Documentos de Hipólito Yrigoyen: Apostolado cívico, obra de gobierno, defensa ante la corte* (Buenos Aires: Talleres Gráficos de la Dirección General de Institutos Penales de la Nación, 1949), 63.

12. For the idea of the social problem, see Zimmermann, *Los liberales reformistas*.

13. See, for example, Ricardo Falcón, *Los orígenes del movimiento obrero (1857–1899)* (Buenos Aires: Centro Editor de América Latina, 1984); Gonzalo Zaragoza, *Anarquismo argentino (1876–1902)* (Madrid: Ediciones de la Torre, 1996); Iaacov Oved, *El anarquismo y el movimiento obrero en Argentina* (Mexico: Siglo xxi, 1978), 11–224; Juan Suriano, *Anarquistas: Cultura y política libertaria en Buenos Aires, 1890–1910* (Buenos Aires: Manantial, 2001); Julio Godio, *Historia del movimiento obrero argentino: Inmigrantes asalariados y lucha de clases, 1880–1910* (Buenos Aires: Editorial Contemporánea, 1973), 55–174; Sebastián Marotta, *El movimiento sindical argentino* (Buenos Aires: "El Lacio," 1960), 1:43–132.

of labor unrest, marked by violence from both government and workers. Between 1902 and 1910 labor strife caused the government to declare a state of siege five times. A new law gave the government the right to expel foreigners whom it considered dangerous.[14]

In the first years of the twentieth century a new labor ideology emerged, Syndicalism (usually referred to in other countries as Revolutionary Syndicalism). The Syndicalists theoretically rejected the bourgeois political system and believed that the revolution would come through the general strike. More than Anarchists, Syndicalists believed in pressing for immediate gains and the importance of organizing unions. Large-scale repression targeted primarily at Anarchists followed the general strikes of 1909 and 1910 and Anarchism never fully recovered. The Syndicalists became the dominant ideological tendency in the labor movement.[15] The Syndicalists fit nicely with the Radicals' desires to cooperate with labor but not to establish formal or bureaucratized relationships. Despite their ideological scorn for bourgeois politics, the Syndicalists proved willing to use the government as an intercessor between themselves and employers. Their nonpolitical stance meant that their growing influence in the working class did not make them necessarily a rival of the Radical Party. Native-born workers could easily be Syndicalists and Radical Party voters.

The same could not be said of the other major ideological force within the labor movement, the Socialist Party, which was formed in 1895. Quite moderate in its programs, it became committed more to reform and good government than to the ideas of Karl Marx. Doctors and lawyers dominated the party leadership and many became related through marriage. Led by Juan B. Justo, a physician who died in 1928, the tight coterie of leaders saw any outsider who could mobilize popular support as a potential threat. This helped lead to an almost-constant shedding of elements of the party, including those who helped form the Communist Party by leaving the Socialist Party in 1917 and 1921, and the largely young and increasingly more conservative Independent Socialists who left in 1927. The Indepen-

---

14. See, for example, Godio, *Historia del movimiento obrero, 1880–1910*, 204–86; Enrique Dickmann, *Recuerdos de un militante socialista* (Buenos Aires: La Vanguardia, 1949), 133–92; Iaacov Oved, "El trasfondo histórico de la ley 4.144 de residencia," *Desarrollo Económico* 61 (April–June 1976): 123–50; Julio Frydenberg and Miguel Ruffo, *La semana roja de 1909* (Buenos Aires: Centro Editor de América Latina, 1992).

15. Hugo del Campo, *Sindicalismo y peronismo: Los comienzos de un vínculo perdurable* (Buenos Aires: CLASCO, 1983), 12–21; Godio, *Historia del movimiento obrero, 1880–1910*, 236–56; Rock, *Politics in Argentina*, 83–91; Marotta, *El movimiento sindical*, 2:25–198.

dent Socialists became, for a brief time, very popular, largely due to their vociferous opposition to Yrigoyen.

The Socialist Party built a solid political base in the city of Buenos Aires by developing support among the popular and middle classes. The party did not limit itself to politics. It sponsored cooperatives and cultural activities. It had influence in the labor movement, but only in the 1920s did it become a major player. The relationship of the party with "Socialist" elements in the labor movement was always difficult, and in 1918 the party passed a resolution that called on its members to join unions but also to keep the labor movement separate from political parties and ideologies. It was seldom so simple. Although the Socialists, or its splinter group the Independent Socialists, presented the only solid opposition to the Radicals in the capital, they failed to build a serious base in other regions of the country.[16]

The Communist Party had its peak strength in the years directly after its formation in 1920. It faded quickly after that but retained a role in the labor movement and among certain immigrant groups, especially through a network of cultural institutions.[17]

The threat of violence from the labor movement—frequently pictured as representing dangerous immigrants, the pressure of the Radicals, and the desires of a faction of the political elite—led to the reform of the electoral system. The reformist faction of the elite felt that the country needed a modern political system, especially the establishment of fair voting. It felt confident, however, that, like its counterparts in many European countries, it could dominate an open political system. The death in 1906 of President Manuel Quintana, with four years left on his term, brought to

---

16. Richard J. Walter, *The Socialist Party of Argentina, 1890–1930* (Austin: University of Texas Press, 1977); Michael F. Mullaney, "The Argentine Socialist Party 1890–1930: Early Development and Internal Schisms" (Ph.D. diss., University of Essex, 1983); Jeremy Adelman, "El Partido Socialista Argentino," in *El progreso, la modernización y su límites (1880–1916)*, vol. 5 of *Nueva Historia Argentina*, 261–90; Horacio Sanguinetti, *Los socialistas independientes* (Buenos Aires: Editorial del Belgrano, 1981); Emilio J. Corbière, *Orígenes del comunismo argentino* (Buenos Aires: Centro Editor de América Latina, 1984); Dora Barrancos, *La escena iluminada* (Buenos Aires: Plus Ultra, 1996); Partido Comunista de la Argentina, *Esbozo de historia del Partido Comunista de la Argentina* (Buenos Aires: Anteo, 1947), 30–70; Alfredo López, *¿Qué pasa en la Confederación General del Trabajo?* (Buenos Aires, 1943), 6–9; Partido Socialista, *Anuario socialista 1930* (Buenos Aires: La Vanguardia, 1929), 53–54.

17. For a good example of the Communist Party attempting to create community, see Hernán Camarero, "Los clubes deportivos comunistas," *Todo es Historia*, November 2004, 16–25. For an excellent discussion of the Communist Party that was published too late to be used, see Hermán Camarero, *A la conquista de la clase obrera: Los comunistas y el mundo del trabajo en la Argentina, 1920–1935* (Buenos Aires: Siglo XXI Editora Iberoamericana, 2007).

power Vice President José Figueroa Alcorta. Figueroa Alcorta used the full power of the presidency to destroy the old ruling coalition and, in 1910, to elect to the presidency Roque Sáenz Peña, who was determined to inaugurate electoral reform.

In 1912 congress passed the legislation that became known as the Ley Sáenz Peña. The law helped bring fair elections by establishing the secret ballot and basing voter rolls on the records created by the military for the draft. Voting became mandatory for all male citizens over the age of eighteen. In addition, the law attempted to tie minority parties to the political system by establishing a form of proportional representation that in each district gave the victorious party two-thirds of the representation and the second-place party one-third.[18] As is to be expected, problems with voting did not suddenly disappear, but elections became generally fair. The law paved the way for the Radical victory.

The Economy and the Radicals

The economy between 1916 and 1930 can be divided into three primary periods: World War I and its immediate aftermath; the 1920s "normality"; and the onset of the Depression. Given the economy's dependence on exports and imports, the impact of outside events was critical.

World War I had a major social and economic effect on the country. In 1913, 203,143 more immigrants entered the country than left. In 1914, the first year of the war, over 63,000 more left than entered. Only in 1920 did once again more immigrants enter than leave and in 1922 the net inflow became sizeable.[19] This temporarily altered the nature of the labor market because there was no longer a constant stream of immigrants coming in search of jobs. As important, a higher percentage of foreigners became accustomed to life in Argentina.

Fewer immigrants arriving and more going home caused the net outflow during and immediately after the war. Those returning home had been called to the colors, had been attracted by booming wartime economies in Europe, or had fled the hard times in Argentina.[20]

18. See sources cited in note 10 above; María Rosa Cicciari and Mariano Prado, "Un proceso de cambio institucional: La reforma electoral de 1912," *Cuadernos del CISH* 6 (segundo semestre de 1999): 95–145.
19. María Silvia Ospital, *Estado e inmigración en la década del veinte: La política inmigratoria de los gobiernos radicales* (Buenos Aires: Centro Editor de América Latina, 1988), 7.
20. Devoto, *Historia de la inmigración*, 353–54.

A combination of bad harvests and wartime-induced changes in the nature of world trade created a severe downturn in the local economy. Employment in the capital shrank dramatically, falling from 343,984 in August 1914 to 292,840 in 1917 before beginning to improve. Simultaneously, inflation created severe problems. According to one study, the consumer price index went up 69 percent between 1914 and 1918 and real wages fell concomitantly. As we shall see, labor unrest escalated.[21]

The end of the war permitted a return of better economic times, though downturns driven by external events occurred in 1920-21 and 1925. Although analysts have had different visions of the 1920s—some see the expansion as being more rapid than others—it was clearly a period of prosperity.[22] In comparison with what came later, it was indeed a golden age. Immigration flowed once again to Argentina, though less strongly than directly before the war, and its sources became more diverse. Employment grew rapidly in the capital, up 33 percent between 1922 and 1929. The cost of living declined 30 percent between 1920 and 1929, and real wages increased 69 percent.[23] Not surprisingly, social tensions fell as well.

After the war, trade became triangular: Argentina's prime buyer of its goods remained Great Britain, and more goods were purchased in the United States, especially cars, agricultural machinery, and general consumer goods. U.S. corporations displayed a great willingness to invest in factories and assembly plants. To a lesser extent companies based in other countries, as well as in Argentina, joined them.

The Great Depression's full impact was not yet visible by the end of the period covered by this book; it was, however, felt. The Depression hit early:

21. *Boletín de servicios*, April 5, 1923, 170; Di Tella and Zymelman, *Las etapas del desarrollo*, 295–355, esp. 317; Oxford Latin America Economic History Database, http://oxlad.qeh.ox.ac.uk/results.php, 9/2/2005; Pablo Gerchunoff and Lucas Llach, *El ciclo de la ilusión y el desencanto* (Buenos Aires: Ariel, 1998), 68–74, 469; Cortés Conde, *La economía argentina*, 30–33; Laura Randall, *An Economic History of Argentina in the Twentieth Century* (New York: Columbia University Press, 1978), 216–18; Díaz Alejandro, *Essays*, 51–53; María Inés Barbero and Fernando Rocchi, "Industry," in *A New Economic History of Argentina*, 271–72.

22. Juan Manuel Palacio, "La antesala de lo peor: La economía argentina entre 1914 y 1930," in *Democracia, conflicto social y renovación de ideas (1916–1930)*, vol. 6 of *Nueva Historia Argentina*, ed. Ricardo Falcón (Buenos Aires: Editorial Sudamericana, 2000), 115–18; Díaz Alejandro, *Essays*, 51–55; Gerchunoff and Llach, *El ciclo de la ilusión*, 78–84; Di Tella and Zymelman, *Las etapas del desarrollo*, 71–101; Robert Edward Shipley, "On the Outside Looking In: A Social History of the 'Porteño' Worker During the 'Golden Age' of Argentine Development, 1914–1930" (Ph.D. diss., Rutgers University, 1977).

23. Comité Nacional de Geografía, *Anuario geográfico argentino 1941* (Buenos Aires: Comité Nacional de Geografía, 1941), 557, 560; Colin Lewis, "Economic Restructuring and Labour Scarcity: Labour in the 1920s," in *Essays in Argentine Labour History, 1870–1930*, ed. Jeremy Adelman (London: Macmillan, 1992), 187.

1928 had been a bad year. Employment in the capital fell slightly from August 1928 to February 1929. As early as mid-1929, prices of agricultural commodities began to drop rapidly and capital began to flow toward New York. In December 1929 the government abandoned the gold standard. In 1930, government revenues from tariffs and port fees declined by 16 percent from the previous year. The value of exports shrank 42 percent from 1928 to 1930. Declines in exports had a severe impact on the ability to import and on certain sectors of the economy.[24]

Working and Living Conditions

Buenos Aires had a modern social structure and a sizeable middle class. According to the calculations of Gino Germani, 38 percent of its population was middle class in 1914, and that had grown to 46 percent by 1936. The figures for the rest of the country were only somewhat lower.[25] The lack of full-scale industrialization meant that the urban popular classes frequently worked in small shops, the service industry, with the government, or in jobs connected with transporting goods or people. Many large factories existed as well.[26]

Although the working and living conditions of the popular classes left a lot to be desired, it is important not to romanticize the problems or the good conditions. Conditions were good enough to continue to attract and hold onto many immigrants. The statistics on return to the other side of the Atlantic make it clear that many more immigrants could have returned home if they had so desired. Especially in the period before World War I, the potential sites for emigration were numerous, but many continued to come to Argentina. Even after the closing of the United States to most immigrants in the postwar period, there were other places to go, but immigrants continued to arrive in large numbers in Argentina. This pattern demonstrates that while conditions were often difficult, immigrants found them better than their alternatives, whether because conditions were better or because they could hope for better lives for themselves or at least their

24. *Boletín de Servicios*, September 1929, 413; Comité Nacional de Geografía, *Anuario*, 404; Díaz Alejandro, *Essays*, 479; Martín Campos, "El cierre de la Caja de Conversión en 1929: Una decisión de política económica," *Desarrollo Económico* 176 (January–March 2005): 537–66.

25. Gino Germani, *Estructura social de la Argentina* (Buenos Aires: Editorial Raigal, 1955), 219–20.

26. See Rocchi, *Chimneys in the Desert*.

children. The belief in upward mobility, even if it was frequently little more than wishful thinking, was extraordinarily important. It gave hope.[27] There was a good deal of intergenerational mobility.

Definite problems existed. Working-class families spent a high percentage of their income on housing, and what they received for their money was frequently extremely inadequate. In a 1929 study done by the Departamento Nacional del Trabajo (DNT) of 680 families, 636 lived in one room. Some of these undoubtedly lived in the infamous *conventillas*, the packed collective housing in the center of the city, though the percentage of people living in these establishments declined over time. The popular classes increasingly moved out of the central part of the city as lots and public transportation became more available, and they frequently built their own houses. The nature of these houses varied, but they were less crowded and permitted families to grow vegetables and, once having paid for the land, to lessen their monthly housing costs.

As Luis Alberto Romero and Leandro Gutiérrez and their students have shown, a new kind of sociability and worldview was developing in the barrios of Buenos Aires with the rise of clubs, political organizations, and neighborhood improvement associations. The development of a real civic culture coincided with the rise of the Radical Party. For example, almost all the professional soccer teams that currently exist developed out of member-based clubs founded in the first two decades of the twentieth century. A spirit of civic engagement flourished and gave inhabitants of the city a multitude of places to turn for help and a sense of belonging. Competing ideas were available. Commercial newspapers had developed and vastly outsold foreign language papers and politically oriented ones. In 1928 three papers claimed circulations of over 180,000 copies. Foreign observers commented on the city's cleanliness and its modernity, the streetcars, and the illusion it gave that it went on forever.[28]

---

27. See, for an excellent discussion of upward mobility among Spaniards, José C. Moya, *Cousins and Strangers: Spanish Immigrants in Buenos Aires, 1850–1930* (Berkeley and Los Angeles: University of California Press, 1998), 259–76.

28. DNT, *Crónica mensual*, May 1930, 3142–46; Ana María Rigotti, "La ciudad y vivienda como ámbitos de la política y la práctica profesional," in *Democracia, conflicto social y renovación de ideas (1916–1930)*, vol. 6 of *Nueva Historia Argentina*, ed. Ricardo Falcón (Buenos Aires: Editorial Sudamericana, 2000), 283–322; Bunge, *Una nueva Argentina*, 351–78; Francis Korn, *Buenos Aires: Los huéspedes del 20* (Buenos Aires: Editorial Sudamericana, 1974), 79–187; Walter, *Politics and Urban Growth*, 1–148; Adrián Gorelik, *La grilla y el parque: Espacio público y cultura urbana en Buenos Aires, 1887–1936* (Bernal, Argentina: Universidad Nacional de Quilmes, 1998); Leandro H. Gutiérrez and Juan Suriano, "Workers' Housing and Living Conditions in Buenos Aires, 1880–1930," in *Essays in Argentine Labour History, 1870–1930*, ed. Jeremy Adelman (London: Macmillan, 1992), 35–51; James A. Baer, "Urbanization and

The diet of the working class tended to be unbalanced. Bread and meat were the foods of chief consumption. Immigrants frequently expressed amazement at the quantity of meat that was eaten. Fruits, vegetables, and dairy products were eaten sparingly, though over the years being discussed it appears that diets became more varied.[29]

Nationwide illiteracy was relatively high: 35 percent in 1914 but falling quickly, reaching 15 percent in 1943. Younger people had much lower illiteracy rates. Argentines and immigrants had similar illiteracy rates, although large variations existed among the different streams of immigrants. Among Argentines the percent of literacy was roughly equal between the sexes, but that was not true in some immigrant groups where many fewer women could read. In 1914 in the capital, illiteracy was 18 percent, while the figure for the native-born stood at 8.5 percent. In that city, illiterate voters were not really a factor, because they represented 4 percent of the registered voters in 1916 and 2.5 in 1930. Nationally they composed 35.5 of registered voters in 1916, but the figure had declined to 22 percent by 1930.[30]

Overview of Politics

The Ley Sáenz Peña of 1912 altered the nature of politics. For the first time the will of the voter truly mattered. The Radicals abandoned their withdrawal from electoral politics and began not only to participate but

---

Mobilization: Housing and Class Identity in Argentina, 1870–1925" (paper delivered at the Latin American Studies Association Congress, 1992); Enrique S. Inda, "La vivienda obrera en la formación del Gran Buenos Aires (1890–1940)," *Todo es Historia*, February 1992, 71–88; Moya, *Cousins and Strangers*, 153–55; Ariel Scher and Héctor Palomino, *Fútbol: Pasión de multitudes y de elites* (Buenos Aires: Documentos del CISEA, 1988), 237–38; American Society of Newspaper Editors, *International Year Book 1929* (New York: Editor and Publisher, 1929), 290; James Bryce, *South America: Observations and Impressions* (New York: Macmillan, 1912), 316–21; André Siegfried, *Impressions of South America*, trans. H. H. Hemming and Doris Hemming (New York: Harcourt, Brace, 1933), 90–95. For an example of the work done by Leandro Gutiérrez and Luis Alberto Romero, see *Sectores populares, cultura política: Buenos Aires en la entreguerra* (Buenos Aires: Editorial Sudamericana, 1995). See also De Privitellio, *Vecinos y ciudadanos*, esp. 107–47.

29. Gutiérrez and Suriano, "Workers' Housing," esp. 41–44; Norberto Ferreras, "Evolución de los principales consumos obreros en Buenos Aires (1880–1920)," *Ciclos* 11, no. 22 (segunda semestre de 2001): 157–80; Moya, *Cousins and Strangers*, 296, 372; Leandro Gutiérrez, "Condiciones de la vida material de los sectores populares en Buenos Aires, 1880–1914," *Siglo XIX* (Monterrey, Mex.) 3, no. 6 (July–December 1988): 41–75.

30. Germani, *Estructura social*, 229–33; Devoto, *Historia de la inmigración*, 300–302; Bunge, *Una nueva Argentina*, 417–23.

also to win. In 1912 and 1914 they won in such key districts as the capital, Santa Fe, and Entre Ríos and did well in several others.[31] The old political elite's hope of continued domination began to pale, in part because they failed to create a unified conservative party. This failure and the Radicals' tactics discussed in the following chapters helped the Radicals become politically dominant.

The electoral reform had an immediate impact: there was a notable increase in voting between 1910 and 1912, the latter being the first election after the reform. Although major differences existed between provinces, participation rates stayed relatively high.[32] The high voter turnouts are in many ways deceiving because they do not include the numerous immigrant males.

In the 1916 presidential elections, the Radicals' candidate, Yrigoyen, won almost 46 percent of the popular vote, but the fragmented nature of the opposition meant that more than 30 percentage points separated Yrigoyen from the second-largest vote getter. In the electoral college the margin was tight; Yrigoyen won only with the help of dissident Radicals from Santa Fe province.[33] The Radicals failed to capture control of the Chamber of Deputies, but they had a sizeable block with 44 deputies out of a total of 116. Their number of seats increased in 1918 and they captured a clear majority in 1920, which they did not surrender until the 1930 coup. The Radicals' lack of acceptance of the opposition and their belief in the prerogatives of the executive branch made cooperation with other parties extremely difficult.[34] Senators were elected for nine years by provincial legislatures, with the exception of the city of Buenos Aires, where they were directly elected. Because of this, the Radicals never achieved a majority in the Senate; when they came close, however, it contributed to the atmosphere that led to the coup of 1930.

The Radicals lacked a clear vision of social transformation, but their idea of the political world changed Argentina in a profound way. They appealed to all citizens to be Radicals (see Chapter 2) and this resonated

31. Mirta Zaida Lobato and Juan Suriano, *Atlas histórico de la Argentina, Nueva Historia Argentina* (Buenos Aires: Editorial Sudamericana, 2000), 287–88.
32. Darío Canton, *Elecciones y partidos políticos en la Argentina* (Buenos Aires: Siglo XXI, 1973), 43–58.
33. Ibid., 267; Waldo Ansaldi, "La trunca transición del régimen oligárquico al régimen democrático," in *Democracia, conflicto social y renovación de ideas (1916–1930)*, vol. 6 of *Nueva Historia Argentina*, ed. Ricardo Falcón (Buenos Aires: Editorial Sudamericana, 2000), 20–22.
34. Centro de Estudios, Unión para la Nueva Mayoría, *Composición de la Cámara de Diputados, 1916–1930, Cuaderno* 21 (October 1991): 2; Mustapic, "Conflictos institucionales," 85–108.

profoundly. As we shall see in subsequent chapters, the Radicals made a concerted attempt to attract the urban popular classes and in that fashion made them part of the system. But by no means was their appeal limited to those sectors of the society; their vision of the party was all encompassing. The society became more inclusive.

Why, given the high percentage of foreigners, were the popular classes seen as such an important potential constituency of the Radicals? Certainly their vision of being all-inclusive contributed, as did their fear of the growth of the Socialist Party. A glance at the 1914 census or a walk around the city of Buenos Aires, however, would have confirmed that the age structure combined with the reversal of immigration during World War I meant that there was going to be a higher percentage of the native born. In the capital the number of eligible voters almost doubled between 1915 and 1930. The reason for this is obvious. In 1914 there were 21,526 foreign males age fourteen through seventeen and 41,624 Argentines. Moreover, if one looks at the age category ten to fourteen, there were 3.6 Argentines for every foreigner. The ratios were higher for the entire country.[35]

The Radicals' acceptance of change, and at times the encouragement of it, had a real impact. As we shall see, this helped set off a strike wave. It also helped encourage a movement for reform in the universities. For some time, students and others had been demanding modernized universities with better curriculums, facilities, and faculty. In 1917 and more acutely in 1918, this erupted in widespread student agitation in the university in Córdoba, with important repercussions elsewhere. This university was the oldest, most traditional, and elite dominated. Many of those who controlled the university were opponents of the Radicals. This gave the Radicals another reason to intervene in the students' favor, which they did. Although the so-called university reform movement was to go on for years, by the end of 1918 important changes had been made. Argentine universities began to have more diverse student bodies and teachers, more modern curriculums, and better facilities. Yrigoyen and the Radicals played an important role in the reforms and received much of the credit. For example, in October 1918 much of the proreform student leadership in Córdoba sent a telegram to Yrigoyen that said, "The reorganization of the University in the form done by the Executive Power of the Nation marks an historic hour in American culture. The University Federation [Federación

---

35. Darío Canton and Jorge Raúl Jorrat, *Elecciones en la ciudad, 1864–2003* (Buenos Aires: Instituto Histórico de la Ciudad de Buenos Aires, 2005), 1:443; Comisión Nacional del Censo, *Tercer Censo*, 3:3, 17, 18, 310.

Universitaria], examining closely this patriotic work, places Your Excellency among the illustrious Argentines. It sends to the first magistrate of the nation its enthusiastic and sincere applause, and it is pleased to invite him in the name of the youth of Córdoba to inaugurate personally . . . the new university era. Córdoba awaits President Irigoyen." The reform movement had repercussions even for those who were unlikely to attend the university. Workers in Córdoba backed the student movement. It stirred stiff opposition as well. The more open universities marked the beginnings of a major societal change.[36]

As Peter Smith has shown on the national level and Gardenia Vidal for Córdoba, the Radical Party over time seemed to produce a new, younger breed of politicians whose roots were in the middle class. The elite use of the term *chusma* (rabble) to describe certain of the Radicals, while reflecting the snobbery of the elite, did derive from the background of some Radical leaders, who had not been born even into the middle class. Pedro Bidegain, a political boss in Buenos Aires and a one-term congressman, had been at one time a blue-collar worker on a railroad. Leopoldo Bard, a key figure in the party in the late 1920s, was accused of being involved with a prostitution ring. The change in electoral practices created a shift in leadership even within the Conservative Party in the Province of Buenos Aires. Local political bosses who could bring voters to the ballot box gained influence at the expense of the traditional elites.[37]

The nature of politics had changed in many ways, but tactics did not suddenly alter. Politics in the capital became "modern" immediately (many contemporaries would have argued that the use of clientelism and the spoils system was not modern, but other contemporary political systems were just as affected by this phenomenon). In many provinces, how-

36. Gardenia Vidal, "La reforma universitaria de 1918 y su repercusión en los resultados electorales," in *La política y la gente: Estudios sobre modernidad y espacio público en Córdoba, 1880–1960*, ed. Gardenia Vidal (Córdoba: Ferreyra Editor, 2007), quote 129–30, and 115–41; Gardenia Vidal, "La modernidad y el espacio público en Argentina: Repensando la Reforma Universitaria de 1918," *Avances del CESOR* (Rosario) 5, no. 5 (2005): 109–31; Adriana R. Chiroleu, "La Reforma Universitaria," in *Democracia, conflicto social y renovación de ideas (1916–1930)*, vol. 6 of *Nueva Historia Argentina*, ed. Richard Falcón (Buenos Aires: Editorial Sudamericana, 2000), 357–89; Tulio Halperín Donghi, *Historia de la Universidad de Buenos Aires* (Buenos Aires: EUDEBA, 1962), 104–46.

37. Peter H. Smith, *Argentina and the Failure of Democracy: Conflict Among Political Elites, 1904–1955* (Madison: University of Wisconsin Press, 1974), esp. 94–95; Vidal, *Radicalismo de Córdoba*, 299–336; Donna Guy, *Sex and Danger in Buenos Aires: Prostitution, Family, and Nation in Argentina* (Lincoln: University of Nebraska Press, 1991), 123; Pablo Fernández Irusta, "El Partido Conservador de la Provincia de Buenos Aires y el proceso de democratización bonaerense, 1908–1918," *Estudios Sociales* 31 (segundo semestre de 2006): 95–136. See also Chapter 3.

ever, the use of traditional political means, from violence to fraud, continued to plague politics. In Mendoza and San Juan, where populist dissident Radicals became important and social tensions were high, violence became far too common.[38] Frequently, Yrigoyen used interventions to change the political balance in recalcitrant provinces and helped to create Radical dominance.

The Radicals came to power with vague goals of implanting political morality and political consolidation. Their initial years were made difficult by the problems produced by World War I and its immediate aftermath. On top of unemployment and inflation, labor agitation increased dramatically. This agitation was caused in part by economic problems, and in part by the new administration's aid to strikes, done with the hope of mobilizing voter support. Also, workers were inspired by the Bolshevik Revolution and the labor unrest that swept the world in its wake. An intense strike wave rolled across Argentina. The capital had 196 strikes in 1918, 367 in 1919, and 206 the following year. The Federación Obrera Regional Argentina IX (FORA IX), the Syndicalist-dominated labor confederation, at its peak in 1920 had 535 member unions and averaged 62,460 monthly dues payers.[39] This was an extremely high number given the size of the labor market and the lack of a system of dues checkoff. Not surprisingly, employers and other elites formed their own organizations to try to counter workers' demands and break unions. Tensions led to the bloody repression of the Tragic Week in January 1919 in Buenos Aires and the even more bloody repression of strikers in Patagonia in 1921 and 1922. As we shall see, this strain led to withdrawal of Radical support for strikes and partially explains the sudden labor peace that developed after mid-1921.

Infighting within the labor movement and the decline in union membership inspired an attempt to create a new confederation that would unite all factions. The Unión Sindical Argentina (USA) was formed in 1922 but could not fulfill the dreams of those who called its first convention. Most Anarchist unions stayed in their own organization, the FORA V, which became known as just the FORA. Syndicalists and Communists dominated

---

38. See, for examples, Pablo Lacoste, "Radicalismo, lencinismo y bloquismo en Mendoza y San Juan," in *Populismo en San Juan y Mendoza*, ed. Pablo Lacoste (Buenos Aires: Centro Editor de América Latina, 1994), 9–40; Pablo Lacoste, *La Unión Cívica Radical en Mendoza y en la Argentina (1890–1946)* (Mendoza: Ediciones Culturales de Mendoza, 1994); Celso Rodríguez, *Lencinas y Cantoni: El populismo cuyano en tiempos de Yrigoyen* (Buenos Aires: Editorial de Belgrano, 1979).

39. DNT, División de Estadística, *Estadística de las huelgas* (Buenos Aires, 1940), 20; *La Vanguardia*, May 1, 1930.

the USA, with the former just able to hold onto power, and friction between the two ideologies became intense. Communist influence in unions had declined considerably by the end of the 1920s.[40] In 1929 as part of a shift in Comintern policy, the Communists withdrew from the USA and formed their own organization. Earlier, irked by the Syndicalists' stand against the participation of labor leaders in politics and other tactics, Socialist-dominated unions had pulled out of the USA and in 1926 joined the two largest railroad unions, the Unión Ferroviaria and La Fraternidad, to form the Confederación Obrera Argentina (COA). The COA had many members because the rail unions were very large.[41]

Even before the withdrawal of first the Socialists and then the Communists, the USA was a pale shadow of the FORA IX. It had 26,290 members in 1923, just 15,656 monthly dues payers in 1926, and only 11,615 in 1928.[42]

The Argentine constitution did not permit the serving of consecutive terms. Yrigoyen wanted to maintain his influence and be reelected in 1928. His choice for a candidate, and it was clearly his choice, was Marcelo T. de Alvear. Scion of an extremely wealthy family whose grandfather had been a hero of the war for independence, Alvear had been a personal friend of Yrigoyen for decades. He had also been a participant in the revolt of 1890 that led to the formation of the Radical Party and had taken part in the Radical revolt of 1893. He spent most of the other years in Europe, especially in Paris, a significant portion of which he spent pursuing a Portuguese opera singer who ultimately agreed to marry him. After the passage of the electoral reform law, Alvear served in congress, and he spent the presidency of Yrigoyen as ambassador to his beloved France. Hoping to dominate politically, Yrigoyen selected as Alvear's running mate Elipidio González, Yrigoyen's key political confidant.

Alvear did not appear to be a man with a lot of political drive. As fre-

---

40. See, for example, *Bandera Proletaria*, March 31, 1923, February 1, March 8, June 7–October 25, 1924; *La Internacional*, March 6, May 10, June 7, October 4, 1924; *El Obrero Municipal*, May 1924, May–October 1925. For the small size of the Communist labor movement by 1929, see Confederación Sindical Latino-Americana, *Bajo la bandera de la CSLA: Resoluciones y documentos del congreso constituyente* (Montevideo: Imprenta La Linotipo, 1929), esp. 256–57, 299.

41. For the Communists, see *La Internacional* and *Bandera Proletaria* for 1929; Robert J. Alexander, *Communism in Latin America* (New Brunswick, N.J.: Rutgers University Press, 1960), 162. For COA, Marotta, *El movimiento sindical argentino*, 3:176–78, 191–204; Hernán Camarero, "Socialismo y movimiento sindical: Una articulación débil: La COA y sus relaciones con el PS durante la década de 1920," in *El Partido Socialista en Argentina*, ed. Hernán Camarero and Carlos Miguel Herrera (Buenos Aires: Prometeo Libros, 2005), 185–217.

42. *El Obrero Gráfico*, June–July 1924; *Bandera Proletaria*, August 31, 1929.

quently happens in such circumstances, however, Alvear displayed a sense of independence, though he never completely broke with Yrigoyen or used the full power of his office to back a political alternative to the segment of the party apparatus controlled by Yrigoyen. Whether this was due to personal loyalty to Yrigoyen, political laziness, or a belief in the limitation of presidential power is not totally clear. As Tulio Halperín Donghi has pointed out, using as evidence a telegraphic exchange in 1920–21 over Argentina's continued presence in the League of Nations, Alvear had an obsequious relationship with Yrigoyen. This demonstrates Alvear's personality as well as Yrigoyen's ability to dominate those who should have been his peers. Yrigoyen, although criticizing Alvear, was careful to remind him of their shared past experiences. Alvear's reply was, in part, "Teacher [Maestro], I believe in you [ti] . . . your explanations are profound and for us untouchable. . . . Whatever will be the path, certainly we will follow you. . . . Teacher, I believe in you."[43]

Alvear won the election with almost 48 percent of the vote, despite spending the campaign in Europe. His total seems underwhelming, but the opposition was so fragmented that no other candidate received even double-digit voter support.[44] The appointment of the cabinet demonstrated that Alvear had a mind of his own. Only one appointee could be called an unconditional ally of Yrigoyen.[45] This declaration of political independence led almost immediately to friction between the close followers of Yrigoyen and those who resented his attempts to dictate policy. At first this primarily manifested itself in jousting for advantage in the Senate but soon began to have much wider ramifications, including major tensions within the party apparatus. The resignation of José Nicolás Matienzo as minister of interior in November 1923 and his replacement by Vicente Gallo marked a sharp turn against Yrigoyen's influence.

In 1924 the party split formally into two wings, the Personalists and the Anti-Personalists. The latter could be seen as Alvearistas but more correctly as those who opposed the dominance of Yrigoyen in the party.[46]

43. Halperín Donghi, *Vida y muerte*, 576. See also 203–5, 571–76.
44. Canton, *Elecciones y partidos*, 268. The Alvear administration has been little studied and no full-scale biography has been written. For a description of Alvear, see, for example, Félix Luna, *Alvear* (Buenos Aires: Libros Argentinos, 1958); Alejandro Cattaruzza, *Marcelo T. de Alvear: El compromiso y la distancia* (Buenos Aires: Fondo de Cultura Económica, 1997); Raúl A. Molina, "Presidencia de Marcelo T. de Alvear," in Academia Nacional de la Historia, *Historia argentina contemporánea* (Buenos Aires: El Ateneo, 1965), 1:sección 2, 271–345.
45. Molina, "Presidencia de Marcelo T. de Alvear," 278.
46. Ibid., 280–81; Roberto Etchepareborda, "La segunda presidencia de Hipólito Yrigoyen y la crisis de 1930," in Academia Nacional de la Historia, *Historia argentina contemporánea* (Buenos Aires: El Ateneo, 1963), 1:sección 2, 350–51; Cattaruzza, *Marcelo T. de Alvear,*

Many of the key leaders were founders of the Radical Party and close to the traditional elite. They could be considered the conservative wing of the party. That characterization, however, is much too simplistic. Yrigoyen's opponents included the populist dissident Radicals in the provinces of Mendoza and San Juan tied to the Lencinas and Cantoni families. In addition, individuals, such as Leónidas Anastasi, played a key role for the Anti-Personalists but cannot be labeled conservatives. Anastasi founded the Anti-Personalist paper *La Acción* and was the president of the Anti-Personalist convention for the capital in 1927. He taught labor law at the universities of Buenos Aires and La Plata and was a lawyer for the Syndicalist-dominated maritime workers' union and the Syndicalist confederation FORA IX.[47] Although tending to be relatively conservative, what held the Anti-Personalists together was their dislike of Yrigoyen's control of the party.

Alvear never countenanced a complete break with Yrigoyen. When Gallo, who tried to use the full power of the government to break the dominance of the Personalists, wanted to oust them from control of the crucial Province of Buenos Aires by an intervention, Alvear balked. He either maintained a loyalty to Yrigoyen or felt that the power of the government should not be used in such a fashion. Gallo resigned, but the pressure to change the electoral calculus by taking over the province remained strong. Alvear never succumbed. Some see a pact between Yrigoyen and Alvear.[48] As we shall see, the Anti-Personalists attempted to woo voters by conventional means, ultimately without a great deal of success.

40; Luciano de Privitellio, "El Concejo Deliberante y el fomentismo en el municipio porteño," PEHESA, *Documento de Trabajo*, April 1996, 3–4; Horacio J. Guido, "Los cismas radicales," *Todo es Historia*, July 1981, 44–46; Carlos Giacobone and Edit Rosalía Gallo, *Radicalismo bonaerense, 1891–1931: La ingeniería política de Hipólito Yrigoyen* (Buenos Aires: Corregidor, 1999), 239; Luis C. Alén Lascano, *Yrigoyenismo y antipersonalismo* (Buenos Aires: Centro Editor de América Latina, 1986), 31–38; Félix Luna, "Los radicales en el gobierno," in Academia Nacional de la Historia, *Nueva historia de la nación argentina* (Buenos Aires: Planeta, 2001), 7:252–53. See also *Crítica*, July 27, November 26, 1923; *La Montaña*, July 29, November 24, 1923; *The Standard*, November 25, 1923 (these are from the clipping books of Alvear); *La Acción*, November 24, 1923.

47. For Mendoza and San Juan, see note 38 above. Luis C. Alén Lascano, *La Argentina ilusionada, 1922–1930* (Buenos Aires: La Bastilla, 1975), 59–79; *La Acción*, September 29 and October 6, 1927; Diego Abad de Santillán, *Gran enciclopedia argentina* (Buenos Aires: Ediar, 1956), 1:185; David Rock, "Machine Politics in Buenos Aires and the Argentine Radical Party, 1912–1930," *Journal of Latin American Studies* 4, no. 2 (November 1972): 242; Walter, *The Socialist Party*, 171–72.

48. Ricard J. Walter, *The Province of Buenos Aires and Argentine Politics, 1912–1943* (Cambridge: Cambridge University Press, 1985), 70–79; Alén Lescano, *Yrigoyenismo*, 46–51; Marcela P. Ferrari, "El voto del silencio: Algunas consideraciones sobre el abstencionismo en la provincia de Buenos Aires, 1913–1931," *Cuadernos del CLAEH* (Montevideo) 83–84, no. 1–2

Yrigoyen reentered the electoral fray in 1928, easily recapturing the presidency. He won 57.4 percent of the popular vote and every province except San Juan. He carried the capital with 54.6 percent.[49] The Anti-Personalist presidential candidate was crushed.

The reelection of Yrigoyen seemed to mark a new moment in the history of the Radical Party. Many of its more conservative members had gone with the Anti-Personalists. The Radicals had won the election with a relatively clear platform calling for the nationalization of the petroleum industry.

Not much changed. In part this was due to Yrigoyen himself. He continued to have a tight hold over decision making, but he was in his mid-seventies and seemed to lack the vigor that he displayed during his first term. The opposition charged that he was senile.[50] Although this was probably untrue, he had a hard time dealing with the massive problems created by the onset of the Depression. As critically, the Radical Party faced a crisis of legitimacy, at least in the minds of many political elites and much of the politicized classes, especially in the capital.[51]

What had happened? Was it just the Depression and Yrigoyen's own growing personal problems? With the splitting of the Radical Party, some came to see the Personalist faction as being increasingly middle class. The Personalists were also about to assume control of the Senate, which for the first time would have left them in full control of all branches of government. This, plus the Radicals' belief that only they were truly Argentine, appeared threatening to many. In addition, many had come to question the liberal ideology that had underlain the society for generations. In March 1930 the Independent Socialists, whose anti-Yrigoyenist crusade was backed by the second-largest-selling newspaper, *Crítica*, easily won congressional elections in the city of Buenos Aires. The Radicals finished a distant second, just ahead of the Socialists.

The electoral defeat in the capital seemed to break a psychological barrier. Anti-Yrigoyen demonstrations became common, frequently led by university students. Street violence and a sense of unease increased. The

---

(1999): 186–90; Leopoldo Bard, *Estampas de una vida: La fe puesto en un ideal "llegar a ser algo"* (Buenos Aires: Talleres Gráficos J. Perrotti, 1957), 122–23.

49. Canton, *Elecciones y partidos*, 269.

50. See, for example, *La Acción*, January 23, 24, March 25, 1928.

51. See, for example, María Inés Tato, *Viento de Fronda: Liberalismo, conservadurismo y democracia en la Argentina, 1911–1932* (Buenos Aires: Siglo XXI Editores Argentina, 2004), 157–82; Loris Zanatta, *Del estado liberal, a la nación católica: Iglesia y ejército en los orígenes del peronismo, 1930–1946* (Bernal, Argentina: Universidad Nacional de Quilmes, 1996), 25–56.

traditional political world seemed to come to a halt. The Personalists' unity was shattered. The Senate met only once in 1930. Non-Yrigoyenist political elites began to conspire with military leaders. In September 1930 a small group of army cadets marched into the city of Buenos Aires; they were wildly cheered and met with little opposition.[52] The Radical government had fallen. The military had forced the first illegitimate change in government since the 1860s. The first experiment in democratic government had failed, and the reinstitution of democracy would prove difficult.

---

52. Walter, *The Socialist Party*, 222; Sylvia Saítta, *Recuerdos de tinta: El diario Crítica en el década de 1920* (Buenos Aires: Editorial Sudamericana, 1998), 236–44; Robert Potash, *The Army and Politics in Argentina, 1928–1945: Yrigoyen to Perón* (Stanford, Calif.: Stanford University Press, 1969), 29–54; Halperín Donghi, *Vida y muerte*, 205–71; Smith, "The Breakdown of Democracy," 3–27; *La Nación, La Prensa, Crítica*, June 1–September 8, 1930.

2

CREATING THE IMAGE: CONSTRUCTION OF THE IMAGES OF YRIGOYEN AND ALVEAR

During Yrigoyen's first inauguration, even before he had his hands on the levers of power, the crowd surged forward and detached the horses from his carriage and pulled it through the streets of Buenos Aires.[1] In 1920 in the traditional end of a campaign rally, when the party's followers marched past a balcony on which Yrigoyen stood to greet them, the marchers from the twentieth ward lowered their banners and knelt before Yrigoyen.[2]

Popular devotion to the Radicals and Yrigoyen was fervent, reflected both in voting totals and street demonstrations. The political style of the Radicals dominated the period of the first opening to democracy and had a major impact for decades. Not surprisingly, this style derived from traditional Argentine politics; the early leaders of the Radicals, with few exceptions, were political veterans. The Ley Sáenz Peña of 1912 did change the nature of politics. For the first time the winning of popular support became essential for political success. The rupture with the past, however, is less dramatic than it appears. The works of Hilda Sabato and Paula Alonso have demonstrated that a tradition of popular involvement in politics existed in Buenos Aires prior to 1912.[3] Still, a change did occur; winning voter approval had become critical.

The Radicals' opponents frequently charged that the party lacked a specific program. This did not mean that they lacked ideas about ways to

---

1. *La Prensa*, October 13, 1916.
2. Marcelo Padoan, *Jesús, el templo y los viles mercaderes: Un examen de la discursividad yrigoyenista* (Bernal, Argentina: Universidad Nacional de Quilmes, 2002), 40.
3. Sabato, *La política en las calles*; Paula Alonso, *Between Revolution and the Ballot Box*.

garner popular support or to govern. Part strategy, part a result of the way that the Radicals viewed themselves, the Radicals presented themselves and their leader, Hipólito Yrigoyen, in a singular fashion that helped make him extraordinarily popular among certain sectors of the population and the center of what could be viewed as almost a cult of personality. The approach of the Anti-Personalist wing of the Radical Party did not differ remarkably, although it was, not surprisingly, less personal.

The rhetoric of the Radicals and of Yrigoyen is important, and this chapter will explore the images that they attempted to create. These images from the era before the full development of radio need to be examined with care. Who read the Radical press or heard the speeches on the street corners? We cannot be certain. The official Yrigoyenist paper, *La Epoca*, does not appear to be designed to have a great deal of popular appeal, and it is written in a style that seems to assume that its readers also read other papers. According to Manuel Gálvez, it did not have a circulation greater than twenty thousand and not even the Radicals read it. *La Acción*, the Anti-Personalist paper, similarly appeared to lack popular appeal. According to the U.S. Department of Commerce, its circulation in 1928 was twenty-five thousand.[4] Even if we know their circulation, how many party affiliates bought them for political reasons but did not really read them? Unlike the Perón era, when few true alternative sources of information existed, under the Radicals there were many. *Crítica* and *La Prensa*, the largest circulating newspapers, were at times furiously anti-Yrigoyen, as were other media organs. *La Fronda*, for example, in 1929 claimed that the Radical victory brought "as a principal consequence an evident predominance of negroid mentality."[5] The public sphere was contested space. There were contradictory messages available, and only those with a predisposition to consume the pro-Radical message were going to be affected by the party's point of view.

Creating the Image of Yrigoyen

The messages about Yrigoyen had a profound impact that is difficult to fully comprehend some eighty years later. Fervor developed among por-

---

4. Manuel Gálvez, *Vida de Hipólito Yrigoyen: El hombre de misterio*, 2nd ed. (Buenos Aires: Guillermo Kraft, 1939), 264; American Society of Newspaper Editors, *International Year Book 1929*, 290.

5. *La Fronda*, July 31, 1929, as cited in Ricardo Sidicaro, *La política mirada desde arriba: Las ideas del diario La Nación, 1909–1989* (Buenos Aires: Editorial Sudamericana, 1993), 111.

tions of the popular sectors that seems almost surreal. Why did Yrigoyen have this impact? Yrigoyen and the party benefited from the image that he and the party crafted for himself. They also received credit for their role in the opening up of the political system. True citizenship had come from the Radicals, and Yrigoyen personified the party. The language of inclusion and democracy that became the political discourse of democracy in Argentina came first from the Radicals, as Daniel James has pointed out. Despite a mythology to the contrary, Juan Perón was not the first person to incorporate popular sectors into the political system.[6] It happened first under the Radicals. Many of the popular classes felt that their inclusion in the political system, and in reality in the social system, was due to the Radicals. The achievement through the efforts of the Radical Party of universal male suffrage had a tremendous impact, wrapping the party in a special aura (whether it deserved all the credit is not really relevant).

The winning of the right to vote should not be underestimated. Pierre Rosanvallon has argued that "universal suffrage is a kind of sacrament of equality among men." He also pointed out that it is a type of rupture with past. The individual becomes truly important. Rosanvallon argued that in France during the Third Republic universal suffrage became the ultimate source of legitimacy. In the Argentina of the Radicals, male suffrage also defined the political system.[7]

Trying to gauge what ideas and attitudes resonated with the average inhabitants of Buenos Aires is difficult because their reception is generally seen through the writings of activists and journalists. Shahid Amin has argued that the reception of the image of Mahatma Gandhi reflected and was shaped by "existing patterns of popular beliefs."[8] In Argentina one can make a similar argument that even though activists wrote party propaganda, the ideas that had an impact were those that fit within the worldview of the average inhabitant.

Language (and I would add symbols) were important. It helped shape what was possible. As Gareth Stedman Jones wrote (about political move-

    6. Daniel James, *Resistance and Integration: Peronism and the Argentine Working Class, 1946–1976* (Cambridge: Cambridge University Press, 1988), 14.
    7. Rosanvallon, *Le sacre du citoyen*, esp. 14, 60, 336, 346–47. In Argentina on paper, male suffrage had existed for a long time; what had changed was that votes really counted. There were real limitations to that suffrage—women and foreigners—but as Rosanvallon has shown, what is universal changes over time.
    8. Shahid Amin, "Gandhi as Mahatma: Gorakhpur District, Eastern UP, 1921-2," in *Selected Subaltern Studies*, ed. Ranajit Guha and Gayatri Chakravorty Spivak (New York: Oxford University Press, 1988), 288–342, esp. 316.

ments): "To be successful, that is, to embed itself in the assumptions of masses of people, a particular political vocabulary must convey a practical hope of a general alternative and a believable means of realizing it, such that potential recruits can think within its terms."[9] The Radicals were able to produce those ideas and symbols and build a fervent following.

Many of the themes that party propaganda stressed are summarized in a short film produced to help Yrigoyen get reelected in 1928. A silent film with a good deal of written material, the movie starts by stressing Yrigoyen's personal charity and then focuses on how the government under Yrigoyen helped orphans, weak children, and mothers; combated usury; and protected the working class. It finishes with a call for votes for Radicals and Yrigoyen because they helped the voter and his family.[10]

Yrigoyen made himself the center of the party. His very personalistic style allowed him to have his hands on all the levers of power. Certainly, one of the key reasons that the Radical Party fractured in the 1920s was the issue of Yrigoyen's dominance. Even the names of the factions, the Personalists (Yrigoyenists) and the Anti-Personalists (anti-Yrigoyenists), reflected the tensions created by the overly large role assumed by Yrigoyen.[11]

Because he does not fit any of the stereotypes about modern popular politicians, the adulation of Yrigoyen is difficult to explain. He limited his public appearances and spoke in public even less often. For example, when he went to Córdoba in 1915 to campaign for the Radical candidate for governor, Yrigoyen installed himself in a hotel and never made a public appearance.[12] He wrote relatively little and his writing is difficult to comprehend. Nevertheless, he became popular and remained so long after his death. His lack of visibility may have helped create the mystique that surrounded him. The Spanish kings of the seventeenth century saw a connection between majesty and invisibility.[13]

On the personal level, Yrigoyen had the ability to captivate people.

---

9. Gareth Stedman Jones, "Rethinking Chartism," in *Languages of Class: Studies in English Working Class History, 1832–1982* (Cambridge: Cambridge University Press, 1983), 96.

10. Film from the Archivo General de la Nación, generously provided to me by Donna Guy, Legajo 1962, tambor 1111, "Obra del gobierno Radical."

11. There were other issues involved, including desire for power and regional conflicts, as well as provincial interests and possibly class interests, because by 1928 the Personalists were more middle class than their rivals.

12. Félix Luna, *Historia integral de la Argentina: Los años de prosperidad* (Buenos Aires: Planeta, 1997), 8:234–35.

13. Peter Burke, *The Fabrication of Louis XIV* (New Haven, Conn.: Yale University Press, 1992), 184. I would like to thank Ariel de la Fuente for suggesting this book to me.

Ramón Columba relates that when a group of Anti-Personalist senators visited Elipidio González when he was vice president, he told them, "You know that if the 'doctor' [Yrigoyen] asked me, I would go naked through the streets. I would not hesitate in doing so."[14]

Despite his unusual style, Yrigoyen clearly fits the definition of charismatic as given by Edward Shils in his discussion of Max Weber:

> According to Weber's usage, charismatic quality may be attributed to religious prophets and reformers, to dominating political leaders . . . who by example and command indicate a way of life to their disciples. . . . Charismatic quality is attributed to expansive personalities who establish ascendancy over other human beings by their commanding forcefulness or by an exemplary inner state which is expressed in a bearing of serenity. . . . Charismatic persons . . . aspire to larger transformations. They seek to break the structures of routine actions and to replace them with structures of inspired actions which are "infused" with those qualities or states of mind generated by immediate and intensive contact with the "ultimate"—with the powers which guide and determine human life. The charismatic person is a creator of a new order as well as the breaker of a routine order.[15]

As we shall see, Yrigoyen saw the coming to power of the Radicals as a sharp break with the past and the new Argentina as a more virtuous nation.

The party focused its attentions on Yrigoyen, and the party apparatus continually glorified him. *La Epoca* constantly lauded him. For example, on the fourth anniversary of his assumption of office, it printed a series of letters praising his activities.[16] Yrigoyen had a hand in creating his own image; according to Manuel Gálvez, every morning the director or the chief editor of *La Epoca* came to his home. Yrigoyen at times submitted ideas for articles and even headlines for certain editorials.[17] One can safely assume that how he was presented reflected, at least in part, his own desires and his political judgment of what would play well to the electorate.

---

14. Ramón Columba, *El congreso que yo he visto* (Buenos Aires: Editorial Columba, 1988), 2:210.

15. Edward Shils, *The Constitution of Society* (Chicago: University of Chicago Press, 1982), 112–13.

16. *La Epoca*, October 20, 1920.

17. Gálvez, *Vida de Hipólito Yrigoyen*, 206, 264.

Yrigoyen was pictured as self-sacrificing and saintlike. It was well known that he lived austerely in a rented, old-fashioned home in a no-longer-stylish neighborhood. The house lacked heat until his last years. He arose early, went to bed early, and never went to the theater or parties. He ate simply, drank little, and wore dark suits, usually black, in the style of the 1880s. No one used the familiar form of address with him except friends from his youth, nor did he ever talk about himself. He never married, though he did have at least six children with several different women.[18]

An article in *La Epoca* the day after his first inauguration said that "the constant and fruitful action of the head of the Unión Cívica Radical doctor Hipólito Irigoyen, devoted in all moments of his life to the work of national reparation from a position of abnegation and sacrifice was like no other in the long trajectory of our agitated civic activities." According to the same article, when he reached the presidency "he did not arrive without effort . . . he arrives after having suffered, on the rough road, the cruelest tortures. He has suffered, without faltering, the acid test. He culminates a life of pain and bitterness and for this his triumph is an example and is a lesson. . . . Crusades are completed thus."[19]

La Epoca showed Yrigoyen to have borne persecution silently. Supposedly, during the interval between presidencies, men operating out of the police station on his block harassed him and even plotted to kill him. Also, the streetcar tracks were moved so that vehicles could not be parked in front of his house. All this he suffered without complaint.[20] He was, according to Antonio Herrero, "so far from the human and the ordinary, he is so severe and ascetic in his nature, based on a new mysticism that could be called a civic mysticism. He is so unusual and singular that even his language contains something biblical and of prophecy."[21]

References were frequently made to Yrigoyen as the apostle of the Radicals. Abraham Heller called him "defender of the humble, decided protector of the workers, of the people, from which springs the power and

18. "Hipólito Yrigoyen en al intimidad: Entrevistado por Luis Pozzo Ardizzi," *El Hogar*, June 13, 1930, in *Grandes entrevistas de la historia argentina, 1879–1988*, ed. Sylvia Saítta and Luis Alberto Romero (Buenos Aires: Aguilar, 1998), 98–102; Gálvez, *Vida de Hipólito Yrigoyen*, 7, 197–207; Felipe Cárdenas (h), "Ese enigmático conductor," in *Los radicales (I)*, ed. Félix Luna (Buenos Aires: Todo es Historia, 1976), 91–92.

19. *La Epoca*, October 13, 1916. It is interesting to note that in 1916 *La Epoca* still used the more traditional spelling of the name, Irigoyen.

20. *La Epoca*, November 17, 27, 1928, February 28, 1929.

21. Antonio Herrero, *Hipólito Yrigoyen: Maestro de la democracia* (La Plata: Talleres Gráficos Olivieri y Domínguez, 1927), 84.

authority of true democracies, Apostle of a noble and holy cause." Leopoldo Bard, describing his first meeting with Yrigoyen, says, "When I left Yrigoyen's house I understood that I had heard the word and shaken the hand of the Apostle of Radicalism."[22] The references to the New Testament are obvious but also perhaps misleading if taken too literally. Bard was Jewish. We have here an adaptation of language stripped of true religious connotation, paralleling the use by militantly atheistic Anarchists of the phrase "martyrs of Chicago." The Radicals had absorbed the Catholic vocabulary of the majority.

As Marcelo Padoan has pointed out, Yrigoyen was compared to Jesus. For example, Antonio Herrero wrote of Yrigoyen, "He, like a new Jesus, shielded by his life of conscientious patriotism, immaculate, irreproachable, disdainful of the slander and hatred of the opponent, has penetrated into the temple of the fatherland and has cast out with whip lashes the vile merchants, reestablishing on its throne, popular sovereignty and civil integrity."[23] Herrero also compared Yrigoyen's thinking to the spirit of Tao and to the philosophy of Lao-tzu.[24]

Yrigoyen became identified with the nation. In an article that first appeared in *La Voz de Quemú* of La Pampa, praise for Yrigoyen was made parallel with the words of the national anthem:

> To the name Yrigoyen, to "victory or death," the same as in the time of Independence. . . .
>
> Citizens! Triumphantly elect the presidential ticket of the Unión Cívica Radical, because it means country, honor and greatness, as in the stanzas of the National Anthem that adorns and runs the words Freedom, Freedom, Freedom. . . .
>
> Argentines! On your feet. . . . Hear the sacred cry of "Yrigoyen, Yrigoyen, Yrigoyen."

The Argentine anthem begins: "Mortals! Hear the sacred cry: 'Freedom! Freedom! Freedom!'"[25]

Yrigoyen is also presented as "the most noble protector of the working class," the "father of the workers," and the "first worker of the country."

22. *La Epoca*, October 26, 1927; Bard, *Estampas de una vida*, 118.
23. Herrero, *Hipólito Yrigoyen*, 83, as cited in Padoan, *Jesús, el templo*, 29.
24. Herrero, *Hipólito Yrigoyen*, 106.
25. *La Epoca*, December 15, 1927; http://www.answers.com/topic/argentine-national-anthem, 6/21/05.

The latter title is particularly interesting, as a similar title was bestowed by a leader of the Unión Ferroviaria, José Domenech, on Juan Perón in 1943 and is usually identified with Perón. In a *La Epoca* article on May Day a section entitled "Yrigoyen, Father of the Argentine Workers" said, "The native worker and the foreigner assimilate in the example of the Father of the Workers, the generous synthesis of patriotism that is persevering labor and civic respect for the national institutions. From these permanent preoccupations of the first worker of the country were born the improvements that today our proletariat enjoys and to whose moral and material elevation has dedicated his best days, Dr. Hipólito Yrigoyen."[26]

A connection existed with the humble. According to the Anarchist intellectual Diego Abad de Santillán, during his second term Yrigoyen walked to the presidential offices daily, greeting the neighbors and even at times the Anarchists as he passed. Propaganda had Yrigoyen winning a special place as president of the humble: "In every home of the humble, Dr. Yrigoyen has an altar in every heart."[27] Practically any public ceremony or Radical Party activity is described as overwhelmed by cheers for Yrigoyen.[28]

The role of charity and caring was highlighted. When Yrigoyen had been a teacher in the 1880s, he had given his salary to charity. Both times when accepting the nomination for president, he promised, if elected, to donate his salary to the Sociedad de Beneficencia, the government-sponsored charity that ran many institutions.[29] He refused his inheritance from Tomasa Alem, just as he refused all inheritances, so that the money could be used for her monument in the cemetery at Recoleta. During his second presidency, he gave forty thousand pesos of his own money to buy land in Humahuaca, Jujuy, to give to the local residents.[30]

On a much smaller scale, he played a role similar to that of Eva Perón in the 1940s. For example, on November 15, 1920, Yrigoyen arrived at the presidential office, the Casa Rosada, at noon. Shortly thereafter, he was informed by the police chief of the damage done by flooding in the working-class neighborhood of Nueva Pompeya, which frequently suffered in-

26. *La Epoca*, September 5, 1927, April 30, 1929; *El Obrero Ferroviario*, January 1944.
27. Diego Abad de Santillán, *Memorias, 1897–1936* (Barcelona: Planeta, 1977), 105–6. I would like to thank James Baer for supplying me with this information. *La Epoca*, October 20, 1928, and September 5, 1927. See also *La Epoca*, November 27, 1929.
28. See *La Epoca*, December 11, 1929, August 12, 1930, for examples.
29. *La Epoca*, February 13, 1918; *Documentos de Hipólito Yrigoyen*, 89; *La Epoca*, March 28, 1928.
30. *La Epoca*, April 10, 1929; Adriana M. Kindgard, "Procesos sociopolíticos nacionales y conflictividad regional: Una mirada alternativa a las formas de acción colectiva en Jujuy en la transición al peronismo," *Entrepasados* 11, no. 22 (principios de 2002): 78.

undations. He immediately set off to investigate the damage with the police chief and his secretary. Besides inspecting the flood damage and demanding that something be done to prevent further such incidents, he visited the local basilica as well as the church school connected to it. In a discussion with the rector of the school, he discovered that state support was small in proportion to the number of boys attending, and Yrigoyen immediately promised to increase it. In addition, learning that many boys did not come to school because they lacked shoes and that many present had worn-out shoes, Yrigoyen ordered the shops of the national penitentiary to provide new footwear, which he paid for out of his own funds.[31]

Yrigoyen pictured himself as close to the Catholic Church. According to Manuel Gálvez, Yrigoyen became the first Argentine president to invoke "God, Divine Providence and the Gospels in his official documents." Yrigoyen argued that congress should not be allowed to permit divorce; according to him, only a constituent assembly should be able to do such a thing.[32] Fairly consistent attempts were made to connect Yrigoyen to the Catholic Church through such things as his visit to the basilica and school in Nueva Pompeya mentioned above and the presence of Yrigoyen, his cabinet, and other high officials at the coronation of the Virgin of Rosario, for which he served as godfather.[33] During the 1928 reelection campaign of Yrigoyen, direct appeals were made to Catholic voters, including a flyer that said, "Remember the attitude of Yrigoyen condemning the project of divorce and sustaining the religious principles and the morals of the Argentine home? . . . Did you know that to achieve electoral support the opponents of Yrigoyen have promised to include in their programs divorce, separation of Church and State and other aggressions against the traditional sentiments of the Argentine people?"[34] *La Epoca* also gave a considerable amount of attention to Catholic attempts to form a labor movement. Nevertheless, although the impact on the average Argentine is unclear, the church hierarchy greeted Yrigoyen's overthrow warmly.[35]

31. *La Epoca*, November 15, 1920. The best discussion of Eva Perón is still Marysa Navarro, *Evita* (Buenos Aires: Corregidor, 1981).
32. Gálvez, *Vida de Hipólito Yrigoyen*, 324, as cited in Arturo Capdevila, "Primera presidencia de Yrigoyen," in Academia Nacional de la Historia, *Historia argentina contemporánea* (Buenos Aires: El Ateneo, 1965), 1:sección 2, 266, 267. The irony of opposition to divorce by a man who did not believe in marriage enough to marry the mother of any of his children is rather striking.
33. *La Epoca*, October 8, 1922.
34. *La Epoca*, January 25, 1928.
35. See, for example, *La Epoca*, August 4, 1920, March 17, 1922, September 5, 1927, April 26, 28, 1929, August 31–September 3, 1930; Zanatta, *Del estado liberal*, 25–31.

The Radical propagandists described Yrigoyen as extraordinarily hardworking: "In the Argentine Republic there is a man who works more than any other . . . even spending money in working for nothing. He is the only worker that is not paid and does not want to be paid. All are paid except him and he works more than the others. That man . . . is untiring. . . . He works and works continually, expending his well-being, his health and his life without asking for anything. . . . That singular worker . . . is your president, Don Hipólito Yrigoyen." During his second term, when stories about his senility circulated, the efforts to show him working hard redoubled. Almost every afternoon, the front page of *La Epoca* contained a listing of that day's work of the president. A not-atypical account went, "Until the time of the close of this edition, the President of the Nation still continued working in his office, exerting an extraordinary labor, not having even a single minute of rest during all of the afternoon."[36]

Yrigoyen is portrayed as the one who bestows rights on the Argentine people. In a manifesto drawn up by the Radical committees of two departments in Corrientes during a political campaign conducted under federal intervention, Yrigoyen gives people their rights: "In the great campaign that approaches, under the guarantees the illustrious chief Don Hipólito Yrigoyen will give us, the Unión Cívica Radical will fight for ideas and not for men." After presenting a program, the statement finishes with a call to fight for social, economic, and political betterment, "under the unstained banner of Argentine Radicalism, that is the party of day laborers and workers, of students and teachers, of honest men and democrats and that has no other head than the eminent American statesman Dr. Don Hipólito Yrigoyen."[37]

The defeat of the Anti-Personalists was shown as transforming the nation: "Moving beyond the year '28 and it seems that we will be separated not by a day but by a century from the ominous men and the indescribable things they did. . . . So great were the crimes and the horrors committed that still the new government has not been able to put the administration in total order."[38]

Lying behind these sentiments was the history of the Radical Party and that of Yrigoyen himself. The Radicals had stood above the political battle; they refused to soil themselves with the political world, which they believed was sordid. They alone stood for good politics and good electoral

36. *La Epoca*, March 28, 1918, February 28, 1929; see also April 10, 1929.
37. *La Epoca*, April 10, 1929.
38. *La Epoca*, December 31, 1928.

procedures. To a large extent it was perceived, and to a certain extent correctly so, that the opening of the political system was owed to the pressure applied by the Radicals. This caused them to have a large political capital when they came to power. They had not been besmirched by the practices of the old system, and the new system began because of their efforts. For example, an editorial in *La Epoca* in August 1920 spoke of the suffering that the party had to overcome: "A true way of the cross of patriotism that [the Radical Party] . . . had to support to follow the righteous path that it has traced, the injuries, the grave insults, the slander," and then the renewed republic brought a society in full liberty and admired by all.[39] Through the achievement of true male suffrage, the Radicals had renewed the country.

It is only during Alvear's presidency, as Yrigoyen readied himself to run for reelection, that we see the total elevation of Yrigoyen into a secular saint. In all probability as the presidential election approached and the break with the Anti-Personalists became definitive, less reason for restraint existed. Previously too much attention to Yrigoyen antagonized elements of the party, but when these broke with Yrigoyen, only those comfortable with his enlarged role remained. During 1927 and subsequent years we see a tighter focus on Yrigoyen in *La Epoca*. He becomes more than ever a larger-than-life figure who embodied patriotic virtues and had a special relationship with the worker. Although beginning during the presidential campaign of 1927–28, this intensified even further during his second presidency.[40] Poems of rather dubious quality sang his praises. This is a typical such poem, entitled "To the Great Argentine President Dr. Hipólito Yrigoyen."

> The Country adorns itself with your name triumphant,
> And the Fatherland praises you deservedly and with love,
> Because always, your slogan was forward!
> And your creed nobility, ideal and ardor.
>
> I that knew to mock the people a moment,
> Learned from your lips the best word,
> The word that says: a brilliant Fatherland
> I will leave as the inheritance of my effort and honor.

---

39. *La Eoca*, August 4, 1920. See also Alonso, *Between Revolution and the Ballot Box*; Félix Luna, *Yrigoyen* (Buenos Aires: Hyspamérica, 1986), esp. 196–268.
40. See, for example, *La Epoca*, January 19, 1929.

> The workers of all the Argentine region
> Today bless your name and the battle that culminates
> In the supreme progress of this immense Nation.[41]

What can explain the behavior and rhetoric of Yrigoyen? Some have posited the influence of the German philosopher Karl Christian Friedrich Krause, as propagated by the Spaniard Julián Sanz del Río. There are distinct parallels, including the idea of a movement identified with the nation. It is also probable that Yrigoyen's austere style was borrowed from that of the followers of Sanz del Río, who dressed in black and avoided cafes and theaters. Nevertheless, Yrigoyen did not promote the ideas of Krause nor call himself a follower of Krause.[42] The influence seems to be mostly stylistic rather than practical. Yrigoyen's style seems to fit his personality, and he appeared highly conscious of what seemed to appeal to the Argentine public.

Yrigoyen's role in expanding citizenship spoke to many. His carefully built image contributed to his popularity. His giving of charity, his supposed suffering, and his austere style spoke to the Catholic heritage of the country. Even those who were not actively Catholic had absorbed the imagery. Above all, Yrigoyen seemed to care for the average citizen, and that should not be underestimated.

It is difficult to find a political figure in Argentina of this period to compare to Yrigoyen. Perhaps the most obvious is Alfredo Palacios, a very different style of politician. A Socialist lawyer with bohemian tendencies, he was a charismatic figure in a more traditional sense. With the reputation as a great orator, he had luxurious and large mustachios and he wore his hat at an angle, frequently with a poncho over his shoulder. He had the reputation as a ladies' man; he fought duels and was nationalistic. He befriended men from all parties and served as a lawyer for the poor at no charge. He constantly gave money away. His independence and flair, however, limited his political impact. He was expelled from the Socialist Party in 1915 for agreeing to fight a duel and only rejoined the party in 1930. His splinter group, the Partido Socialista Argentina, did fairly well

41. *La Epoca*, March 14, 1929. For another example, see *La Epoca*, August 17, 1930.
42. Arturo Andrés Roig, *Los krausistas argentinos* (Puebla, Mexico: Editorial José M. Cajica Jr., 1969), esp. 168–69, 184, 223, 227; Karl Christian Friedrich Krause, *Ideal de la humanidad para la vida*, commentaries and introduction by Julián del Río, 2nd ed. (Madrid: F. Martínez García, 1871); Juan López Morillas, *El krausismo español: Perfil de una aventura intelectual* (Mexico: Fondo de Cultura Económica, 1956), esp. 54–55; Luna, *Yrigoyen*, 51–52.

in the 1916 and 1918 congressional elections; although Palacios did better than his fellow party members, even he failed to win a seat. In 1916 he received over thirty-three thousand votes, while the others on his slate obtained between seven thousand and nine thousand votes. A study has indicated that his support did not come from workers. Without a sizeable political apparatus, Palacios could accomplish nothing. Still, Palacios had enough charisma to reemerge as a major political figure in the 1930s and once again briefly in the 1960s.[43]

In some ways a better comparison to Yrigoyen—even if very different—was the popular poet Almafuerte (Pedro B. Palacios, 1854–1917). He constantly addressed his beloved *chusma* (rabble) and wrote about Christianity in an anti-Catholic manner. He lived alone and in poverty. He gave away much of his salary to the poor and did not go to parties. He constantly questioned authority and those who did not do as they should. His verses appealed to different groups. The young Radicals in the 1890s liked one, Anarchists liked another, and the Socialists liked a third. He had a deep impact on students and on the intellectual milieu of Anarchism and Socialism. Roberto Giusti, speaking of his student days at the beginning of the twentieth century, recounts a conversation in which a friend proposes that Almafuerte teach ethics and metaphysics at the university. The friend's reasoning was simple: "Because he is a great fellow who says bad words.... We need men like him." Alfredo Palacios speaking in the Senate in 1938 said, "Our great Almafuerte is a poet of the metaphysical type and of a character ethical and apostolic.... The pain of the many was his own pain; he loved the oppressed, the persecuted; he lived for them and died among them." A critic publishing in the 1960s compares him to Saint Francis of Assisi. Probably much more resonant of his impact was that the first plaza in the working-class suburb Berisso (outside of La Plata) was named for him in 1937 and a statue was erected to him there in 1943. According to Danny James's account, a working-class woman residing in Berisso, María Roldán, wrote a poem in 1947 that was greatly influenced by Almafuerte. His impact on the popular psyche was deep. The reasons why this man and his poetry spoke so well to so many are not easy to

43. See, for example, Víctor García Costa, *Alfredo Palacios: Entre el clavel y la espada* (Buenos Aires: Planeta, 1997); Columba, *El congreso que yo he visto*, 1:120–68; Walter, *The Argentine Socialist Party*, 74–78, 130–49; Darío Canton and Jorge Raúl Jorrat, *Elecciones en la ciudad, 1892–2001* (Buenos Aires: Instituto Histórico de la Ciudad de Buenos Aires, 2001), 2:219.

fathom.⁴⁴ But the image of inclusion, of suffering, of charity and austere living appealed to many, just as the image of Yrigoyen did.

In Uruguay and Chile the opening up and the "modernization" of the political systems during the first two decades of the twentieth century produced larger-than-life leaders who can be compared to Yrigoyen. Superficially José Batlle y Ordóñez of Uruguay (president 1903-7, 1911-15) resembled Yrigoyen. Symbolically their differences can be summed up by Batlle's action after the ceremony to hand over power to his successor in 1907. Unlike Yrigoyen when the crowd wanted to detach the horses from his carriage and pull it, Batlle refused to let them and left his carriage and walked home. Like Yrigoyen he developed a close relationship with elements of the union movement, supporting some strikes and even openly saying that workers had the right to strike. His support for labor, while inconsistent, appears to be more consistent than that of his Argentine counterpart. He did share with Yrigoyen an aversion to regularizing the relationship of unions with the state. Batlle also depended on a well-organized political party, the Colorados, and large-scale use of patronage. Patronage opportunities increased with the rapid expansion of the scope of the state, including the beginnings of a welfare system. Batlle had the advantage of leading one of the two traditional parties, although being the leader of a traditionally nonideological party meant that he always had powerful opposition within the organization. Nevertheless, the Colorados had been the dominant political party for decades prior to his presidency, and during his first term the opposition party, the Blancos, were crushed militarily.⁴⁵ Batlle had a clearer vision of the kind of society that he wanted Uruguay to be than Yrigoyen did for Argentina.

44. Almafuerte, *Obras completas* (Buenos Aires: Ediciones Antonio Zamora, 1954); Héctor Adolfo Cordero, *El profeta del hombre: Pasión de Almafuerte* (Buenos Aires: Julio E. Rossi e Hijos, 1958), esp. 30-31, 114-15; Roberto F. Giusti, *Visto y vivido: Anécdotas, semblanzas, confesiones y batalles* (Buenos Aires: Editorial Losada, 1965), 83; Alfredo L. Palacios, *Almafuerte* (La Plata: Universidad Nacional de La Plata, 1944), 8-9; Julio G. de Alari, *Almafuerte: Su vida y su obra* (Buenos Aires: Editorial "Agora," 1965), esp. 7; Ricardo Santiago Katz, *Almafuerte: Un maestro y periodista combativo* (La Plata: El Autor, 2005); Daniel James, *Doña María's Story: Life, History, Memory, and Political Identity* (Durham, N.C.: Duke University Press, 2000), 252-53.

45. Milton I. Vanger, *José Batlle Ordóñez of Uruguay: The Creator of His Times, 1902-1907* (Cambridge, Mass.: Harvard University Press, 1963), esp. 276; and *The Model Country: José Batlle Ordóñez of Uruguay, 1907-1915* (Hanover, N.H.: University Press of New England, 1980); Benjamín Nahum, *La época batllista: 1905-1930* (Montevideo: Ediciones de la Banda, 1975); Francisco R. Pintos, *Batlle y el proceso histórico del Uruguay* (Montevideo: Claudio García y Cía, n.d.); Mark Healey, *In the Spirit of Batlle: The Shaping of the Political Arena and the Great Uruguayan Exception*, Working Paper 21 (Durham, N.C.: Duke–University of North Carolina Program in Latin American Studies, 1996); Fernando López D'Alesandro, *Historia*

Arturo Alessandri opened up politics in Chile by breaking tradition with his personal campaigning, but the effectiveness of appeals to the working class was limited because illiterates lacked the vote. Still, his use of his magnetic personality and his speaking ability allowed him to win a tightly contested presidential election in 1920. Once in office he toured factories and spoke to workers. He also intervened in strikes on the side of workers. Like his counterpart in Argentina, as we shall see, despite these actions he faced a continuing wave of labor unrest and violence; only a little later than Yrigoyen did he lose patience with strikes and had them put down. Alessandri failed to achieve very much politically because of a stalemate with congress and opposition from key factions of the army. The resonance of his opening up of the political system and his personal flair and speaking abilities allowed him to cast a long shadow, despite a lack of political mooring. His political beliefs seemed to have been based to a large extent on what worked for him. He veered from traditional beliefs to a reformist stance and back to conservative positions. Still, due to his charisma and his role in opening up the political system, Alessandri was reelected to the presidency in 1932 and his son won the presidency in 1958. Alessandri fits the traditional image of a charismatic politician much better than does Yrigoyen.[46]

Beyond Yrigoyen's Image

The popularity of Yrigoyen and his party did not rest totally on image; it also depended on the concrete. The creation of ties between leaders and followers is a complex development that includes the material, the cultural,

---

de la izquierda Uruguaya (Montevideo: Ediciones del Nuevo Mundo, 1988), 2:primera parte; Carlos M. Rama, "Batlle y el movimiento obrero y social," in Batlle: Su vida, su obra, ed. Jorge Batlle (Montevideo: Editorial "Acción," 1956), 37–59; Ruth Berins Collier and David Collier, Shaping the Political Arena: Critical Junctures, the Labor Movement, and Regime Dynamics in Latin America (Princeton, N.J.: Princeton University Press, 1991), 273–88; Tulio Halperín Donghi, Historia contemporánea de América Latina, 13th ed. (Madrid: Alianza Editorial, 1990), 334–37; Juan A. Oddone, "The Formation of Modern Uruguay, c. 1870–1930," in The Cambridge History of Latin America, ed. Leslie Bethell (Cambridge: Cambridge University Press, 1986), 5:463–74.

46. See, for example, Simon Collier and William F. Sater, A History of Chile, 1808–1994 (Cambridge: Cambridge University Press, 1996), 202–14; Paul W. Drake, Socialism and Populism in Chile, 1932–52 (Urbana: University of Illinois Press, 1978), 45–55; Peter DeShazo, Urban Workers and Labor Unions in Chile, 1902–1927 (Madison: University of Wisconsin Press, 1983), 179–94; Ricardo Donoso, Alessandri, agitador y demoledor: Cincuenta años de historia política de Chile, 2 vols. (Mexico: Fondo de Cultura Económica, 1952–54).

and the ideological. As Ariel de la Fuente has stated in his excellent work on nineteenth-century caudillos, "The material exchanges took place in a context of emotional attachment and cultural identification between leaders and followers, a tie constructed, in part, through the representations the followers had of their caudillos."[47]

Yrigoyen and the Radicals called on the nationalism of their fellow citizens. In its campaigns, the Radical Party employed the country's semi-mythic past by using gauchos on horseback and similar images.[48] A key way of enlisting nationalistic sentiments was through Yrigoyen's independent stance on foreign policy. Particularly noteworthy was Argentina's pugnacious neutrality during World War I, in which Yrigoyen aggressively demanded that both sides take into account Argentina's interests, especially when faced with incidents arising from naval warfare. Yrigoyen also refused to allow Argentina to participate in the League of Nations unless all nations, including the defeated ones, were permitted to join. Argentina had an independent foreign policy and appeared to be standing up for itself.[49] Usually this nationalism did not descend into xenophobia, despite important exceptions, especially the events of the Tragic Week of 1919 and the massacres in Patagonia in 1921 and 1922. In both cases, foreigners became primary targets and scapegoats.

Nevertheless, both branches of the Radicals attempted to rally electoral support from various immigrant groups and their descendants, including Jews, Italians, Spaniards, and Syrio-Lebanese. For example, during the campaign of 1928 special committees of Jews were established to support the presidential candidates of both branches of Radicalism, including one committee whose mission was to publish a periodical.[50] The largely Span-

---

47. Ariel de la Fuente, *Children of Facundo: Caudillo and Gaucho Insurgency During the Argentine State-Formation Process (La Rioja, 1853–1870)* (Durham, N.C.: Duke University Press, 2000), 4.

48. See, for example, *La Epoca*, March 19, 1928, or August 30, 1930.

49. Roberto Etchepareborda, *Biografía, Yrigoyen/1* (Buenos Aires: Centro Editor de América Latina, 1983), 127–59; Luna, *Yrigoyen*, 225–39; Joseph S. Tulchin, *Argentina and the United States: A Conflicted Relationship* (Boston: Twayne, 1990), 34–42; Luis C. Alén Lascano, "El principismo argentino ante la primera guerra mundial," *Res Gesta* (Rosario) 37 (1998–99): 5–21; Carlos A. Goñi Demarchi et al., *Yrigoyen y la gran guerra* (Buenos Aires: Ediciones Ciudad Argentina, 1998); María Monserrat Llairó and Raimundo Siepe, *Argentina en Europa: Yrigoyen y la Sociedad de las Naciones (1918–1920)* (Buenos Aires: Ediciones Macchi, 1997). For some of the sentiments behind these policies, see exchange between Yrigoyen and Alvear in Halperín Donghi, *Vida y muerte*, 571–76.

50. See, for example, Cámara de Diputados, *Diario de sesiones*, v, December 22, 1922, 436; *La Epoca*, March 22, 31, June 1, 13, 26, July 15, 1922, June 24, July 27, August 22, October 28, November 25, 1927, January 5, 19, February 19, March 7–14, 25, 1928; *La Acción*, December 1–2, 1927. Also see Chapter 5.

ish small grocery store owners had a special relationship with the Radicals in Buenos Aires.[51] The contradiction between nationalism and appeals to the immigrant communities is less great than it first appears. The locally born children of foreigners tended to be proud Argentine patriots. The schools did a good job of inculcating nationalism. Most of the nationalistic appeals were not of the type that foreigners would necessarily find repellant.

Yrigoyen always tried to maintain personal contacts. For example, in 1920 he received a delegation of workers from the naval arsenal asking for higher wages. After talking with the head of the arsenal, the president promised that in the new budget they would receive increases. Similarly, he involved himself in an initiative of the Asociación Amateurs de Football to create a tournament with teams from both the capital and the interior by presenting a cup, "Copa presidente de la Nación," to be awarded to the victor. According to *La Epoca*, he did so because he was disposed to support all initiatives "intended to [increase] the patriotic ties of the Argentine people and maintain Argentineness." On a not unusual day in January 1929, he received three workers' delegations.[52]

Reliance on a personalistic approach, rather than a bureaucracy, can be seen in Yrigoyen's use of the police chiefs of Buenos Aires as his chosen intercessors with labor. Police chiefs served as his confidants, hearkening back to traditional practices in which police powers and political activity had combined. Yrigoyen had in his youth served as such a police commissioner. In a contemporary attack on the political system, Rafael Bielsa said, "The so-called police chiefs are not, in general, anything but *comisarios de campaña* [rural police commissioners] who act on a large scale but with the same organic vices and the same lack of competence as those others."[53] As we shall see, police chiefs regularly negotiated with unions. For example, a strike at the West Indian Oil Company refinery in Campana was ended with the help of both the *intendente* (mayor) and the police chief of Buenos Aires. Campana is more than fifty kilometers northwest from the city of Buenos Aires and therefore far outside their jurisdiction.[54]

51. Rock, "Machine Politics," 241–42; *La Vanguardia*, December 26, 1926.
52. *La Epoca*, November 17 and August 21, 1920; *La Prensa*, January 8, 1929.
53. Rafael Bielsa, *El cacique en la función pública: Patología política criolla* (Buenos Aires: Imprenta Nacional de Lajouane y Cía, 1928), 17.
54. *La Epoca* and *La Prensa*, January 5–12, 1921. See also *La Epoca*, October 27, 1922, and *La Prensa*, February 1, 1930. The role of the police did not end with the Radicals. Some railroaders made their first contact with Juan Perón through the police. Luis Monsalvo, *Testigo de la primera hora del peronismo* (Buenos Aires: Editorial Pleamar, 1974), 64–65.

The career path of Yrigoyen's confidant Elipidio González epitomizes the reliance on the police chief. He went from minister of war to unsuccessful candidate for governor of Córdoba; appointed police chief of Buenos Aires during the crisis of the Tragic Week of 1919, he held that position, except for a short interval, almost until his election as vice president. During Yrigoyen's second presidency, he was minister of interior. One of his predecessors, Julio Moreno, went from police chief of Buenos Aires to minister of war.[55]

The use of the police commander as a crucial political operator was not limited to the capital. For example, in 1929 in La Rioja Manuel Alfaro dominated one of the key Radical Party factions. He had come to the province with an intervention sent by Yrigoyen and had been made police chief of Famatina, where he built the base of his political power. He continued to depend on the aid of the national government. He began the election campaign in 1930 with twenty-five thousand pesos and thirty-eight jobs given to him by the national government.[56]

Key to the use of police chiefs as political operatives was a sense that power was individual and personalistic and not restrained by form. At the center of a web of personal connections was Yrigoyen himself, a man who had not forgotten his own experience as a police commissioner. Police chiefs mattered, and their importance had little to do with fighting crime. Direct involvement created personal linkages, favors that needed to be returned.

To what other concrete factors can we ascribe the popularity of Yrigoyen and the Radicals among sectors of the middle and working classes? The ill-defined concept of *obrerismo* was crucial. Opposition groups often used the term scornfully, but the tactic seemed to have resonated with its intended audience, the native-born popular classes. What was *obrerismo*? It was the idea that the Radicals, especially Yrigoyen, had a special relationship with the working class, though Alvear, or at least the Anti-Personalists, used the concept as well. Class relationships should not be based on conflict (unlike the idea in Socialism), but rather there existed a certain paternalism. Yrigoyen and his party gave the impression that they cared about the workers. This was the first time that the working class had been actively wooed from the seat of power. The nature of the appeals varied

---

55. Adolfo Enrique Rodríguez, *Historia de la policía federal argentina, 1916–1944* (Buenos Aires: Editorial Policial, 1978), 7:13, 35–36.

56. Ricardo Mercado Luna, *Los rostros de la ciudad golpeada* (La Rioja: Editorial Canguro, 1995), 15; Persello, *El partido radical*, 69.

over time, but what remained constant was the desire to keep the relationship ad hoc. No major attempt was made to formalize the relationship between either the state or the party and unions. Although proposals were initiated to legally define the relationship between unions and the government, the impression is left that no major effort to enact them was made.[57]

As we shall see in subsequent chapters, Yrigoyen depended on his personal ties to union leaders. These union leaders often met directly with Yrigoyen. This ensured a personal connection that frequently became a deep personal loyalty. Francisco García, the longtime leader of the Federación Obrera Marítima, worked well with Yrigoyen and remained loyal, despite efforts by the Anti-Personalist Radicals to woo him away. When García died in March 1930, the minister of interior and former vice president, Elipidio González, attended his wake, an unprecedented gesture in that period.[58]

Symbolic tokens of Yrigoyen's concern for the workers were important. He recognized them as components of the body politic. A delegation of the Sociedad Rural, which represented many of the largest landowners, went to see Yrigoyen about a strike in the meatpacking houses. The president did not receive them, and the establishment daily *La Nación* lamented that they had not received the same consideration as strike leaders, who when they come are received and sent away with strong attacks on the companies.[59]

Certainly, part of the *obrerismo* strategy was the reaction to strikes and to unions, discussed in subsequent chapters. Yrigoyen's tolerance of certain stoppages in the years prior to the general strike of mid-1921 was part of this tactic, as was his relationship with key labor organizations in later years. We can see the potential impact by sentiments expressed by politicians. A Personalist Radical deputy argued in August 1924, "On social matters, Dr. Irigoyen has made true radicalism, something like that attempted by radical socialism in France. And without going further, I remind the deputies of the left of his behavior with respect to the great maritime strike." We can also see it in the support for Yrigoyen by some unions through the September 1930 coup.[60]

In addition, gestures were made to the working class, some of which had only symbolic value, while others had significant impact. For example,

   57. See Chapters 4 and 5.
   58. See Chapter 4; and *Bandera Proletaria*, March 22, 1930.
   59. *La Nación*, December 19, 1917, as cited in Sidicaro, *La política mirada desde arriba*, 59.
   60. Cámara de Diputados, *Diario de sesiones*, v, August 29, 1924, 126; see Chapter 7.

after a large railroad accident in 1927, the unions organized a funeral for the workers killed. Alvear and his minister of public works, Roberto M. Ortiz, attended. Elipidio Gónzalez, the vice president, was also present, but his words indicated that he was not there as vice president: "I come in the name of the [Radical] Committee of the Capital . . . that recognizes as its only and indisputable head Dr. Hipólito Yrigoyen, great friend and enthusiastic and decided protector of the railroaders."[61]

The Radicals could claim, as did *La Epoca* in October 1917, that the conflict between capital and labor was taking place for the first time under the severe but impartial eye of the government. At times this kind of gesture could have a real impact. Herrero wrote that Yrigoyen replied to those asking that he use the army to end a railroad strike as follows: "That privileges have ended in the country and that from today onward the armed services of the Nation will not move except in defense of the honor and integrity [of the Nation]."[62] Also, the Yrigoyen administration helped set up an extensive consumer cooperative for employees of the state railroads.[63] These gestures had importance, indicating or attempting to indicate an interest in workers.

The attempts of the Radical Party and the government to alleviate some of the more immediate problems of the poor can also be labeled as *obrerismo*. World War I helped create both unemployment and inflation. Food prices soared 60 percent between 1916 and 1920; bread of the second quality cost twenty-three centavos a kilo in 1914 and forty-two centavos in 1920. The party and then the government took action. As early as 1913 the party sold bread (*pan radical*) for less money and of a lower quality than that commercially available. Even after the party came to power, its bread was sold in municipal markets and in bread stores owned by affiliates. The government arranged that wheat be made available to millers and flour to bakers at set prices; bread was sold throughout the country at thirty centavos a kilo. To block a sudden run-up of sugar prices, by decree the government blocked further exports of sugar, expropriated large quantities through legislative action, and removed tariffs on imported sugar. Sugar was sold to the public at low cost through sale at public markets and at police stations. The police tried to make sure that even the poorest received their fair share of the sugar. The government proclaimed its intervention

---

61. *La Acción,* July 18 and 19–27, 1927.
62. *La Epoca,* October 3, 1917; Herrero, *Hipólito Yrigoyen,* 104. See also *La Epoca,* December 27, 1917.
63. *La Epoca,* April 9, 1922, October 11, 1928, May 24, 1929.

in the sugar market with typical flair. Two-part posters appeared in Buenos Aires. In one part a worker was seated behind a plate with two sugar cubes. In the other the worker had before him a full sugar bowl. The legend on the poster declaimed, "Thanks to the action of the Radical Government the price of sugar dropped from 90 to 43 centavos a kilo."

Through pressure on manufacturers, the government obtained cheap shoes to sell. The *intendente* (mayor) of Buenos Aires arranged for the sale of inexpensive shoes and suits to municipal employees and initiated a consumer cooperative. He also offered overcoats for sale at reduced prices. He arranged to have cheaper meat brought into the city and worked to have prices posted in markets so that consumers could more easily find the best buys. In the minds of the Radical politicians, the political benefits outweighed the political costs in sugar-growing areas and elsewhere.[64]

Similarly, the government responded to rising rents in the capital and the accompanying political agitation. In 1916 the average monthly rent for a one-room apartment stood at 15.94 pesos, 21.14 in 1917, 28.66 in 1919, and 37.77 in 1920. In response, legislation passed in June 1921 froze all rents nationally for two years at the level of January 1, 1920.[65] It is difficult to judge the overall impact of these measures on the soaring costs of living, but clearly the combined weight of the gestures did not go unnoticed by the urban popular classes. In all probability these measures helped create an emotional bond between the popular classes and the Radicals.

The Radicals did use legislative gestures to win support. In both 1919 and 1921 the administration presented bills that would have regulated both unions and labor conflict. Neither made it out of committee. How serious were the Radicals? The legislation was unpopular with organized labor, and in 1919, the labor confederation FORA IX threatened a general strike. In 1921 the Radicals had a majority in the Chamber of Deputies but never

64. DNT, *Crónica mensual*, April 1922, 844; Ferreras, "Evolución de los principales consumos obreros," 162–65; *La Epoca*, April 17, 1917, August 6, 19–20, 1918, September 3, November 5–8, 1919, May 28–November 23, 1920, especially June 2, 14, July 3, 10, 13–23, August 18, 27, November 6, 8, 12; Walter, *Politics and Urban Growth*, 73; María Celia Bravo, "Cuestión regional: Azúcar y crisis cañera en Tucumán durante la primera presidencia de Yrigoyen," *Ruralia* 4 (October 1993): 53–54. Quotation from *Revista Azucarera*, no. 207 (1920): 89, as quoted in Bravo, "Cuestión regional," 58–59n36.

65. Ministerio del Interior, *Memoria del Ministerio del Interior presentada al honorable Congreso de la Nación, 1921–1922* (Buenos Aires, 1922), 531 (hereafter Ministerio del Interior, *Memoria year*); *La Epoca*, October 12, 1922; James A. Baer, "Buenos Aires: Housing Reform and the Decline of the Liberal State in Argentina," in *Cities of Hope: People, Protests, and Progress in Urbanizing Latin America, 1870–1930*, ed. Ronn Pineo and James A. Baer (Boulder, Colo.: Westview Press, 1998), 143–46; Walter, *Politics and Urban Growth*, 73.

got the legislation to the floor, indicating a lack of interest in doing so.[66] The Radicals demonstrated more interest in legislation intended for targeted audiences. For example, in 1919 the railroad worker pension plan was amended, with both the key unions and management supporting the changes, unlike the original scheme, which they had opposed. It was further amended in 1921 to create a fund to build houses for railroaders and in that way helped to alleviate the decided shortage of decent affordable housing.[67] The other major pieces of such legislation that passed were a 1921 pension law for workers in public utilities and a 1918 bill that attempted to control (largely unsuccessfully) work done at home in the capital. The Radicals proposed a flurry of labor legislation in 1921 and 1922, but despite what appeared to be intense interest from many sectors, none were approved during Yrigoyen's administration. A version of the large social welfare program initiated by Yrigoyen, but passed under Alvear, created a wave of protests from workers and employers alike. It was never successfully implemented, as we will see in Chapter 4.[68]

The Alvear administration, despite its problems with getting bills through congress, did have some success with labor legislation: a pension plan for bank employees, legislation forcing the payment of salaries in money and not goods, a law intending to protect women and children factory workers, and a law ending night work for bread bakers. In the second administration of Yrigoyen, a law was enacted that set the work day at eight hours.[69]

How effective these laws were intended to be is difficult to say. In 1926 the enforcement agency, the Departamento Nacional del Trabajo (DNT),

---

66. DNT, *Boletín*, November 1921, 9–89; Ministerio del Interior, *Memoria 1920–21*, 448–51; Ministerio del Interior, *Memoria 1921–22*, 346–458; Walter, *The Socialist Party*, 159–60, 168; Ernesto A. Isuani, *Los orígenes conflictos de la seguridad social argentina* (Buenos Aires: Centro Editor de América Latina, 1985), 98–108; Ricardo Falcón, "La relación estado-sindicatos en la política laboral del primer gobierno de Hipólito Yrigoyen," *Estudios Sociales* 4, no. 10 (primer semestre de 1996): 75–78, 84; Centro de Estudios, Unión para la Nueva Mayoría, *Composición de la Cámara de Diputados*, 2.

67. Isuani, *Los orígenes conflictos de la seguridad social*, 83–94; Paul Goodwin, *Los ferrocarriles británicos y la UCR*, trans. Celso Rodríguez (Buenos Aires: Ediciones La Bastilla, 1974), 173; laws 9.653, 10.650, and 11.173, *Anales de legislación argentina* (Buenos Aires: La Ley, 1942–53), 2:930–31, 1081–86, 3:82; Horowitz, "Occupational Community," 67–69.

68. Isuani, *Los orígenes conflictos de la seguridad social*, 99, 100, 122–23; José Panettieri, *Las primeras leyes obreras* (Buenos Aires: Centro Editor de América Latina, 1984), 78; Juan Guillermo Torres, "Labor Politics of the Radicalism in Argentina (1916–1930)," (Ph.D. diss., University of California, San Diego, 1982), 186–89; Cámara de Diputados, *Diario de sesiones*, 1921, 1922.

69. For a listing of such laws see, Luis Ramicone, *Apuntes para la historia: La organización gremial obrera en la actualidad* (Buenos Aires: Editorial Bases, 1963), 66.

complained that it had fewer resources, including employees, than it had had in 1914, despite having much more to do. The number of employees stayed the same between 1920 and 1927, but two sources differ on whether the DNT had more employees in 1914 or in 1929.[70]

The impact of legislation on workers' lives may have been limited, but the gestures remain important. The government gave the impression that it cared. The spirit of the Radicals can be seen by a speech given by Senator Pablo Torello, a Radical from Buenos Aires province: "I will say to the senator [Mario Bravo—Socialist senator from the capital] that the only hope that the workers of the country have today is in the constructive work that we did when we proposed and passed the railroad pension laws, those of the railroad pay scales [escalafones], that of the work day. . . . We were the only ones capable of beginning a policy of protecting the country's workers with the efficiency that is well known."[71] When Pedro Bidegain, the Radical boss of Buenos Aires's sixth ward, was feted at the end of his term in congress, he was praised as someone who dedicated himself to the problems of workers.[72]

The Radicals, and especially Yrigoyen, struck a chord with large sections of the populace. They would help when help was necessary, and they managed for many to identify the party with the nation itself. Yrigoyen created an image of himself as saintlike, generous, austere, sober, and concerned about the poor. His appeal is not necessarily apparent some eight decades later, but it was real enough. It spoke to millions. Why?

Emile Durkheim suggested that "we see society constantly creating sacred things out of ordinary ones. If it happens to fall in love with a man and if it thinks it has found in him the principal aspirations that move it . . . this man will be raised above the others and, as it were, deified." Barry Schwartz has argued that George Washington became such a great hero, even in his own times, because he personified the heroic archetype of his society. One can make a similar argument about Yrigoyen, though he probably had more of a hand in shaping his image than did Washington. Yrigoyen's austerity and charitable works appealed to the Catholic ethos that existed during this time when the influence of the church was grow-

70. Ministerio del Interior, *Crónica Informativa*, September 1926, 61; Néstor Tomás Auza, "La legislación laboral y la complejidad del mundo del trabajo: El Departamento Nacional del Trabajo, 1912–1925," *Revista de Historia del Derecho* 17 (1989): esp. 98–99; Hernán González Bollo, "Ciencias sociales y sociografía estatal: Tras el estudio de la familia porteña, 1889–1932," *Estudios Sociales* 9, no. 16 (primero semestre de 1999): 37.
71. *La Epoca*, July 31, 1929.
72. *La Epoca*, June 24, 1930.

ing.⁷³ The austerity also appealed to those influenced by the culture of Anarchism and Socialism. Yrigoyen also personally embodied the achievement of true citizenship and equality. In part his success was due to his sincerity. He seemed to think of himself in the terms in which he was described. Yrigoyen seemed to care about the average person, their nation, and at the same time appeared selfless. He also inspired pride. This gave the Radical Party a special place in the political landscape. The resemblance to the public discourse about Juan Perón is large, but Juan was never pictured as saintlike; that was reserved for Evita, but she was not abstemious. The Peróns built on the Radicals' rhetorical and symbolic traditions, but it is important to remember that the Radicals never controlled political discourse as the Peróns did.

Alvear

Alvear was a very different figure than Yrigoyen. The way he lived his life was far from austere. From an extremely rich family, he enjoyed his wealth and even while president continued to live a good life. He walked up the Avenida de Mayo to the Café Tortoni to hear poets, walked down the fashionable Calle Florida, and went swimming in Mar del Plata. According to Félix Luna, he attended massive numbers of official functions with the idea that it was a key part of a president's job. Alvear embodied the concept of Anti-Personalistic behavior. He maintained a hands-off style and allowed his ministers a great deal of discretion. Some have attributed this to a desire for a "European"-style government—that is, giving power to the cabinet ministers—but it is not at all clear what Alvear did much of the time.⁷⁴ Even in the columns of the supportive press, Alvear was not presented as being engaged in carrying out political activities for long periods. It is possible that he did much behind the scenes. Still, his cabinet ministers often worked at cross-purposes; it became difficult to discuss the administration's policy because there seemed to be more than one. It is not at all clear how much Alvear really wanted to govern.

73. Emile Durkheim, *The Elementary Forms of Religious Life* (New York: Free Press, 1965), 243–44, as quoted in Barry Schwartz, "George Washington and the Whig Concept of Heroic Leadership," *American Sociological Review* 48, no. 1 (February 1983): 21; see also 18–33; Roberto Di Stefano and Loris Zanatta, *Historia de la iglesia argentina: Desde la conquista hasta fines del siglo xx* (Buenos Aires: Grijalbo Mondadori, 2000), 354–407.

74. Korn, *Buenos Aires*, 128–29; Luna, *Alvear*, esp. 69–70; Cattaruzza, *Marcelo T. de Alvear*.

Alvear did prefer to use bureaucracies. In many senses Alvear could not use personalism. His base of support existed because he was willing to share power and because he was not Yrigoyen. Because both Alvear and Yrigoyen and their supporters came from the Radical Party, it is not terribly surprising that they shared ideas and ways of expressing themselves.

Some incidents of this have already been discussed. The Alvearistas also attempted to use *obrerismo*. Despite its reputation to the contrary, Chapter 6 will make it clear that the Alvear administration, in some areas, went much further than did that of Yrigoyen in attempting to create an ongoing relationship with labor, especially the railroaders. Efforts in other arenas, however, such as the port of Buenos Aires, were undermined by the contradictions within the administration. Nevertheless, the administration did attempt to build support through unions.

Like his predecessor, Alvear made gestures about caring for the popular classes. For example, after Alvear visited the state workshops along the Riachuelo River, he ordered that a plan be drawn up to build houses for the workers that would be rented to them at low cost.[75] Alvear met regularly with union delegations, though probably less frequently than Yrigoyen, because in many cases he left this to his cabinet members. For example, in 1927 he met with representatives of La Fraternidad, the railroad engineers' and firemen's union, and the railroad companies to help finalize an agreement on salary increases.[76] Alvear also decreed that May 1, Labor Day, was to be a holiday for government employees.[77]

Unlike the Personalists, however, the Anti-Personalists lacked a good grasp of the symbolic. When Alvear toured the Aguila factory that made coffees and chocolates, one of those who accompanied him was the head of the antiunion Asociación del Trabajo, Joaquín Anchorena.[78]

The Alvear administration, particularly while José Tamborini was minister of interior (1925–28), was not afraid of the big gesture that cost little but aimed at pleasing large numbers of the popular classes. The presidential pardon of Eusebio Mañasco is a good example. Mañasco, the leader of a union representing workers on the mate plantations in San Ignacio, Misiones, had been sentenced to life imprisonment for the murder of an

---

75. *La Acción*, November 2, 1923.
76. *La Acción*, August 26, 1927; *La Epoca*, August 26, 1927; *El Obrero Ferroviario*, September 1, 1927. See, for other examples, *La Confraternidad*, August, December 1923.
77. Mariano Ben Plotkin, *Mañana es San Perón: Propaganda, rituales políticos y educación en el régimen peronista (1946–1955)* (Buenos Aires: Ariel Historia Argentina, 1993), 83.
78. *Boletín de Servicios*, November 20, 1923, 584.

Allan Stevenson in 1921. Mañasco's supporters claimed that he had been convicted on the basis of coerced testimony. In 1927 the USA, the Syndicalist labor confederation, launched a campaign to pressure the supreme court to overturn the sentence or to have Alvear issue a pardon. Agitation became intense and mixed with that against the execution of Nicola Sacco and Bartolomeo Vanzetti in Massachusetts. Almost the entire Left joined the campaigns, and a giant rally was held in February. The Anti-Personalist political apparatus clearly favored freeing Mañasco. The coverage in *La Acción,* the Anti-Personalist daily, was favorable to freeing him and a pardon appeared almost inevitable once the supreme court only reduced his sentence. A convention of Anti-Personalists of the capital pressed for a pardon. Alvear received a delegation from the USA, and they asked that a pardon be granted along with the traditional ones given on Independence Day, July 9. After leaving, the delegates expressed their certainty that Mañasco would be freed. There was some talk of a general strike, but *La Acción* claimed that "the workers of the country have a profound faith in the president. It is not a case of idolatrous and sentimental devotion that would turn out to be depressing for its unconditionalism but an act of justice, thoughtful and serene, based on the tranquil analysis of the leader's work." On the eighth, the freeing of Mañasco made the front page of *La Acción* and the Anti-Personalists continued to milk the situation. On the thirteenth, *La Acción* described Mañasco's visit to the paper and displayed two photographs of him surrounded by its employees. The paper claimed that the Anti-Personalists "are not indifferent to the worries and desires of the laboring masses." The Communists responded more cynically (and more accurately); they viewed the pardon as *obrerismo,* done with the hope of collecting votes in the upcoming presidential election. They also saw the hand of Leónidas Anastasi, the head of the Anti-Personalist apparatus in the capital and the former lawyer of the shipboard workers' union, as behind the pardon. Whatever the role of Anastasi, the accusation was correct, especially because *La Acción* stressed that Mañasco would not be a Communist Party candidate in the elections but would continue to support the USA.[79]

79. *La Vanguardia,* December 27, 1926; *La Acción,* February 12–July 13, 1927, esp. February 12–25, May 3, June 29, July 1–13; *La Internacional,* April 9, July 9, 16, 1927; *Bandera Proletaria,* July 9, August 17, September 3, 1927; Marotta, *El movimiento sindical,* 3:226–40. Possibly there existed a role for Mexican diplomacy as well. Pablo Yankelevich, *Miradas australes: Propaganda, cabildeo y proyección de la Revolución Mexicana en el Río de la Plata, 1910–1930* (Mexico City: Instituto Nacional de Estudios Históricos de la Revolución Mexicana, 1997), 333.

From April through August 1927 large-scale agitation roiled Argentina as workers protested the pending execution of Sacco and Vanzetti. A series of general strikes was called, despite the lack of cooperation between various elements of the Left. Still, unions and left-wing organizations tapped something heartfelt. The autobiography of José Peter, a key Communist leader among the meatpackers in the 1930s and 1940s, makes clear that his participation in this movement radicalized him. The Anarchist José Grunfeld had a similar experience. One could undoubtedly multiply these experiences. From the point of view of the Anti-Personalists, the agitation presented a minor opportunity because they could do nothing about the fate of Sacco and Vanzetti. The strikes were tolerated. According to *La Prensa,* directly prior to the general strike of August 10 the police chief met with union leaders just to urge them to call for serenity in the demonstrations. *La Acción* seemed sympathetic, even indicating that it might favor a boycott of American goods. A cartoon that appeared on August 5 suggested that Alvear had a better idea than the governor of Massachusetts, implying that the pardon of Mañasco was the example to follow.[80]

The Alvear administration's *obrerista* ideas were at least partially undermined by its staffing. Many of those around Alvear—Leopoldo Melo, friend and Anti-Personalist presidential candidate in 1928; Foreign Minister Angel Gallardo; Naval Minister Manuel Domencq García; and the *intendente* of Buenos Aires, Carlos Noel—were conspicuous members of the Liga Patriótica, a militant right-wing, antilabor group. Alvear even appointed Manuel Carlés, the leader of the organization, to be the interventor of the Province of San Juan. Noel had also been active in the antiunion Asociación del Trabajo since its founding, and after his appointment as *intendente* the association offered a banquet in his honor in the upper-class bastion of the Jockey Club. Many in the union movement found these ties disquieting and even occasionally denounced them. The memberships complicated the administration's relationships with labor leaders.[81]

80. *La Prensa,* April 1–September 1927, esp. August 10; *La Epoca,* April 1–September 1927; *La Acción,* April 1–September 1, 1927, esp. August 4–11, September 1; *Bandera Proletaria,* June 5, 1926, April 16–September 3, October 22, 1927; *La Chispa,* August 21–September 15, 1927; *La Confederación,* July, August 1927; José Peter, *Crónicas proletarias* (Buenos Aires: Editorial Esfera, 1968), 34–45; José Grunfeld, *Memorias de un anarquista* (Buenos Aires: Nuevohacer, 2000), 93.
81. Luis María Caterina, *La Liga Patriótica Argentina: Un grupo de presión frente a las convulsiones sociales de la década de '20* (Buenos Aires: Corregidor, 1995), 90–91, 285; Sandra McGee Deutsch, *Counterrevolution in Argentina, 1900–1932: The Argentine Patrotic League* (Lincoln: University of Nebraska Press, 1986), 103, 185–86; Molina, "Presidencia de Marcelo T. de Alvear," 341; *Boletín de Servicios,* November 20, 1922, 533; *Bandera Proletaria,* February 21, 1925; *La Unión del Marino,* December 1922, March 1923.

Alvear never attempted to create personal popularity. Although there were efforts to build political support among the popular classes, these did not fare particularly well. Despite real improvements in working conditions in certain industries and an overall good economy, Yrigoyen and his allies crushed the Anti-Personalists in the 1928 elections. A contributing factor to the Personalists victory lay in their opponents' inability to grasp the importance of the symbolic.

Rejection of the Opposition

A crucial element of the political culture of all elements of the Radical Party was their unwillingness to accept opposition forces as truly legitimate. This contributed to the military coup of September 1930 because the unwillingness to accept opponents grew as the Radicals came closer to controlling all branches of government.[82] Despite operating within a democratic system, the Radicals viewed all opposition as unpatriotic. Only they understood the nation and strived for its betterment. They constructed a vision of the political system that portrayed themselves as true representatives of the people; opposition forces were portrayed as the other. A Radical Party manifesto of March 1916 proclaimed, for example, "The Unión Cívica Radical is the Nation itself, struggling for twenty-six years to free it from usurper and regressive leaders. It is the Nation itself and for being so, all those who fight for the elevated ideas that animate its goals fit within it."[83] Or in the manifesto announcing the return to electoral participation in 1912, "The Unión Cívica Radical being the genuine expression of citizenship in its most sacred desires and aspirations, all well intentioned citizens ought to identify with it, in all activities and unite under its banners, increasing their ranks until they overcome the many obstacles that oppose the freeing of the republic from so many troubles and oppressions."[84]

The Yrigoyenist paper, *La Epoca,* referred during the 1928 presidential campaign to the key opposition (the Anti-Personalists) as the "traitors." During the same campaign, the Personalist senator for Santa Fe, Armando

---

82. See the argument on the causes of the coup in Smith, "The Breakdown of Democracy," 3–27.
83. "Manifesto de la Unión Cívica Radical al pueblo de la República," March 30, 1916, as reprinted in Halperín Donghi, *Vida y muerte,* 559.
84. Horacio A. Varela and José Camilo Crotto, "Al pueblo de la República," August 30, 1912, in *Documentos de Hipólito Yrigoyen,* 45.

Antille, proposed that the Anti-Personalists' heads should be placed on pikes, clearly a reference to the events in Argentina during the dictatorship of Juan Manuel de Rosas in the first half of the nineteenth century. The Anti-Personalists (part of the same rhetorical tradition) replied in kind. Discussing a provincial election in Entre Ríos in 1927, *La Acción* referred to the Personalists as "slaves," implying that they were subservient to Yrigoyen.[85] In the final days of the 1928 presidential campaign, *La Acción* printed attacks on the mental health of Yrigoyen, calling him senile. On the day before the election, the paper characterized the choices as follows: "Order, peace and work are the themes that embody the ticket of the Unión Cívica Radical [Anti-Personalists]. . . . Demagoguery, scandal and corruption is the program of the Personalist horde [montonera] [Yrigoyenist]."[86] Clearly, here is a world in which the concept of loyal opposition does not exist. Only we (whichever group of Radicals is speaking) truly represent the nation.

Conclusion

Yrigoyen and his faction of the Radical Party built tremendous popular support around the figure of Yrigoyen himself. For many, he did become an almost saintlike figure to whom Argentina owed full democracy and dignity. He protected the worker and cared about all Argentines. Despite his unconventional style, he did have charisma. Upon his death *La Voz del Interior*'s headline proclaimed, "The Supreme Star of Democracy Has Concluded Its Magnificent Arc." Underneath it proclaimed, "Great Personage of Democracy and Liberty, Without Fear, Without Stain, and Without Blemish."[87]

---

85. *La Epoca*, April 11, 30, 1928; Padoan, *Jesús, el templo*, 32–33; *La Acción*, June 6, 1927.
86. *La Acción*, January 23, 24, March 25, 31, 1928. *Montoneras* were the irregular forces so common in the civil wars of the nineteenth century. The term was being used as an insult here.
87. *La Voz del Interior* (Córdoba), July 4, 1933. I would like to thank Fernando Rocchi for providing me with this edition.

THE LIMITS OF PATRONAGE

Clientelism and the hiring of supporters have been seen as essential to the popularity of Yrigoyen, both by contemporary observers and by later historians.[1] The Radicals, both Personalists and Anti-Personalists, hired their followers in large numbers. The question remains, however, whether we can ascribe a significant portion of Yrigoyen's popularity to this practice. Undoubtedly, it contributed, but, for example, was it sufficient to overcome the memory of the slaughter of workers during the Tragic Week of January 1919? The importance of clientelism in producing Yrigoyen's popularity is questionable. Despite a reputation of abstaining from large-scale patronage, the Anti-Personalists behaved similarly to the Personalists, but the Anti-Personalists failed to achieve mass popularity.

Despite myths to the contrary, employment mania and the spoils system did not begin or end with the Radicals. Ariel Yablon has shown that patronage was crucial in obtaining jobs in the 1880s.[2] As early as 1910, *La Nación* criticized the Conservative government for engaging in "Empleomanía." There were too many employees and costs were too high. The following year landowners in the Province of Buenos Aires complained that in the Conservative provincial government "funds are devoted to patronage, subsidies, pensions, exorbitant official salaries, etc."[3] These are words that could easily have been written later in reference to the Radicals. In 1918 *La Prensa* blamed the spoils system on President Roque Sáenz

---

1. The classic argument is in Rock, *Politics in Argentina*.
2. See, for example, Ariel Yablon, "Patronage and Party System in Buenos Aires, 1880–1886" (paper delivered at the Conference on Latin American History, 2005).
3. Sidicaro, *La política mirada desde arriba*, 27; quotation from *Review of the River Plate*, October 20, 1911, 1009–10, taken from Hora, *The Landowners*, 125.

Peña but claimed that in Yrigoyen's first year he refrained from behaving similarly, although in 1918 he laid off a large number of customs workers for partisan reasons. In 1925 *La Nación* claimed that before 1916 to get a job one only needed the help of an influential person.[4]

Giving jobs helped provide workers for the Radical machine's electoral efforts, but it is difficult to give it credit for much more than that. An examination of the scope and the context for clientelism makes this clear.

Bosses and Machines

Urban political machines developed in response to several kinds of interlocking needs. The rise of political participation created a desire among elites to find ways to mobilize voters belonging to the lower-middle and working classes in nonthreatening fashions.[5] They wanted to tie the voters to the party and in that way achieve political success. The potential voter had desires as well. In societies in which steady, well-paying jobs were in short supply and in which the government was a crucial and attractive source of employment, the political boss or patron became a good source of jobs. Some authors have argued that political client-patron relations take place only in peripheral or semiperipheral states and not in industrialized countries. Clearly this is not the case, because the industrial Chicago of Upton Sinclair's *The Jungle* or of Mayor Richard J. Daley had political bosses and client-patron relationships.

Political bosses appeared where there was rapid urban growth, little stability, and groups that felt excluded from society. They provided jobs. As Simon Sabiani, a political boss of Marseille, said, "I will hire my friends!" The political patron also intervened with the faceless bureaucracy for those who lacked the ability or the confidence to do it themselves (for example, getting someone released from jail for a minor infraction).[6]

---

4. *La Prensa*, March 1, 1918; *La Nación*, January 28, 1925.
5. Nicos Mouzelis, "On the Concept of Populism: Populist and Clientelist Modes of Incorporation in Semi Peripheral Politics," *Politics and Society* 14 (1985): 332.
6. For the quote, Paul Jankowski, *Communism and Collaboration: Simon Sabiani and Politics in Marseille, 1919–1944* (New Haven, Conn.: Yale University Press, 1989), 69; Luigi Graziano, "Patron-Client Relationships in Southern Italy," *European Journal of Political Research* 1, no. 1 (March 1973): 4–5; P. A. Allum, *Politics and Society in Post-war Naples* (Cambridge: Cambridge University Press, 1973), 10, 209; Alex Weingrod, "Patrons, Patronage, and Political Parties," *Comparative Studies in Society and History* 4 (July 1968): 383; Amy Bridges, *A City in the Republic: Antebellum New York and the Origins of Machine Politics* (Cambridge: Cambridge University Press, 1984), 132–37; S. N. Eisenstadt and L. Roniger, *Patrons, Clients, and Friends: Interpersonal Structure of Trust in Society* (Cambridge: Cambridge University Press, 1984), 191; Upton Sinclair, *The Jungle* (1906; repr., New York: Bantam, 1981);

Patronage became important in big-city politics, from Chicago to New York to Marseille, in the late nineteenth and early twentieth centuries. As in Buenos Aires, public employment offered stability in a world where there was little. In addition, cities grew very fast and needed numerous workers to provide even minimally acceptable living conditions. Increasing attention was being paid to public health. In our worry about the pollution produced by the automobile, we forget the mess left by its predecessor, the horse, which made street cleaning in the summer a necessity, not a luxury. Therefore, aside from political demands, there existed extremely practical needs at the urban level. Because Buenos Aires was the national capital, political bosses in the city also could place people in the rapidly expanding workforce of the national government. The opportunity for vast exercises in patronage was created by the lack of effective civil service systems. In Argentina, there are indications that bosses could provide jobs in the private sector, although little solid information exists. According to Marcela Ferrari, just prior to the Radical era in the city of Zárate, the Conservative boss obtained jobs for his followers in local factories. In sectors in which the government had a large role, such as public utilities, it is likely that bosses would have the ability to place people.[7]

Client-patron relationships help to explain hierarchical arrangements in which a certain level of reciprocity exists. What was reciprocal in all this? The patron (boss) offers a job, intervention with the bureaucracy, or material help and in return the client gives his vote and general support. As William Foote Whyte explained about the North End of Boston, which he called Cornerville, "The Cornerville political organization can best be described as a system of reciprocal personal obligations. . . . Everyone recognizes that when a politician does a favor for a constituent, the constituent becomes obligated to the politician." It is a reciprocal, if uneven, relationship. As one of Whyte's informants said, "A Republican governor will probably be elected this fall, and, in that case, if the Republicans in Cornerville make a good showing, the workers will get taken care of."[8] The

---

Mike Royko, *Richard J. Daley of Chicago* (New York: Dutton, 1971); John M. Allswang, *Bosses, Machines, and Urban Voters*, rev. ed. (Baltimore: Johns Hopkins University Press, 1986).

7. Marcela P. Ferrari, "Los que eligen. Colegios electorales y electores en tiempos de la 'República verdadera,' 1916, 1922, 1928," *Estudios Sociales* 24 (primer semestre de 2003): 53. According to de Privitellio, *Vecinos y ciudadanos*, 225, Arturo Jauretche said in his interview in the Instituto Di Tella Oral History Program that private companies were important sites for patronage.

8. William F. Whyte, *Street Corner Society: The Social Structure of an Italian Slum*, 4th ed. (Chicago: University of Chicago Press, 1993), 240, 86. Although the political culture that Whyte describes may seem far from that of Buenos Aires, I suspect that it was less far than one might suspect. Most of the people he observed were first-generation Italian Americans

clientele provided votes and support in return for favors. Support could mean many things but probably included joining the party, attending at least some meetings, and helping with election preparations. Although we do not have a great deal of direct evidence of this in Buenos Aires, this type of obligation helps explain the extraordinary turnouts noted by David Rock in the internal elections inside the Radical Party in the 1920s. In 1927, sixty thousand people voted in internal election in Buenos Aires. It was just ten thousand fewer votes than the Radicals had won in municipal elections the previous year.[9] Numerous people received jobs from the Radicals, and their presence would be noted. This relationship was, of course, hierarchical and asymmetrical, because the boss held most of the cards; he could give that job to someone else.

The subaltern part of this relationship did not lack resources. Voting was secret and debts owed to the local caudillo, the ward heeler, did not necessarily translate into votes for a candidate. As a local party boss exclaimed in Montevideo, "I have obtained at least 50 pensions; I have gotten many people out of jail; I have obtained the installation of at least 30 telephones; and have helped at a minimum 30 or 40 people get jobs. But if they have all voted for us that I don't know. As you know people are very ungrateful."[10] This observation on completing the reciprocity is not unique.[11]

In the first decades of the twentieth century, political bosses in Buenos Aires bore little resemblance to their counterparts in traditional rural regions. A patron in a traditional rural economy is endowed with a degree of deference and a wider control of economic resources than an urban political boss in a twentieth-century city could have. In cities, alternate sources of power exist, as do other sources of jobs. In addition, in rural areas the patron uses his or her wealth as the base of their power, though

---

and therefore of a familial background not dissimilar to many in Buenos Aires. Also see Gardenia Vidal, "Los partidos políticos y el fenómeno clientelístico luego de la Ley Sáenz Peña: La Unión Cívica Radical de la Provincia de Córdoba, 1912–1930," in *La construcción de las democracias rioplatenses: Proyectos institucionales y practicas políticas, 1900–1930*, ed. Fernando J. Devoto and Marcela P. Ferrari (Buenos Aires: Editorial Biblos, 1994), esp. 190–91.

9. Rock, "Machine Politics," esp. 251; Ismael Bucich Escobar, *Buenos Aires ciudad* (Buenos Aires: Editorial Tor, 1936), 217–18. Rock sees the large participation as a sign of deep involvement and the decentralization of the party. I am not sure that this is true; the large number of participants might have been just fulfilling their clientelistic duties.

10. Germán Rama, *El club político* (Montevideo: ARCA, 1971), as cited in Francisco Panizza, "El clientelismo en la teoría contemporánea," *Cuadernos del CLAEH* (Montevideo), April 1988, 69.

11. See, for example, Whyte, *Street Corner Society*, 163, 169.

the possibility of tapping state power exists. Urban political bosses are part of a larger entity, a political party, and they have a finite goal, electoral victory, from which wealth and power flow. Their strength comes from success in political mobilization, the delivery of votes, and their power rests on access through their party to the state.

The role of urban political bosses, in at least some areas in Latin America, also differed from those in the Buenos Aires of the Radicals. In Rio de Janeiro in the 1920s patronage was essential to politics and the mayor was a presidential appointment, just as in Buenos Aires. Voter turnouts were low, however, fraud was still a problem, and no political parties existed. Politics was extraordinarily hierarchical. Bosses seemed to control their votes and did it in large part through the giving of jobs. Bosses almost always held elective office or senior government jobs. Things were more complex in Buenos Aires from 1916 to 1930. Parties played a crucial role; more opportunities existed for finding help in the complex civil society; and economic opportunities were greater. The availability of nongovernmental jobs is what differentiates the Buenos Aires of Yrigoyen and Alvear from the patronage networks described in greater Buenos Aires in recent years.[12]

The Radical urban bosses' role resembled that of their counterparts in the United States and southern Europe, providing jobs and services in return for political support. The political system in which the Argentines operated differed, as did the nature of their clientele, but to a large extent the nature of the job was similar. Where the role of the political boss in Buenos Aires differed most from that of their urban counterparts in other countries is in the scope of the opportunities available to them. The same

---

12. For differentiating traditional clientelism from its more modern, urban variety, see, for example, Ernest Gellner, "Patrons and Clients," in *Patrons and Clients in Mediterranean Societies*, ed. Ernest Gellner and John Waterburg (London: Duckworth, 1977), 5; Graziano, "Patron-Client Relationships," 20–22; Luigi Graziano, *A Conceptual Framework for the Study of Clientelism*, Western Societies Program, Occasional Paper no. 2 (Ithaca, N.Y.: Center for International Studies, Cornell University, 1975), esp. 23–31; Weingrod, "Patrons, Patronage, and Political Parties," 380–81; Wayne A. Cornelius Jr., "Contemporary Mexico: A Structural Analysis of Urban Caciquismo," in *The Caciques*, ed. Robert Kerr (Albuquerque: University of New Mexico Press, 1973), esp. 140. For a discussion of the centrality of patronage in Latin America, see Richard Graham, *Patronage and Politics in Nineteenth-Century Brazil* (Stanford, Calif.: Stanford University Press, 1990). For Rio, see Michael L. Conniff, *Urban Politics in Brazil: The Rise of Populism, 1925–1945* (Pittsburgh: University of Pittsburgh Press, 1981), 60–77. For modern greater Buenos Aires, see Javier Auyero, *Poor People's Politics: Peronist Survival Networks and the Legacy of Evita* (Durham, N.C.: Duke University Press, 2001); Steven Levitsky, *Transforming Labor-Based Parties in Latin America: Argentine Peronism in Comparative Perspective* (Cambridge: Cambridge University Press, 2003).

party always ran the municipal government and the national government, because the president appointed the *intendente* or mayor. *Intendentes* had the right to make all municipal appointments.

Political bosses in Buenos Aires did operate in a competitive atmosphere in which there were numerous suitors for their clientele. The citizens of Buenos Aires had options in finding help, in giving their loyalty, or in establishing a larger identity. Ethnic organizations—mutual aid societies and the like—proliferated. As Leandro Gutiérrez and Luis Alberto Romero have demonstrated, in the 1920s an array of neighborhood institutions flourished and offered the Buenos Aires resident aid and a sense of belonging. Fans or members of soccer clubs—such as River Plate, the Boca Juniors, and myriad others—could claim an identity beyond that of their street or family.[13] Labor unions also offered a sense of identity. Anarchists and Socialists created an alternative cultural world for their members.[14]

Although political organizations had delivered votes prior to the opening of the political system, the Radicals needed to create their own machine once they had their hands on the levers of power. Moreover, the nature of the process had changed. Voters had to be convinced to go to the polls and vote for a specific party.

Slightly over a month after assuming the presidency, Yrigoyen appointed as *intendente* of Buenos Aires the president of the Radical Party's organization in the city. Simultaneously, he appointed a special twenty-two-person city council whose members were important party functionaries in each of the twenty wards into which the city was divided. The party apparatus had become the municipal government.[15]

In the city of Buenos Aires, and across most of the nation, the Radical Party was extraordinarily well organized. In the city, each ward had its own committee and many had subcommittees as well. The party sponsored libraries and cultural activities. Ties were forged with community organizations. The amount of activity that each ward committee carried out in

13. For an example of the work done by Leandro Gutiérrez and Luis Alberto Romero, see *Sectores populares*. See also Privitellio, *Vecinos y ciudadanos*, 107–47; Juan Suriano, "Vivir y sobrevivir en la gran ciudad: Hábitat popular en la Ciudad de Buenos Aires a comienzos del siglo," *Estudios Sociales* 4, no. 7 (segundo semestre de 1994): 62–63.
14. See, for example, Dora Barrancos, *Anarquismo, educación y costumbres en la Argentina de principios de siglo* (Buenos Aires: Editorial Contrapunto, 1990), and *La escena iluminada*; Suriano, *Anarquistas*; Ricardo O. Pasolini, "Entre la evasión y el humanismo: Lecturas, lectores y cultura de los sectores populares: La Biblioteca Juan B. Justo de Tandil, 1928–1945," *Anuario del IEHS* 12 (1997): 373–401; Privitellio, *Vecinos y ciudadanos*, 81–82.
15. Privitellio, *Vecinos y ciudadanos*, 48–49.

periods between electoral campaigns varied tremendously, depending on the leadership. A crucial function of the committees was to organize the propaganda for elections. With radio still in its infancy, electoral campaigns were labor intensive. Campaign workers needed to place posters on walls, canvass voters, and organize demonstrations.

As had been true prior to 1912, election campaigns provided a type of diversion. At a time when little cheap entertainment existed for the popular classes, electoral campaigns provided just that, along with information on public affairs. All parties carried out similar activities, but the Radical Party's campaigns were larger, more complex, and therefore had more entertainment value. Perusal of *La Epoca* during any campaign shows a roughly similar set of activities. By describing briefly a few events toward the end of the March 1919 campaign for a senator and two seats in the Chamber of Deputies, we can get some idea of their potential role in people's lives. For example, the sixteenth ward, Belgrano, announced street rallies for Wednesday, Thursday, and Friday at 9 P.M. with four different speakers each time. On Saturday the rally was indoors in the hall of the Sociedad Italiana and the crowd was to be addressed by five Radical congressmen. Other wards scheduled similar events. On another night, wards ten, eleven, thirteen, fourteen, nineteen, and twenty held rallies in their respective districts and then the attendees converged at 11 P.M. in the plaza in front of the congress building, where several speakers addressed them. After the rally the crowd—led by the senatorial candidate, Vicente Gallo, and the president of the Radical Party for the capital, José Tamborini— marched to the party headquarters singing the national anthem. A similar rally was held the following night. The Friday before the election, the campaign culminated with a giant rally. Each ward committee held a meeting in its own district before the attendees walked or took streetcars, some specially arranged, to locations on the Avenida de Mayo, the grand avenue linking the Plaza de Mayo, the historic center of the city, with that of the Plaza del Congreso. The crowd then marched up the avenue, passing by Yrigoyen, who stood on a balcony. Who went to these rallies? Charges circulated that government workers were forced to attend, many wearing uniforms, such as mailmen, but according to a recent study by Aníbal Viguera, the crowds were mixed. Photos showed well-dressed attendees.[16]

16. Sabato, *La política en las calles;* Rock, *Politics in Argentina,* 55–60; Rock, "Machine Politics," 233–56; Aníbal Viguera, "Participación electoral y practicas políticas de los sectores populares en Buenos Aires, 1912–1922," *Entrepasados* 1, no. 1 (comienzos de 1991): 23–25; *La Epoca,* March 12–22, 1919. See photographs during any electoral campaign in *La Epoca.*

What role did political bosses, the caudillos, play in Buenos Aires? They acted as the intermediary among the party, the state, and the average inhabitant. The bosses gave support in a society that provided little in the way of social services. Their power came from their connection to a political party that needed them to turn out voters. The party made sure that the bosses had the tools to do their work, and in return the boss expected his "clients" to vote correctly and to help with the business of doing politics.

The district committees of the Radical Party distributed low-cost food, such as bread (the famous *pan radical*), meat, cheese, and milk. Children received toys on Epiphany. The committees and the party paper provided free or low-cost medical care and free legal advice. Classes of various types were offered. In October 1927 the party committee of the eighth ward gave clothes to more than eight hundred poor children. The following year Federación Obrera Irigoyenista, which had been formed to push for the nationalization of the petroleum industry and the creation of a national agricultural bank and an Argentine merchant marine, celebrated Columbus Day and Yrigoyen's reelection by giving clothes, shoes, school utensils, toys, and candy to poor children.[17]

The Radical political bosses also operated through the many formal and informal organizations that sprang up in Buenos Aires. Some of the supposedly politically neutral neighborhood associations had ties to political parties, including the Radicals. Soccer clubs were membership organizations and many had political ties. A striking example is Almagro, which usually played in the second division. It was definitively founded in 1916 because of a split in another club between Radical and Conservative members. Its president between 1919 and 1927 was Miguel Ortíz de Zárate, who was elected to the Chamber of Deputies in 1928 and 1938 on Radical slates. In 1924, according to the sporting magazine *El Globo*, almost all members of Almagro were Radicals and Ortíz de Zárate controlled the local Radical committee with the help of the votes from its members. Rómulo Trucco, who had been elected to congress as a Radical, succeeded Ortíz de Zárate as president of Almagro. Arturo Frondizi, the future Radical president of Argentina, played in the youth divisions of the club in the 1920s.[18]

17. Rock, "Machine Politics," 252; Héctor Iñigo Carrera, *La experiencia radical, 1916–1922* (Buenos Aires: Ediciones La Bastilla, 1980), 1:264; Privitellio, *Vecinos y ciudadanos*, 82; *La Epoca*, October 13, November 3, 1927, January 6, May 5, 1929, June 6, 1930; Library of the Instituto Ravignani, Colección Emilio Ravignani, Serie 2, Caja 10b, 104, 105; Ferreras, "Evolución de los principales consumos obreros," 165.

18. See Leandro Gutiérrez and Luis Alberto Romero, "Ciudadanía política y ciudadanía social: Los sectores populares en Buenos Aires, 1912–1955," *Indice* 5, no. 2 (April 1992): 85; Ricardo González, "Lo propio y lo ajeno: Actividades culturales y fomentismo en una asocia-

As in other countries, a few of the caudillos had links to criminal organizations and undoubtedly financed some of their operations in this manner.[19] A good example of a Personalist Radical caudillo was Pedro Bidegain from the sixth ward, San Carlos Sur, who sat on the city council from 1921 to 1923 and in the Chamber of Deputies from 1926 to 1930. We know more about him than most of his peers because he replied to attacks in writing. Bidegain was born, raised, and married in the ward. At age sixteen he went to work for the Ferrocarril Oeste, became a fireman, and was on his way to becoming an engineer when he quit to go into business. He had been an active member of the engineers' and firemen's union, La Fraternidad. Apparently, Bidegain had no great success as a businessman, but in 1924 he owned a bus company. Although he claimed in his 1929 pamphlet that he only held a public sector job in 1922, in 1930 he had a supervisory job at the municipal slaughterhouse. There was some controversy about when he started working for the Radical Party and charges were made that he had previously worked for the Socialists or the Conservatives or both; in any case, he began his Radical Party labors prior to Yrigoyen's presidency. An opponent in the sixth ward accused him of keeping control of the local Radical organization by padding the membership with Socialists and using public employees as party workers. A key power base for Bidegain was the important soccer club San Lorenzo de Almagro. The club's internal elections in 1924 could be pictured as a contest between Personalist and Anti-Personalist Radicals, and in 1926 Bidegain used the club's membership lists to ask for support for his candidacy for the Chamber of Deputies. He was able to win the club's presidency. Bidegain's brother and nephew also played key roles in the club. San Lorenzo's current stadium is officially named for Bidegain but is commonly known by another name. He also participated in the founding of an important social club in the barrio.[20]

---

ción vecinal, Barrio Nazca (1925–1930)," in *Mundo urbano y cultura popular*, ed. Diego Armus (Buenos Aires: Editorial Sudamericana, 1990), 93–128; *La Internacional*, November 22, 1924; *La Vanguardia*, April 27, 1926; Sanguinetti, *Los socialistas independientes*, 36; Sitio Oficial Club Almagro, Historia en tres colores, http://www.calmagro.com.ar/historia.htm, 2/2/2007; Almagro-Historia-Apéndice: Presidentes del Club, http://cablemodem.fibertel.com.ar/almagro/historia/apenpres.html, 1/26/07; H. Cámara de Diputados de la Nación, *Nomina de Diputados de la Nación por distrito electora: Periodo 1854–1991* (Buenos Aires: Secretaría Parlamentaria, Dirección de Archivo, Publicaciones y Museo, 1991), 103, 112. In the United States political bosses used and developed out of clubs; see Royko, *Richard J. Daley*; Whyte, *Street Corner Society*.

19. Rock, "Machine Politics," 249; Gerardo Bra, *La organización negra: La increíble historia de la Zwi Migdal* (Buenos Aires: Corregidor, 1999), 65; Norberto Folino, *Barceló, Ruggierito y el populismo oligárquico* (Buenos Aires: Ediciones de la Flor, 1983). The latter is a discussion of a Conservative boss.

20. Richard J. Walter, "Municipal Politics and Government in Buenos Aires, 1918–

A neighborhood paper in the 1930s had this to say about a caudillo active in the 1920s in a neighboring barrio: "As a neighbor he was always one of the enthusiastic proponents of the area. [He was] the founder of the old Development Association, a member of School Council, president of various school associations, athletic leader, organizer of patriotic and popular celebrations, collaborator in all culture activities."[21]

The public face of the boss was seconded by a more private one. The boss interceded with the bureaucracy or the police. For example, Dr. Francisco Raynoli wrote on March 23, 1924, to Vicente Gallo, the minister of interior, on the letterhead of the capital committee of the Unión Cívica Radical Principista complaining that his client Ernesto Cosolino (or Gozzolino) had been held unfairly by the police for eleven days, then had been released, and almost immediately rearrested. On March 27 Gallo received a reply from the police stating that Cosolino had a record and that he had been arrested for carrying arms.[22] Although Raynoli did not receive the type of response he desired, without his connections there would have been no response. At times political intervention could be much more mundane, such as seeking to obtain the necessary paperwork to sell something.[23]

A key function of the caudillo was to help people get jobs. For example, in La Plata after a federal intervention had thrown out the Conservatives, Radical Party followers crowded around the home of the Radical leader Luis Monteverde hoping to obtain a job.[24] Such wholesale granting of jobs occurred much more frequently in the provinces than in Buenos Aires, but in either case, obtaining employment was usually a more private affair.

In an interview in the 1970s, Francisco Pérez Leirós—who dominated the Unión Obrera Municipal (UOM), the Socialist-controlled municipal workers union during the 1920s and 1930s—claimed that for a laborer to

---

1930," *Journal of Interamerican Studies and World Affairs* 16, no. 2 (May 1974): 182; Pedro Bidegain, *Mi radicalismo* (Buenos Aires, 1929); *La Internacional*, March 6, November 22, 1924; *La Vanguardia*, April 27, 1926; *Crítica*, January 24–February 4, 1929; Concejo Deliberante de la Municipalidad de Buenos Aires, *Actas*, March 23, 1922, 504–7; Enrique Díaz Araujo, *1930 conspiración y revolución* (Mendoza: Universidad Nacional de Cuyo, Facultad de Filosofía y Letras, 1998), 3:225–31; Luciano de Privitellio, "Inventar el barrio: Boedo 1936–1942," *Cuadernos de Ciesal* (Rosario) 2, no. 2–3 (1994): 118–20; Eduardo Rubén Bernal, "Pedro Bidegain, un hombre de Boedo," *Desmemoria* 13–14 (1997): 82–101; Mundo Azulgrana, Estadio Pedro Bidegain, http://www.gasometro.com.ar/casla/estadio.php, 3/21/2008.
21. *Boedo*, October 31, 1939, as quoted in Privitellio, "Inventar el barrio," 120.
22. Archivo General de la Nación, Ministerio del Interior, 1924, Legajo 15, no. 6129.
23. See, for example, Colección Emilio Ravignani, Serie 4, Caja 1, 150.
24. Ferrari, "Los que eligen," 52.

get a job with the city he needed a recommendation from someone in office; he also reported that posts were even sold.[25]

In 1925 the Socialist Party paper, *La Vanguardia,* claimed that a Radical Party boss was overheard complaining to the *intendente's* private secretary about the delay in hiring a worker and stating that those who had paid had gotten their posts immediately. According to the article, this was confirmed when the secretary of hacienda received a letter accusing a man named Roulet of offering for sale posts as laborers and working through the *intendente's* secretary. After a fistfight between Roulet and an accuser, the charges were proved, at least to the satisfaction of the paper. Similar accusations were later made against the national administration.[26]

Sales of jobs undoubtedly occurred, but much more common was the obtaining of posts through political connections. Men and women received jobs as political rewards or favors to politicians and sometimes lost them when political fortunes reversed. The UOM regularly objected to the connections needed to get a job. For example, it complained that a group of laborers and masons who worked for the city as supernumeraries were fired on March 17, 1927. The union believed that it could not have been for lack of funds because replacements were hired directly afterward, but the fired workers lacked patrons.[27]

How extensive were the ties between government jobs and the party political apparatus? We have solid evidence coming from a December 1922 interpellation of the minister of interior on the issue of government employees taking part in electoral activities. Adolfo Dickmann, a Socialist Party deputy, read off the names of the Radical committee for the second ward and all held government posts. He also claimed that almost all the members of the national and capital committees of the Radicals were government employees. No one contradicted him.[28]

Jobs were considered something that successful politicians distributed among their followers and friends. When some Radicals broke with the party in 1924, their former associates made accusations. In Córdoba, a prominent Anti-Personalist, Arsenio Soria, had obtained employment for his friends, including as manager of a branch of the Banco Hipotecario

25. Francisco Pérez Leirós, Instituto Di Tella Oral History Program, 29.
26. Reprinted in *El Obrero Municipal,* November 1925. See also *La Nación,* March 28, April 4–8, 1930.
27. *El Obrero Municipal,* October 1922, April 1927.
28. Cámara de Diputados, *Diario de sesiones* v, December 21, 1922, 360–67, December 22, 1922, 423–78, esp. 438–39.

Nacional, with a normal school, and as a doctor with the State Railroads.[29] In general, the giving of jobs was a normal part of the political process. For example, in 1943 the former president of the Unión Ferroviaria, José Domenech, accused the State Railroads of being a dumping ground for political workers in the era before 1930: "Those railroads constituted a refuge for the people of [political] committees, placing them there, granting them a salary and not giving them work; even the case of office workers who did not know what a typewriter was." Others just went to their offices once a month to pick up their salary. *La Prensa* claimed that in the workshops of the State Railroads in Tafí Viejo a handful of bosses could just place their people.[30]

The existence of patronage was well known, but it was seen as wrong and rarely talked about directly. Most information available today is therefore indirect.[31] We do, however, have some letters kept by the historian Emilio Ravignani, who held a key position in the city administration between 1922 and 1927, that show that he became the center of a web of patronage. Most of the letters are those he received, but they do permit some idea of the process of patronage. Some made reference to actions taken, while a few others had penciled notations on them. Letters requesting jobs came from cabinet ministers such as Minister of Interior Nicolás Matienzo and Naval Minister Manuel Domecq García but also from the president's wife, Regina P. de Alvear. Radical Party organizations requested jobs for individuals but also for groups of deserving job seekers. Prominent Anti-Personalists Vincente Gallo, Leónidas Anastasi, and Reinaldo Elena asked for jobs for individuals, but so did members of the opposition, including prominent Socialists, the Personalist boss Pedro Bidegain, the Communist city councilor José Penelón, as well as the Conservative councilor Adolfo Múgica.[32] Personal connections did matter. Personalist deputy and fellow historian Diego Molinari wrote requesting a job

---

29. Vidal, *Radicalismo de Córdoba*, 356–57.
30. Unión Ferroviaria, *Libros de actas de la Comisión Directiva*, Acta 8, July 2, 1943, 13; *La Prensa*, January 8, 1925.
31. The records of the Radical clubs, if they still exist, are unavailable or of little value for this type of discussion. Mar del Plata is one of the few places where records exist. Elisa Pastoriza and Rodolfo Rodríguez, "El radicalismo perdedor: Las bases sociales de la UCR en el municipio de General Pueyrredón en la década de 1920," in *La construcción de las democracias rioplatenses*, ed. Fernando J. Devoto and Marcela P. Ferrari (Buenos Aires: Editorial Biblos, 1994), 247–68. Another, Berisso, whose records were generously lent me by Mirta Zaida Lobato, contains no information of this type.
32. Colección Emilio Ravignani, Serie 4, Caja 1, 40, 46, 234, Caja 2, 3, 10, 12, 274, 299, 305, 307, 309, 397, Caja 3, 20, 47, 54, Caja 4, 246, 335, Caja 5, 16, Caja 9, 54, 214, 215.

for a Secundino Potti, about whom he had spoken to Ravignani at the institute.[33]

Asking for jobs for people is not the same as obtaining the positions, but the pursuit of employment was often successful. For example, a letter of November 1926 from Socialist city councilor Miguel Briuolo spoke of sending the names of two women for jobs, as was already agreed on. Briuolo also mentioned one more woman as decided on and added that he was supplying another name in case there was room for her.[34] Arrangements were frequently complex. On October 1, 1927, a Carmen Oliva sent a letter to Ravignani to inform him and thank him because she had been appointed as a teacher after being recommended to an Arturo Demarco by Elena, to whom she had been sent by Ravignani. He would have already known, as he had received letters from the other two. Demarco was president of something called the Biblioteca Popular Dr. Leopoldo Melo (Melo being a key Anti-Personalist) and a member of school council 19, which had influence over schools in a neighborhood in the city. Teachers frequently received posts in this fashion.[35] Even important people could not be assured that a recommended person would obtain a post. Lieutenant Colonel José Sarobe, secretary of the minister of war, asked for a job for an Emilia Frigoni, but it was noted that no vacancies existed. A short time later a Juan González, whom Sarobe had also recommended, did receive a post.[36] It is clear from the numerous requests received, even from political allies, that it would have been impossible to fulfill all of them. The municipal administration did not heedlessly and unendingly create new positions. A feature that made the system of patronage unusual, by world standards, is the sharing of positions with the opposition. The reasons for this will be discussed below.

We will see in Chapter 6 an aspect of clientelism when the Anti-Personalists appointed labor leaders to government posts with the idea of helping create new and politically friendly unions among both municipal and national government workers. Individual labor leaders also received jobs from the government or the party, though one does have to be careful about the charges flung by ideological opponents. For example, Luis

---

33. Ibid., Serie 4, Caja 5, 53. Presumably the historical institute that now bears Ravignani's name and where the letters are stored.

34. Ibid., Serie 4, Caja 6, 209.

35. Ibid., Serie 4, Caja 6, 38, 70, 178. See also Serie 4, Caja 1, 30, 31, 54, 65, Serie 2, Caja 6, 37.

36. Ibid., Serie 4, Caja 8, 116, 143.

Lauzet, an important Syndicalist, printer, and writer for the *Bandera Proletaria*, who had served on the Federal Council of the FORA IX, went to the International Labor Organization conference in Geneva as a technical advisor to the government delegation. He had originally been nominated by a union and appointed as a worker delegate. The Socialist paper pointed out that the union did not exist and the original appointment had to be withdrawn. He was expelled from the printers' union for going to Geneva against the wishes of his confederation, but he received a high position in the Anti-Personalist paper *La Acción*.[37] According to the Communists, in 1926 Francisco Rosanova, who led the railroad union during some of the 1917 strikes, was a high employee of the Ministry of Public Works and an advisor to that minister and to the minister of interior. In 1920 the maritime workers' union claimed that the editor of the Anarchist paper, *La Protesta*, Luis María López, was a customs employee. Charges also circulated that a secretary of the union of shipbuilding carpenters received a job in the Ministry of Public Works. Clearly attempts were made to woo union leaders by giving them jobs.[38]

Why was government employment so important? Blue-collar jobs were frequently unstable and ill paying. Stable and well-paying jobs with the government were therefore extremely attractive to blue-collar workers. By the mid-1920s the wages of blue-collar municipal and national employees were markedly higher than in comparable employment in the private sector. This was also true for petty clerks and other semiskilled white-collar employees.

Employment with the City of Buenos Aires

The political system of the city of Buenos Aires made it an ideal site for patronage. The executive power, the *intendente* or mayor, was appointed by the president, served at his approval, and reflected his desires. The *intendente* had wide powers. He set the budget and had the right to make all

---

37. Cámara de Diputados, *Diario de sesiones* 11, June 18, 1925, 166–67; *La Internacional*, May 8, August 4, 1925, July 23, 1927; *Bandera Proletaria*, May 9, 1925; Ministerio del Interior, *Memoria 1924–25*, 569–83; Sebastián Marotta, *El movimiento sindical argentino*, 2:238; Oscar Troncoso, *Fundadores del gremialismo obrero/2* (Buenos Aires: Centro Editor de América Latina, 1983), 231–32.

38. *La Internacional*, October 9, December 25, 1926; *Boletín de Unión del Marino*, March 6, 1920; *La Acción*, July 25, 1927.

appointments to municipal posts. The modern structure of the city government was created in 1917 when a law was passed establishing an elected city council and giving the council the power to approve budgets and even the *intendente's* salary. As important, the council could make the *intendente's* life difficult, slowing key measures and even embarrassing him.[39] The council played a crucial role because the balance of power in municipal politics, unlike almost anywhere else in Argentina, remained divided between several parties. At no time between 1918 and 1930 did one party control the intendency and have a majority on the council.[40] This made governing a game of coalition building. Although the party that controlled the presidency and thus the intendency claimed for its followers the lion's portion of the spoils and the right to purge opponents when regimes changed, it also shared jobs with opposing parties. The reasons why spoils were shared, unlike in machine-run cities in the United States, lay in the political structure. In the United States the paramount goal of a political boss was to control the office of the municipal executive, an impossibility in Argentina because the *intendente* was the president's man. Even dominance of the city council was difficult given the proportional nature of the electoral system. Division of the spoils oiled the waters.

Municipal workers and other government employees became important due to the very small numbers required to elect city councilors and congressmen. In 1920 a party received a seat on the city council with only 5,601 votes. Turnout for congressional elections was higher and the two-thirds/one-third division of seats made the numbers needed to win a seat in congress much higher than for the city council, but still it remained relatively low.[41] In 1928 the program of the Socialist Party's capital branch focused on municipal workers, and an editorial in *La Prensa* in 1930 commented on how the two branches of the city government competed for the favor of the municipal workers in their search for votes.[42]

39. Joel Horowitz, *Argentine Unions and the Rise of Perón* (Berkeley: Institute of International Studies, University of California, Berkeley, 1990), esp. 44–45; Privitellio, "El Concejo Deliberante y el fomentismo," esp. 11; Walter, *Politics and Urban Growth;* Austin F. McDonald, *Government of the Argentine Republic* (New York: Thomas Y. Crowell, 1942), 415–25.

40. Walter, "Municipal Politics and Government," 180; Horowitz, *Argentine Unions,* 44. The Radicals had effective control of the council and of course the intendency in 1929. *La Nación,* April 16, 26, 1929.

41. Law 10.240 in *Anales de legislación argentina,* 2:1039–40; Bucich Escobar, *Buenos Aires ciudad,* 213–20, esp. 216. For congress see Ministerio del Interior, Subsecretaría de Informaciones, *Las fuerzas armadas restituyen el imperio de la soberanía popular* (Buenos Aires: Imprenta de la Cámara de Diputados, 1946), 1:368–434.

42. *La Prensa,* October 29, 1928, July 17, 1930.

In other words, a few votes were important, and government workers had to vote. For example, the city's secretary of hacienda in November 1928 directed the heads of the sections under his authority to remind their subordinates of their duty to vote in the upcoming elections. The memo stated that employees were to present their voting books (*libretas*) to their supervisors to prove that they had voted; the supervisors were to submit to the secretary the names and the reasons why employees had not voted.[43] In 1922 the governor of the Province of Buenos Aires, José Luis Cantilo, decreed that all provincial employees had to present their voting books to their superiors the day after the election; if they had not voted this would be placed in their files and would make promotions more difficult.[44] It may have been difficult to control how government employees voted, but they could be coerced into voting.

Usually coercion was not necessary because municipal workers had a large stake in the outcome. The city council not only set wages and established working conditions but also acted as a sounding board for worker complaints. Councilors spent inordinate amounts of time discussing these issues. The good treatment of municipal workers after the establishment of the popularly elected city council was due in large measure to patronage. If a boss gets jobs for his clients, it pays to treat them well. The governing force in the city, the Radical Party, had a critical stake in such treatment. But so did other parties, because they also had supporters in the workforce and a say in the conditions, because of the *intendente*'s need to work with the council.

The numerous Socialists and Communists who worked for the municipality indicate that the job recommendations from those parties frequently met with success. Socialists controlled the dominant municipal workers' union, the UOM. Although the Socialists frequently protested the use of patronage and called for following the strict regulations, they benefited from the existing system. For example, in 1924 a Socialist council member protested the large number of workers in the Dirección de Paseos, which had 217 supernumerary employees. An opposing councilor retorted that 30 were Socialist militants, to which charge the Socialists did not reply.[45] Clearly they received a share of the spoils.

The unique relationship that the city had with the national government limited the scope and size of the city's workforce. The national government

43. *La Prensa*, December 1, 1928.
44. Ferrari, "El voto del silencio," 179.
45. Concejo Deliberante, *Actas*, June 21, 1923, 944–45.

controlled the schools, the police, and the waterworks. Still, Buenos Aires had a wide range of employees. For example, in 1926 it employed 416 doctors, 91 veterinarians, 55 midwives, 35 engineers, and 13 architects, as well as jewelers, tailors, dressmakers, clerks, and manual laborers. In early 1922 almost three-quarters of the city employees were blue-collar workers who did an entire range of activities, from street sweeping to more skilled occupations. The UOM did complain that the number of blue-collar jobs did not expand sufficiently to meet the city's growing needs, particularly for street cleaning, despite an overall increase in the number of employees. Workers were frequently misclassified and worked at white-collar jobs but were paid as laborers.[46] This reflected the need of patronage to provide what in the eyes of the recipients was respectable employment.

With one major exception, the ethnic composition of the municipal workforce did resemble the larger population. According to the census of municipal workers taken in June 1926, 42 percent of the workforce was Argentine, 20 percent Spanish, and 17.8 percent Italian. The only large anomaly, which points to the importance of a spoils system, was the 13.2 percent of all municipal workers who were naturalized citizens and therefore could vote in national elections. In 1914 just 2.4 percent of the city's foreign-born population was naturalized.[47] Why so many foreign municipal employees who could not vote? The worker hired might not be the one being rewarded for political loyalty; the worker might be a relative or friend of the person being rewarded. In addition, the noncitizen could provide crucial services to the organization, at least as important as a vote. Many foreign-born municipal employees were eligible to vote in municipal elections and may have done so.[48] As we have seen, some jobs could be bought and therefore whether the person voted did not matter. Some might have been hired outside of the spoils system.

A dizzying ascent in the number of municipal workers began before the Radicals came to power in 1916. In 1906 the city employed 5,353 workers and by 1914 there were 11,732 workers. The Yrigoyen years did not see

---

46. Municipalidad de la Ciudad de Buenos Aires, *Censo de personal administrativo y obreros de la Municipalidad de la Ciudad de Buenos Aires* (Buenos Aires, 1928), 22–23; Concejo Deliberante, *Actas*, February 24, 1929, 207; *El Obrero Municipal*, August 1, 1924, December 1, 1929. The official classifications only at times reflected reality. See, for example, Concejo Deliberante, *Actas*, June 22, 1923, 980.

47. Municipalidad de la Ciudad de Buenos Aires, *Censo de personal*, 21; Germani, *Política y sociedad*, 281.

48. Male foreigners who met certain financial standards were eligible to vote in municipal elections.

a comparable rise, although there was an increase, which pushed the number of employees to almost 15,000. During most of the first Yrigoyen presidency economic times were extremely bad and, as discussed below, he did get an opportunity to replace many workers with his own choices. A real surge came during the Alvear years, with number of employees reaching almost 22,000. This does not fit the traditional image of Alvear as being above such tactics. The rapid pace of hiring continued during the second term of Yrigoyen, with employment reaching almost 26,000 workers in 1930. As I have shown elsewhere, subsequent governments continued the enlargement of the municipal payroll at a very fast rate.[49] Clearly the Radicals were part of a larger political culture and it would be difficult to attribute their success to a trait that they shared with all contemporary governments.

Was the rapid increase in city employees just a response to the growing needs of a developing urban area? Buenos Aires, after all, had the reputation of being a clean and well-maintained city, at least in its central areas.[50] The city's population almost doubled between 1909 and 1936, and the number of municipal employees almost quadrupled.[51] The complexity of providing municipal services increases as the population goes up and with it the areas of dense habitation. How did the number of employees compare with cities elsewhere? If one compares the number of employees per hundred thousand inhabitants that Buenos Aires had in 1926 with North American cities the previous year, the figure for Buenos Aires, 1,121, was similar or lower. New York had 1,122 workers per 100,000 inhabitants, Chicago 1,192, and Los Angeles 1,765.

The comparisons are not really fair, however, because the numbers for Chicago include all municipal employees (including teachers, police, and firemen), and those for New York and Los Angeles exclude teachers, but include police and fire personnel, none of whom are included in the Buenos Aires municipal budget.[52] In 1927 in Buenos Aires there were 6,746 subaltern members of the police force or 342 for every 100,000 inhabi-

---

49. Joel Horowitz, "Bosses and Clients: Municipal Employment in the Buenos Aires of the Radicals, 1916–1930," *Journal of Latin American Studies* 31 (1999): 643. For an example of a traditional view of Alvear, see Rock, *Politics in Argentina*, 221–32.
50. Bryce, *South America*, 316–21.
51. Walter, *Politics and Urban Growth*, appendix A1; Horowitz, "Bosses and Clients," 643.
52. Municipalidad de la Ciudad de Buenos Aires, *Censo de personal*, 19; *Revista de Estadística Municipal*, August 1930, 43; Leonard White, *Trends in Public Administration* (New York: McGraw-Hill, 1933), 244–45.

tants.⁵³ So the number of municipal employees in Buenos Aires was really much higher than in New York or Chicago. If one could include in such calculations other excluded groups, the ratio for Buenos Aires would be much greater than for comparable cities.

The comparison with Chicago is particularly interesting because Chicago had and has a reputation for being machine run and dominated by patronage, but, in the number of jobs available, Buenos Aires easily surpassed it. The different political systems, however, make it difficult to directly compare the number of employees. In the United States, many jobs would be hidden in the county and state systems, which had no parallel in Buenos Aires. Radical Party bosses in Buenos Aires had access to the national bureaucracy, and therefore had an even wider venue for placing their clients.

Perhaps the best evidence of the existence of a patronage system was the major effort to improve municipal working conditions, especially in the area of salaries. During the last years of Conservative rule, despite the flurry in hiring of municipal workers, working conditions and wages were extraordinarily bad. In 1909, 46 percent earned sixty pesos per month or less. The lack of attention to patronage is further indicated by the large number of Spaniards (nonvoters) who held unskilled jobs. It is not that the Conservatives were above such activities, as they amply demonstrated in Buenos Aires province, but because votes could be obtained in other manners and the amount of political mobilization was limited, there was little need to reward blue-collar workers.⁵⁴

In a competitive situation, it makes little sense to give supporters jobs and then treat them badly. As pointed out above, a political boss has no guarantee that his "client" will stay loyal, especially because of the secret ballot. Some of the improvements occurred due to the efforts of the UOM, but that organization's leverage remained limited. The UOM, created in early 1916, had close ties to the Socialist Party. Increasing conflict with the new Radical administration led to a major strike in 1917 that was essen-

---

53. Rodríguez, *Historia de la policía federal argentina*, 7:170; *Revista de Estadística Municipal*, August 1930, 43.
54. Municipalidad de la Capital, *Anuario estadístico de la Ciudad de Buenos Aires 1910 y 1911* (Buenos Aires, 1913), 445 (hereafter Municipalidad de la Capital, *Anuario estadístico, year*); Rock, *Politics in Argentina*, 133; Folino, *Barceló, Ruggierito*; Ana María Mustapic, "El Partido Conservador de la Provincia de Buenos Aires ante la intervención federal y competencia democrática: 1917–1928," Instituto Torcuato Di Tella, Centro de Investigaciones Sociales, Documento de Trabajo 95, 1987. For the nature of politics prior to 1912, see, for example, Privitellio, *Vecinos y ciudadanos*, 28–44; Alonso, *Between Revolution and the Ballot Box*; Sabato, *La política en las calles*.

tially crushed; five thousand to seven thousand workers lost their jobs, though subsequently many did regain them. This gave the Radicals an opportunity to hire their own. The union recovered in the next few years and was able to negotiate with the city executive.[55]

After initial strikes that lent it credibility, the UOM refrained from calling stoppages and depended on support from the Socialists on the city council and the embarrassment it could cause the municipal executive branch by publicizing bad treatment of employees. The UOM's biggest threat, however, was its potential to expand the base of the Socialist Party.

The next few years saw major improvements in the municipal workers' conditions. Although the UOM claimed credit, politics played a larger role. Both major parties in the capital had a stake in improving the municipal workers' conditions: the Radicals because so many workers were party clients, the Socialists because of ideology and the UOM's close ties to that party. Even minor parties, such as the Communists, played a role. José Penelón, a key Communist leader, served two terms on the council and was the municipal workers' most vociferous protector.[56]

The city council passed and the *intendente* signed a series of improvements in working conditions. Some came in response to national legislation; others were local initiatives. Workers began to receive Sundays or an equivalent day off; they also became eligible for paid vacations and a forty-four-hour week. The retirement plan for municipal workers was placed on a more regular footing and widened to include blue-collar workers. Some categories of employees failed to receive these benefits, and the union and some on the city council continually complained.[57]

The biggest changes came in salaries and other monetary reimbursements, which coincided with the establishment of a city council elected by a wide electorate, as the councilors bragged. In the sanitation division, a peon made 60 pesos a month in 1919, 80 in 1920, 88 in 1921, and 100 pesos in 1922. In 1924 a minimum wage of 160 pesos a month was established and remained constant until 1930, when it was raised to 165 pesos. The average municipal employee in 1914 earned 118.69 pesos per month and 185.96 in 1924.[58]

55. See Chapter 5.
56. See any Concejo Deliberante, *Actas*, while Penelón was a councilor.
57. *El Obrero Municipal*, April 1924, July 1925, December 1927, April 1, 1929, April 15, 1930; *La Confederación*, July 1926; Concejo Deliberante, *Actas*, April 23, 1929, 274–80; Municipalidad de Buenos Aires, Departamento Ejecutivo, *Memoria del Departamento Ejecutivo de la Municipalidad de la Ciudad de Buenos Aires, Año 1935* (Buenos Aires: Guillermo Kraft, 1936), 191–92.
58. Concejo Deliberante, *Actas*, May 24, 1921, 850–63, February 22, 1922, 113–32, esp.

After the establishment of a minimum salary, the scale for city workers was much higher than for the average wage earner. In 1925, 85 percent of blue-collar city workers earned from 160 to 180 pesos. According to Adolfo Dorfman, in 1924 the average salary in Buenos Aires stood at 118.30 pesos. There is some possibility that Dorfman's figure is low, but a 1928 study by the DNT indicates that it is more or less accurate. The study examined the budgets of 1,198 workers' families and found that their average monthly expenses were 169.65 pesos per month and they earned 170.03 per month. The family of four had two wage earners.[59] Therefore, municipal workers, particularly those holding nonskilled jobs such as street sweepers, did much better than their counterparts employed elsewhere. In the years after 1924 a higher percentage of municipal workers earned over the municipal minimum.[60]

Although not counted in the city budget as salaries, many workers earned money in addition to their wages. Starting in 1923 the city paid a 15 percent bonus to white-collar employees who earned low salaries and had at least ten years of seniority. Later, white-collar employees with more seniority received a 20 percent bonus. In 1926 blue-collar workers earning fewer than 250 pesos a month and having more than ten years of service were given a 10 percent bonus.[61] When this program started, the overwhelming majority of those eligible were not Radical appointees. Starting in 1929 those who made less than 300 pesos a month and had worked ten years received 5 pesos a month for every child under fifteen. In 1929 the bonuses represented 4.4 percent of the total amount of salaries.[62] Municipal workers also enjoyed the benefits of a pension system. The political parties took care of their clients.

The municipal budget soared between 1910 and the end of the Radical control of the city. Municipal expenditures stood at some 33.6 million

---

131, December 27, 1923, 3159–60; *El Obrero Municipal*, May 1923, January 1924; Municipalidad de Buenos Aires, *Presupuesto general de gastos y cálculo de recursos para el ejerció 1920–1930* (Buenos Aires, 1920–30); *Revista de Estadística Municipal*, April/June 1933, 92.

59. *Revista de Estadística Municipal*, April/June 1924, 92; *El Obrero Municipal*, January 1926; Adolfo Dorfman, *La evolución industrial argentina* (Buenos Aires: Editorial Losada, 1942), 241, as cited in Di Tella and Zymelman, *Las etapas del desarrollo*, 369; DNT, *Crónica Mensual*, November 1923, 1171, June 1929, 2796–801.

60. See, for example, Municipalidad de la Ciudad de Buenos Aires, *Censo de personal*, 19–20.

61. See Municipalidad de Buenos Aires, *Presupuesto*, 1920–1930; *El Obrero Municipal*, 1920–30.

62. *El Obrero Municipal*, January 19, 1929; Concejo Deliberante, *Actas*, December 30, 1929, 3096–97; *Revista de Estadística Municipal*, August 1930, 50.

pesos in 1910 and at 37.4 million in 1916, the year Yrigoyen took office, though they had been higher before World War I. In the subsequent presidential election year, 1922, the budget was 68.6 million pesos, but the increase had not been steady. By 1928 the budget had risen to some 87.7 million pesos and by 1930 to 99 million.[63] The budget increased faster than the population, and during World War I and its immediate aftermath the cost of living rose precipitously, peaking in 1920 but then falling.[64] Therefore, inflation cannot account for the rapid expansion of the budget. The increase occurred because of growing political demands. A significant portion was due to the surge in the number of municipal workers and the amount of wages and the improvements in working conditions, but also to the activist and expansive city government.[65] In the years between 1910 and 1930, the overall budget almost tripled, but the outlay for salaries increased almost 5.5 times.

In 1916 salaries consumed more than 40 percent of the budget. The Radical Party's taking control of the city did not have an immediate impact. It is only between 1919 and 1921, in the midst of vast labor upheaval, the establishment of the popularly elected city council, the emergence of the UOM, and a postwar economic recovery, that per capita spending reached prewar levels. The surge comes in both the general budget and salaries. This confirms Rock's observation of a turn to political patronage in this era, but the timing may not be due so much to a decided change in strategy as to a shift in budgeting realities. The initial years of the Alvear administration saw some budget restraint (though the percentages spent on salaries were much higher than during the first years of the Yrigoyen administration). Especially as the presidential election of 1928 approached, the percentage spent on city employees surged, reaching more than 60 percent in 1927 before shrinking slightly under Yrigoyen. There can be no doubt that keeping employees happy became more important over time.[66] These figures do not include the bonuses based on seniority and on the number of children. The municipal government now spent its money on employees rather than capital projects.

63. *Revista de Estadística Municipal*, April/June 1933, 90.
64. Adolfo Dorfman, *Historia de la industria argentina* (Buenos Aires: Solar/Hachettte, 1970), 267.
65. See Walter, *Politics and Urban Growth*, for the nature of growth.
66. *Revista de Estadística Municipal*, August 1930, 50, April/June 1933, 88, 90; Municipalidad de la Capital, *Anuario estadístico 1915–1923*, 50.

The National Government

Parallel to the situation at the municipal level was that of the national government. The chaotic nature of the budgeting process, however, makes it impossible to have a firm grasp of the size of the national bureaucracy. For example, in 1923 a study of the pension fund for national employees lamented that a census of such workers was needed to understand the scope of the fund's problems and that each year since 1906 the fund's annual report had called for such a study.[67] In other words, not even the pension board knew the size of the government workforce. An examination of annual budgets fails to give us solid figures because many workers were outside budget lines and in the 1920s congress frequently failed to pass a new budget.[68] Some growing state operations—such as the state petroleum company, YPF, or the State Railroads—were not included in the budget.

Ana Virginia Persello has made an analysis of the budgets (without the armed services) and has noted 60,109 employees in 1914, 69,427 in 1923, 87,932 in 1927, and 94,898 in 1929.[69] Between 1914 and 1923, employment increased by 9,318, or 15.5 percent. This includes the entire first Yrigoyen presidency; although in all probability shrinkage occurred during the economic downturn caused by World War I. Under Alvear, the increase appears much larger; from 1923 to 1927 employment grew by 18,505 or 26.6 percent. These figures demonstrate that conventional wisdom about patronage and the two presidencies is not correct.

Are there other figures available? According to a study published in 1915, there were over 110,000 total government employees in 1914 with 80,323 in the budget (including groups such as the military). At the end of 1919, 96,000 were paying into the government pension fund. According to an official publication, national employment, including supernumeraries, had reached 152,856 (112,369 without uniformed military personnel) in 1922. A 1924 census of government personnel arrived at a figure of 112,220. Another calculation of the number of national employ-

---

67. José H. Porto, "Caja Nacional de Jubilaciones y Pensiones Civiles: Estudio financiero," in *Investigaciones de seminario de Facultad de Ciencias Económicas de la Universidad de Buenos Aires* (Buenos Aires: Talleres Gráficos A. Baiocco y Cía, 1923), 3:486.
68. José Antonio Sánchez Román, "Economic Elites, Regional Cleavages, and the Introduction of the Income Tax in Argentina" (unpublished paper, 2003).
69. Ana Virginia Persello, "Administración y política en los gobiernos radicales, 1916–1930," *Cuadernos del CISH* 8 (segundo semestre de 2000): 137.

ees, without conscripts, gave the figure as 124,688 for both 1929 and 1930.[70]

In 1926 the Department of Hacienda did a census of blue-collar workers in a number of different divisions of the government, coming up with a total of 14,150. When seniority of workers was shown, the largest group was hired between 1923 and 1925, under Alvear. Hiring during World War I had been limited. Unfortunately, this type of information does not account for worker turnover, which may have been high.[71]

In 1935 the pension board for public employees did a study of those paying into the fund, dividing them into four categories, white-collar employees (*empleados*), blue-collar workers (*obreros*), police, and teaching personnel. Again, by examining seniority, an idea of hiring patterns can be discerned, but turnover makes an accurate picture impossible. In all four categories it appears that World War I had limited the number of new employees and hiring peaks were found during the last years of the first Yrigoyen administration, the last years of Alvear's term, and Yrigoyen's second term. According to this study, there is not a marked difference between the Alvear and Yrigoyen years.[72]

Unfortunately, the very disparate sources for the overall number of national employees make it difficult to do a full analysis of the increase, but it was important and occurred under both Yrigoyen and Alvear. Expansion of state jobs, however, does not prove clientelism. A significant part of the increase reflected the widening scope of government. For example, the state petroleum company, founded after the discovery of oil in 1907 and reorganized as YPF in 1922, had 6,380 employees by December 1930.[73]

70. Francisco Stach, "Empleados nacionales civiles en la República Argentina: Su situación social y económica," *Boletín del Museo Social Argentino* 4 (1915): 535; Departamento de Hacienda, *Memoria correspondiente al año 1919* (Buenos Aires: Talleres Gráficos Argentinos, 1920), 265; A. E. Bunge, "Personal de los servicios públicos desde 1903 hasta 1923," Dirección General de Estadística de la Nación, Informe no. 3, serie A, no. 1, August 10, 1923, 3; Caja Nacional de Jubilaciones y Pensiones Civiles, *Memoria correspondiente al año 1927* (Buenos Aires: Talleres Gráficos de L. C. López y Cía., 1928), 69; Mario Sáenz, *El presupuesto de 1938* (Buenos Aires, 1938), 62. For figures before the Radicals, see Ariel Yablon, "Patronazgo en la ciudad de Buenos Aires, 1880–1916" (paper delivered to the Latin American Studies Association Congress, 2003).
    71. Departamento de Hacienda, *Memoria correspondiente al año 1926* (Buenos Aires: Talleres Gráficos de G. Pesce, 1927), 271, 276.
    72. Caja Nacional de Jubilaciones y Pensiones Civiles, *Informe y balance técnico-actuarial al 30 de junio de 1935* (Buenos Aires: Guillermo Kraft, 1937), 99–102.
    73. Yacimientos Petrolíferos Fiscales, *Desarrollo de la industria petrolífera fiscal, 1907–1932* (Buenos Aires: Jacobo Peuser, 1932); Carl E. Solberg, *Oil and Nation in Argentina* (Stanford, Calif.: Stanford University Press, 1979); Orietta Favaro, "Estado y empresas públicas, el caso YPF, 1922–1955," *Estudios Sociales* 9, no. 16 (primer semestre de 1999): 73.

Is there evidence of clientelism and where? All indications are that some sectors were staffed more by political appointments than others. As mentioned above, the State Railroads had such a reputation. When Yrigoyen became president for the second time, the new administration charged that Alvear's had placed clients on the State Railroads and used this claim to justify layoffs, which according to press accounts numbered over a thousand. According to *La Prensa*, however, by December 1929 the number of State Railroad employees in the capital had doubled during Yrigoyen's presidency, reaching 3,600. The company needed to rent much more office space. Similarly, in January 1929 in the station of the port of Buenos Aires where the railroad discharged river traffic, there had been 48 State Railroad employees costing 7,550 pesos per month, and by October the number had increased to 304 with a cost of 47,910 pesos per month.[74]

State Railroad employment does not follow a pattern that can logically be ascribed just to patronage. The number of employees increased rapidly between 1916 and 1930, growing from 16,827 workers to 26,680. It was not, however, a simple upward line. Employment declined in 1917 and hit bottom in 1918 with 13,313 employees before increasing between 1919 and 1921. The number of employees stood at 18,707 in 1921 before shrinking to 16,977 in the presidential election year of 1922. If patronage were the prime consideration, an election year would not be a good time to do this. During this period the size of the rail network stayed relatively stable, only increasing slightly. The employment downturns of 1917–18 and 1922–23 can be tied to a decrease in rail traffic. The number of employees increased steadily from 1924 through 1930, but this, at least in part, reflected the sizeable increase in track mileage. Passenger and freight traffic increased dramatically between 1916 and 1929, 115 and 81 percent, respectively, and less sharply, but significantly, from 1924 to 1929. The number of workers per kilometer increased during the Radical governments but was usually lower than it was for the private railroads. Silvana Palermo has argued that the staffing of the railroads was not a product of clientelism. The total number of workers employed by the State Railroads supports this thesis. Total numbers, however, do not explain distribution or who was hired. An organization with few employees can be totally staffed by those with political connections.[75]

74. *La Prensa*, December 2, 1928, February 9, 15–17, December 4, 1929; *La Nación*, April 21, 1929; *Crítica*, February 9, 1929.

75. Ministerio de Obras Públicas, Dirección General de Ferrocarriles, *Estadística de los ferrocarriles en explotación 1916–1940/1941* (Buenos Aires: Talleres Gráficos del Ministerio de

In Buenos Aires, public school teachers were national employees and, as we have seen, frequently gained employment through patronage. A curious anomaly existed: most elementary school teachers were women and therefore could not vote. Similar to the case with immigrants, this did not mean that they lacked political connections. Male members of their families voted and the teachers could participate in the work of political campaigns. The number of teachers in the capital grew from 3,229 in 1908 to 5,222 in 1917, 7,644 in 1922, and 14,434 in 1929. This is a spectacular rise, but the number of teachers rose only twice as fast as the increase in the number of students, which went from 97,584 in 1908 to 232,377 in 1929.[76] The student-teacher ratio was 16:1 in 1929. Nationwide a similar pattern occurred in primary schools run by the national government; the number of teachers increased from 9,039 in 1915 to 29,479 in 1930, and students went from 326,281 to 691,750. The student-teacher ratio fell from 36:1 to 23:1.[77] The number of teachers does not seem excessive, although clearly patronage appointments were crucial.

The mail and telegraph offices had the reputation of being a center for clientelism, yet the number of employees did not grow remarkably. They had 15,015 employees in 1914, 20,949 in 1922, 25,137 in 1929, and 27,639 in 1930. Censuses of workers were done in 1930 and 1934 and from these we can tell how long they worked in this division of the government (we cannot judge who had been laid off during this period or had left their jobs for other reasons). The figures show that considerable hiring was done under both presidents. The amount of work done did increase; more mail and telegrams were sent, indicating that at least some of the job growth was created by need. Evidence of clientelism does exist. A special investigative committee established after the 1930 coup found that on June 30, 1930, 1,753 workers were authorized to be hired outside the budget for the department of mail and telegraph. In 1930, 82 percent of the employees were born in Argentina and 78 percent of the foreign-born had been naturalized. This was clearly out of alignment with the general population.[78]

Obras Públicas, 1924–43). Silvana Palermo, "Democracia, progreso y modernidad: El radicalismo y la expansión de los Ferrocarriles del Estado" (paper delivered at the Latin American Studies Association Congress, 2001); and "Railways and the Making of Modern Argentina" (Ph.D. diss., SUNY, Stony Brook, 2001).

76. Barrancos, *Anarquismo, educación*, 315.

77. Comité Nacional de Geografía, *Anuario*, 500, 516.

78. Persello, "Administración y política," 138; A. E. Bunge, "Personal de los servicios públicos"; *La Epoca*, August 28, 1930; Comité Nacional de Geografía, *Anuario*, 477, 480–81;

It is impossible to calculate the number of excess workers that state institutions employed, because it would be necessary to calculate exact functions for all parts of the governmental structure. Bloated sectors did exist. According to Hector Otero's examination of the Ministry of Agriculture, Alvear's minister, Tomás Le Bretón, came to the post with the idea of reducing the number of employees. The ministry was infamous as a site for patronage, especially the Defensa Agrícola, which was supposed to eradicate locusts. The jobs with the Defensa were frequently political; many were stationed in the capital. This started prior to the Radicals coming to power. After one year in office, Le Breton had reduced the number of employees in his ministry from 4,681 to 2,246 and 222 positions remained to be filled.[79]

The easiest time to see the nature of appointments is during changes in administration. Followers are rewarded, and when hostile changes take place, political enemies are punished or at least lose their jobs in order that the faithful might be rewarded. For example, in a city council debate in 1923, a Socialist councilor accused Yrigoyen of placing people in all types of posts because of their support for Radical committees; most appointments came in January and February 1922, just prior to the April presidential elections. He accused the municipal secretary of hacienda of preparing his own candidacy for the Chamber of Deputies by dispensing jobs and thus obtaining the support of the party convention.[80]

The change in administration in 1928 from Alvear to Yrigoyen produced a major purge of personnel. The Yrigoyenists claimed that numerous unnecessary people had been appointed to positions. For example, in the municipal administration women had been appointed as street sweepers and "they only swept their salary at the end of the month." When dismissals mounted in the Ministry of Agriculture, *Crítica* charged that replacements lined the halls of the ministry hoping for a job. The importance of clientelism is indicated by one division in which all foreign-born workers who had been employed less than ten years and had not been

---

Dirección General de Correos y Telégrafos, *Censo general del personal* (Buenos Aires: Casa OUCINDE, 1930), 22–23, 397; and *Memoria 1934* (Buenos Aires: Talleres Gráficos de Correos y Telégrafos, 1935), 178; Archivo General de la Nación, Fondo Documental, Ministerio del Interior, Serie Comisión Investigadora de la presidencia de H. Irigoyen, documento 3, 74. Slightly different figures exist for the number of employees but the trends are consistent.

79. Héctor Horacio Otero, "La reorganización administrativa durante el segundo gobierno radical (1922–1928): El caso del Ministerio de Agricultura" (Tesis de Licenciatura, Universidad de Buenos Aires, 1996), 103–15; Vidal, "Los partidos políticos," 201.

80. Concejo Deliberante, *Actas*, June 21, 1923, 947. A Radical denied the latter charge.

naturalized were to be fired. Those with more seniority had to become citizens as soon as possible.

Both *La Prensa* and *La Nación* attacked the layoffs. The latter in March 1929 claimed that some ten thousand had been purged from the bureaucracy. Some solid figures were given: 3,343 in the Ministry of Agriculture; 1,148 in mail and telegraph; 721 in customs; and 500 municipal employees. The number of city workers is undoubtedly an underestimation, because figures from the municipal personnel office emerged during a city council debate in 1932. The council had just reopened after being closed following the September 1930 coup. During Yrigoyen's shortened second term, 926 firings took place and 1,951 retirements, many of which were forced. The Depression was not a factor, because 6,828 were simultaneously named to municipal jobs, which produced an increase of 3,951 employees. Gregorio Beschinsky, an Independent Socialist councilor, claimed that two classes of people lost their jobs between 1928 and 1930: those fired because their positions were needed for someone else and those fired for political vengeance.[81] Employment was clearly tied to politics.

As in the municipal government, national government employees received relatively high salaries. In 1921, the minimum was set at 160 pesos a month, or 6.40 per day.[82] This meant that for almost all unskilled and semiskilled jobs, government employees earned much more than did their counterparts in the private sector. Government workers also had a pension system. These are clear signs of politicians trying to do right by their clientele.

This was not always true. The administrative ineptitude of the government at all levels—municipal, provincial, and national—created numerous incidents in which public employees were not paid for months. This produced suffering and work stoppages and indicates the fragility of the ties of those in authority to their clients.[83]

During the entire Radical period, except for 1920, the national govern-

---

81. See especially *Crítica*, January 3, 1929; *La Prensa*, October 17, December 1, 6, 1928, January 9–11, February 9, 14, 1929; *La Nación*, March, 25–27, April 21, 1929; *La Epoca*, November 30, December 1, 1928, March 26, April 2, 1929; Concejo Deliberante, *Actas*, March 4, 1932, 58–98, esp. 62–65, June 28, 1932, 2213–32.

82. Persello, "Administración y política,"140.

83. See, from among many examples, *La Epoca*, March 1917; *La Prensa*, October 10–13, 1925, February 6–12, 1929; *Crítica*, May 20, 1929; Ferrari, "El voto de silencio," 186; Nicholas Biddle, "Oil and Democracy in Argentina, 1916–1930" (Ph.D. diss., Duke University, 1991), 225; Joel Horowitz, "Argentina's Failed General Strike of 1921: A Critical Moment in the Radicals' Relations with Unions," *Hispanic American Historical Review* 75, no. 1 (1995): 67–68.

ment ran a large deficit, despite a sharp increase in revenues. In 1916 the government spent some 374 million pesos, in 1922, 614 million, and in 1927, 1,049 million. Expenditures declined the next year before rising in 1929 and 1930. Pensions, salaries, and general administration took an ever-increasing share of the budget. This was partially compensated for, much as it was in the municipal government, by a shrinking percentage of expenditures going to public works. The percentage dropped quickly during the first years before recovering considerably between 1926 and 1930, but was still lower than in the period before the Radicals won power. The Radical attention to patronage had a long-term cost, decreasing investment in public works.[84]

According to many sources, the use of jobs as political tools was even more intense in the provinces. Gardenia Vidal reports that in 1929, a year after the Radicals won the governorship of Córdoba, 95 percent of the employees of the Ministerio de Gobierno had been replaced. In the Province of Buenos Aires in 1917, the year that the Radicals took over the province, the number of employees stood at 15,884 and by 1927 there were 25,583. La Prensa claimed that the increase occurred despite a vigorous purge of employees and that these figures did not include supernumeraries and squads of laborers whose numbers seemed to multiply around election time. Salaries also increased. It would not be unfair to suspect a similar pattern for other provinces.[85] Patronage was common across Argentina.

Conclusion

Clientelism existed; it consumed a significant percentage of budgets in salaries and benefits. It is what allowed the Radical bosses to organize extensive political machines. Followers would be rewarded and afterward they would be expected to continue political work. It is difficult to believe, however, that one can assign Yrigoyen's popularity to patronage. Too many politicians of all stripes practiced it, but they failed to build a wide electoral

---

84. Comité Nacional de Geografía, *Anuario*, 395–96; Dirección General de Finanzas, *El ajuste de los resultados financieros de los ejercicios de 1928 a 1936* (Buenos Aires: Gerónimo J. Pesce y Cía, 1938), 146; Adriana Montequín, "Sector público y sistema tributario argentino, 1914–1932," *Ciclos* 5, no. 9 (segundo semestre de 1995): 150–51.

85. Vidal, *Radicalismo*, 176–77; Hora, *The Landowners*, 158; *La Prensa*, February 2, 1927; Persello, "Administración y política," 126–27. The total figures in *La Prensa* and Hora are slightly different.

base. The best example is the struggle between the Personalists and the Anti-Personalists. Both used extensive patronage, but only the Personalists in the figure of Yrigoyen created true loyalty. In addition, in the municipality of Buenos Aires patronage was shared among all parties and at least in the era prior to the Radicals coming to power, this was also true at the national level.[86]

Large patronage systems were a common feature of the early twentieth century, as people looked for stable employment and politicians searched for support. People needed help with an increasingly bureaucratic world. What makes Argentina stand out is not the existence of such systems, nor the fact that the Radicals used them to help create political machines, but rather that no truly successful civil service reform has occurred. The Radicals use of patronage was part of a historical pattern and they practiced patronage skillfully, but it is difficult to ascribe their popularity to it.

---

86. Ariel Yablon, "'Empleomanía': Prácticas políticas y denuncias en corrupción de Buenos Aires, Argentina, 1880–1910" (paper delivered at the Latin American Studies Association Congress, 2006).

4

WHEN BOSSES AND WORKERS AGREED: THE FAILURE OF SOCIAL WELFARE LEGISLATION

Since the development of the first social security system by Otto von Bismarck in Germany, such legislation has had dual aims: to tie workers to the social and political system and to better their conditions. The Radical governments of Yrigoyen and Alvear had such goals in mind when they tried to create an overarching pension system. They wanted to simultaneously increase their popularity and address some of the severe problems that the popular classes faced. Despite being astute politicians, the Radicals failed to line up organized support and were forced to abandon the project.

As Eduardo A. Zimmermann has amply demonstrated, Argentine elites were more than aware of the social question.[1] Why then did the Radicals fail to implement such policies? The long-term implications were profound, altering the nature of politics and failing to institutionalize worker relationships with the state. An overarching social security system was not even created under Perón.[2]

It was not that the Radicals did not try, but rather that they failed miserably to sell the project. In 1923 the Alvear administration enacted a pension plan that had been initially proposed by Yrigoyen. The Radicals clearly intended to use the measure to build popular support, tie workers to the political system, and lessen social turmoil, but the plan backfired, produc-

---

1. Zimmermann, *Los liberales reformistas*.
2. Juan Perón did not create a comprehensive social security system, in part, because of the vested interest of strong unions in the existing system of *cajas de jubilación*. See Mariano Plotkin, *Mañana es San Perón*, 218–22.

ing the opposite effect. Instead of rallying support behind the government, the measure produced the almost impossible—unions and business owners agreed in their dislike of the legislation. They prevented its being put in place and subsequently such legislation became difficult to pass.

What type of structural impediments prevented the implementation of such laws? The importance of Syndicalist and Anarchist ideologies in the labor movement played a role. Unions offered no support to such efforts and even opposed them. The Radical Party's extremely personalistic approach to attracting support also contributed. These explanations, however, are an oversimplification. The Radicals were at times as eager for legislation as were the Socialists, and the Syndicalists were inconsistent in their opposition to government involvement in labor affairs. The Anarchists were marginalized by the 1920s. Employer groups claimed that they supported such plans. Nevertheless, the political dynamics of Argentine society made it very difficult to construct a large social welfare program.

Why did the Radicals, both supporters of Alvear and of Yrigoyen, so badly misread the political climate? What did they hope to gain? What led to the overwhelming opposition from both ends of the social spectrum? What were the end results of the massive opposition? Were the Radicals really so bad at reading the political climate, or did they perhaps have an understanding of the potential voters that surpassed that of the opposition but failed to comprehend the institutional realities?

History of the Legislation

The desire for informal ties between the state and the private sector had doomed earlier attempts to create a special place for workers in the legal system. In 1904 Interior Minister Joaquín V. González proposed a comprehensive law—465 articles—that called for, among many other things, limits on the length of the workday, controls on working conditions, established norms for unions, and tribunals of arbitration and conciliation. It met opposition from almost all sectors, including unions of almost all stripes and the Socialists, some of whom had been involved in drawing up the law. The industrialists also opposed it.[3]

When in mid-1919 labor unrest rolled across Argentina, placing the

3. See, for example, Zimmermann, *Los liberales reformistas*, 178–86; Maricel Bertolo, *Una propuesta gremial alternativa: El sindicalismo revolucionario* (Buenos Aires: Centro Editor de América Latina, 1993), 30.

THE FAILURE OF SOCIAL WELFARE LEGISLATION   97

government of Yrigoyen under tremendous pressure, one response was to introduce legislation that called for conciliation and arbitration of labor disputes and legally defined what unions were. The unions responded vociferously. The FORA IX held a special congress that threatened a general strike and called for propaganda against the bill and a mass demonstration. The rally, sponsored by the FORA IX, the Socialist Party, and the International Socialists (later to become the Communists), drew an estimated 140,000 people in the capital and 100,250 in the interior.[4] Increased agitation went against Yrigoyen's political needs and the legislation died.

In mid-1921 a cluster of proposals for pension plans, covering wide numbers of workers, was introduced in congress.[5] Earlier retirement plans *(cajas de jubilación)* had been restricted to specific and strategic groups of workers, such as railroaders and government employees. In August 1922, shortly before giving up the presidency to Alvear, Yrigoyen presented the key proposal to congress; in the message that accompanied it, he makes clear some of the reasons why he favored this type of legislation. Yrigoyen argued that the social progress that had been achieved through the intervention of the state needed to be advanced and amplified. In speaking of retirement plans, the message stated:

> It is indispensable to extend these benefits, in order to assure the country its permanent tranquility and continual progress in the harmonious whole of all its spheres and activities.
>
> A few days ago the capital of the republic witnessed the beautiful spectacle of a demonstration of many thousands of Argentines and foreigners who displayed as their only emblem the national flag. They paraded, making manifest a culture that . . . is pleasing and patriotic to put in writing.
>
> Immediately, it calls attention that to this imposing demonstration came for the first time united, bosses and workers already without signs of angry protest, but on the contrary, demonstrating their confidence in the ratification that they looked for from the public powers.

---

4. Walter, *The Socialist Party*, 159–60; Marotta, *El movimiento sindical argentino*, 2:270–75; Rock, *Politics in Argentina*, 196–98. Also see, for example, *El Obrero Ferroviario*, June–July 15, 1919; *La Unión del Marino*, September 1919; *La Organización Obrera*, August 2–16, November 22, 1919.

5. Isuani, *Los orígenes conflictivos de la seguridad social*, 87.

By pointing out that supporters carried the Argentine flag, Yrigoyen is arguing that pension laws had public support and would lessen social tensions (unsaid is the implication that otherwise demonstrators would march with red or red-and-black banners of those on the Left who Yrigoyen would claim placed ideology above the nation). The lack of differentiation between workers and employers fit in very nicely with Radicals' beliefs and in any case promised harmony. Implied in this and all other contemporary pension legislation was the expectation that strikes would become more rare, because those who struck could lose their jobs and therefore their rights to pensions. The existing pension laws, such as that covering the railroads, could have had that impact but did not, primarily because unions protected the workers.[6] Yrigoyen and the Radicals hoped to gain political support because the legislation would improve the living conditions of large sectors of the population, but also because it would help lessen social agitation.

On September 28, 1923, two pieces of pension legislation passed the Chamber of Deputies. Augusto Bunge, a Socialist deputy, had proposed one, law 11.286. It called for the creation of a commission to draw up an overarching piece of social security legislation. No such legislation ever saw the light of day and one can hypothesize that this surprised almost no one. The other, what became law 11.289, was presented by the committee on work legislation. The Radicals pressed hard to get the law passed during that session. They limited debate over the vigorous objections of Bunge, and in protest both the Socialists and the Democratic Progressives walked out of the chamber prior to the vote. A Radical deputy practically crowed "that the workers and employees [empleados] know these things. The deputies [the opposition] only come to the chamber to name investigative commissions." He was implying that the Radicals accomplished things and would therefore reap the political benefits. The motion passed easily and quickly. The debate rarely rose above this level of discourse.[7]

What did the law entail after it cleared both houses of congress? It created four separate funds, intended to benefit both blue- and white-collar workers in industrial operations, commerce, the merchant marine, and

6. Cámara de Diputados, *Diario de sesiones*, vi, September 23, 1923, 897. See also, for question of strikes, Isuani, *Los orígenes conflictivos de la seguridad social*, 87–88.
7. For what becomes 11.286, see Cámara de Diputados, *Diario de sesiones*, vi, September 21, 1923, 370–91, September 23, 1923, 855. For 11.289, Cámara de Diputados, *Diario de sesiones*, vi, September 23, 1923, 855–914, for quote 914. When amendments were presented from the Senate, once again no debate was permitted; see ibid., viii, November 22, 1923, 542.

printing and journalism. The law covered retirement and disability. Both employees and companies would contribute 5 percent of salaries or wages to the funds. In addition, workers were to pay a month's remuneration to their fund. The boards that controlled the pensions were to be elected by employers and enrollees, and the chair, who would hold the decisive vote, would be appointed by the president with approval of the Senate. Fifty percent of the money collected was to be invested in government bonds, and the other half would be loaned to enrolled members to buy housing.[8] If the law had been successfully implemented, it had the potential for at least partially addressing the shortage of decent affordable living space.

As critics soon pointed out, and correctly so, the law was badly drawn up, although subsequent regulations could have prevented many of the problems. The law set no standard age for retirement or required length of service. The regulations included only permanent employees but failed to define adequately who these were. Very small firms were exempt from the legislation, which presented potential problems because smaller firms would have a competitive advantage and large companies could escape the burden of the pension funds by putting out work to small-scale operations. Although intending to recognize work done prior to the enactment of the law, how workers could prove that they had worked for thirty years in jobs that qualified remained unclear. The Socialists constantly challenged the financial viability of the pension funds, probably for good reason.[9]

Motivations for Enactment

What lay behind the desire for such a law? No doubt sincere concern for the well-being of the workers and employees should not be discounted. The constant references in the congressional debates to the existence of similar plans in Europe seem to indicate a desire to be on par with other countries. In addition, considerable support for some such bill existed. Groups claiming to represent both employees and employers presented petitions to congress and held demonstrations before and after the legislation passed. Some of these were well-established organizations, while oth-

8. DNT, *Crónica Mensual*, December 1923, 1185–86.
9. Cámara de Diputados, *Diario de sesiones*, VIII, n.d., 1923, 675–78. For regulations, see *Boletín de la Unión Industrial Argentina*, January 15, 1924, 14–15, February 15, 1924, 9–13, April 15, 1924, 38–40. The Socialists' comments appear in most of the debates on the law. Although I can claim no expertise in actuarial matters, their arguments appear to make sense, and the other pension funds were unsound, as critics brought up constantly.

ers were created for the purpose of supporting pension legislation. For example, in July 1922 one such group planned a march and a presentation of a petition to Yrigoyen and to congress. A number of large firms closed their doors in order to have their employees participate. Yrigoyen received a delegation and later, along with several of his ministers, went out on the balcony of the Casa Rosada to greet the demonstrators. Support for pension legislation seemed particularly strong among retail establishments. As late as April 27, 1924, *La Prensa* believed that more people supported the legislation than opposed it.[10]

What caused the Alvear administration and its allies in congress (the split between Personalists and Anti-Personalists was still incipient) to push for the rapid passage of this legislation and to continue to back it even after its unpopularity with key sectors became clear? It is necessary to remember how difficult it is to retroactively judge the sentiments of unorganized elements of society. Most of the popular sectors were unorganized; support for unions had declined greatly from the heady times of 1917–21. How completely the organizations that claimed to represent the economic elites did so is questionable.[11] It is hard to believe that not only did the professional politicians of the Radical Party misjudge the public mood so completely—that is always possible—but that if sentiments were so adverse that they would continue to back the plan as they did. Why did they not just cut their losses?

The administration's thinking remains obscure. David Rock has presented a very attractive theory that the government, unable to consolidate its debts by floating bonds, decided to create funds with this law. His source was the *Review of the River Plate*. Few of the sources I examined, however, mentioned this as a reason or protested against what would be a forced loan, although Alvear did face a budget crisis.[12]

---

10. See, for example, *La Prensa*, March 8, April 27, June 14, 1924; *Boletín de Servicios*, July 5, 1922, 274–75, July 20, 1922, 309; *Nuestra Palabra*, May 1, 1923; *La Epoca*, April 13, July 7–29, esp. 7–10, October 27, 30, 1922, February 9, March 15, 1924; Cámara de Diputados, *Diario de sesiones*, I, June 23, 1924, 555–67, IV, August 27, 1924, 784–93, VI, September 25, 1924, 657; U.S. Military Attaché Report, Buenos Aires, 3278, February 6, 1924, *U.S. Military Intelligence Reports: Argentina, 1918–1941* (Frederick, Md.: University Publications of America, 1984).

11. See, for example, Jorge Schvarzer, *Empresarios del pasado: La Unión Industrial Argentina* (Buenos Aires: CISEA/Imago Mundi, 1991), 56–57.

12. Rock, *Politics in Argentina*, 227; Cámara de Diputados, *Diario de sesiones*, IV, August 27, 1924, 765–66 (this is a dialogue between Bunge and the Minister of Hacienda Víctor M. Molina); *Bandera Proletaria*, February 21, 1925, as quoted in Godio, *El movimiento obrero argentino (1910–1930)*, 159; Colin Lewis, "Social Insurance: Ideology and Policy in the Argentine, 1920–66," in *Welfare, Poverty, and Development in Latin America*, ed. Christopher Abel and Colin Lewis (London: Macmillan, 1993), 179–81.

Other explanations were more common. The key seems to have been the desire to harvest votes; this helps explain the speed with which the legislation passed, because congressional elections were scheduled for March 1924. Agitation for and against the pension plan did intensify in the period leading up to the elections.[13] The Radical press tied support for what became law 11.289 to the concept of *obrerismo*. For example, when Vice President Elipidio González broke a tie vote in the Senate on a portion of the bill, a headline in *La Epoca* read, "A definition of a social and *obrerista* policy."[14]

Reactions to the Law

The Radicals achieved one of those rare moments in which labor and organized groups of employers agreed on a basic issue. They believed that the legislation not only failed to meet their needs but also hurt their members. The reasoning behind this consensus revealed disagreements.

Reactions of unions and the Left to the pension plan were complex. Ideology, nature of the industry represented, and the state of the organization all had an impact. So did the existence of already-functioning pension plans; unions in industries with pension plans did not feel compelled to take strong positions on 11.289.[15]

The Socialist response to the law was multifaceted. The Socialist Party led the opposition to law 11.289 in congress, vigorously fighting it from 1923 until its repeal in 1926. The party was a significant force in the congress, holding nine seats in 1923, and in the congressional elections of 1924 the Socialists did extremely well and doubled the size of their delegation. It is unclear whether the pension legislation had an impact.[16] Its spokesmen bore the brunt of the partisan fighting in congress and were, as usual, determined, hardworking, prepared, and loquacious. Unions dominated by party members remained, on the whole, unenthusiastic about using strikes to prevent its implementation. A key reason for Socialist opposition was the same as the Radicals' reason for supporting the law.

13. See, for example, *La Epoca*, March 14–23, 1924; Cámara de Diputados, *Diario de sesiones*, VI (1925), January 21, 1926, 629.
14. *La Epoca*, November 27, 1923.
15. The unions did not have control of the pension funds, nor did the legislation attempt to consolidate existing *cajas*; therefore, any kind of parallel to union opposition to the creation of a unified pension plan under Perón does not work.
16. Walter, *The Socialist Party*, 188–89, 192; *La Epoca*, April 4, 1924.

The Socialists believed that the Radicals wanted the law in order to reap political benefits. They felt that the Radicals were indulging in demagoguery, or what they called *política criolla*.[17]

Also, the Socialists argued that the law was inadequate. All workers needed to be included and only a measure like the one that they proposed would be acceptable, because it would cover workers when they changed jobs. In addition, they harped on some of the inadequacies of the law: its lack of financial viability and the lack of an upper limit on pensions. They believed that the legislation would push many employers, especially in the garment industry, to move to a putting-out system based on home production, in order not to have direct employees and thereby escape paying into the system. They also worried that women would be forced to pay into the system but would spend time working for small firms that were not included or that they would not work the required thirty years and therefore not be able to draw a pension. A key issue for the Socialists, as it was for the entire Left, was the workers having to contribute such large sums from meager wages.[18]

The attitude of the UOM (whose members already had a pension plan) represents well the attitudes of many Socialist-dominated unions. The UOM supported the idea of pensions but believed that the law was inadequate, as it failed to cover enough people. Although joining demonstrations against the law, it failed to support the general strike.[19]

In 1924 the Syndicalists were the most important ideological tendency in the labor movement, controlling the Unión Sindical Argentina (USA). They had developed a pragmatic approach, dealing with government figures, particularly on issues of collective bargaining, but preferring that their contacts with the state not be institutionalized. In part, they opposed the pension plan because all such laws were bad. In January 1924 the Central Committee of the USA claimed that "the pension law was prompted by the goal of distracting the attention of the workers from other more fundamental problems and like all things inspired by the bourgeoisie, it cannot offer to the wage earner advantages from any aspect." Later, the USA claimed that legislation was the chain that enslaved men. Usually it

17. See, for example, *Nueva Era* (Avellaneda), February 9, 1924; *La Vanguardia*, May 7, 1924; Cámara de Diputados, *Diario de sesiones*, VI, September 26, 1924, 768; *El Obrero Gráfico*, October/November 1923.

18. Cámara de Diputados, *Diario de sesiones*, VI, September 23, 1923, 907–9, IV, August 27, 1924, 786–89, V, August 28, 1924, 30–63, VI, September 18, 1924, 110–51, September 26, 1924, 767–72; *La Vanguardia*, April 30, 1924.

19. *Bandera Proletaria*, December 22, 1923; *El Obrero Municipal*, January–May 1924.

stressed problems with the law. The legislation would divide the working class into those who would receive pensions and those who would not. It also argued that the law would reduce the already-low wages and raise prices. Employers should bear the full burden. They also feared that the legislation would deter strikes and other kinds of agitation, because loss of jobs could mean loss of pension rights.

The Syndicalist furniture makers' union rejected the law: "We reject it not because we, the workers, do not deserve to enjoy a stipend that would allow us a rest and have a life, more or less human, in old age, but because we know through our long experience in our struggle in the labor movement that what least preoccupies the bourgeoisie and the State is arranging our future situation." It later referred to the pension plan as the "theft law." The paper of the shipbuilders declared, "The thieves are not only in the wilderness. In the pension fund and in the shelter of law 11.289 they seek to assault all workers' salaries."[20] In the maritime industry, divisions between officers and crew over the pension law—the officers wanted a pension plan—led to initial neutrality on the issue within the Federación Obrera Marítima (FOM). When the union opposed the law, it created a split with the officers.[21] Although the Socialists opposed law 11.289, they liked the idea of pension plans, but the Syndicalists opposed the idea, as well as the details.

The Communists vociferously rejected the pension law. They played a significant role within the labor movement, controlling the USA's Buenos Aires organization, the Unión Obrera Local (UOL), and were a strong force within the USA itself. The Communists came close to controlling the USA's first ordinary congress in April 1924. Although more delegates supported the Communists than the Syndicalists, the latter represented more union members and won because voting was based on membership.[22] The Communists attacked the law because it lowered workers' wages, but their stand went further. They rejected the idea completely. Before the law was passed, the paper of the Communist-controlled retail clerks' union argued that their members would not live long enough to collect pensions. Orestes

20. *Bandera Proletaria*, January 19, 1924; *Bandera Proletaria*, February 21, 1925, as quoted in Godio, *El movimiento obrero (1910–1930)*, 158; *Acción Obrera*, February and September 1924; *El Constructor Naval*, June 1925. See also, for example, *Bandera Proletaria*, January 12–26, May 11, June 21, 1924; *Acción Obrera*, June 1924; Cámara de Diputados, *Diario de sesiones*, IV, August 27, 1924, 805.
21. See Chapter 6.
22. Jacinto Oddone, *Gremialismo proletario argentino*, 2nd ed. (Buenos Aires: Ediciones Líbera, 1975), 433–34.

Ghioldi, a rising star within the party, proclaimed that a pension law remained impossible until the revolution and the establishment of the dictatorship of the proletariat. The Communists also chastised all other ideological tendencies for not doing enough to block the law.[23]

Not surprisingly, the Anarchists opposed the pension law, as they did all laws. The Anarchist confederation's strike committee proclaimed, "Following its full principals, the FORA is against the laws because in them rests the political and economic power of the government, [and] against capitalism as well, because it is one of the strong pillars of the [government] and the biggest enemy of the working class." Another wing of Anarchism made clear that it opposed the law, not only because the pension plan was intended to fill the treasury of the government but also because it was designed to prevent strikes by imposing penalties for abandoning work.[24]

In opposing the law, the Left and the labor movement were not alone. Employer organizations joined them, including the Bolsa de Comercio; the Confederación del Comercio, de la Industria y de la Producción; the Asociación del Trabajo (AT); and the Unión Industrial Argentina (UIA). The four organizations formed a commission to study the law and make recommendations on the enabling regulations. The commission moved to all-out opposition. The leading organization of industrialists, the UIA, in the January 15, 1924, edition of its *Boletín*, very carefully said that while it had favored pension plans because they displayed social solidarity and even eased social tensions, this law lacked thought and that not even regulations would permit its quick implementation. The AT even went so far as to print union objections to the law, an unusual step for an organization whose primary objective was to break unions.[25]

Industrialists objected that the legislation had been hurried and lacked clear definitions and rules, making it impossible to carry out (a complaint not unlike that of the Socialists). The government's postponement of the enforcement of the legislation and the issuing of new regulations did not quiet the complaints. In fact, they intensified. The employers complained about the additional costs, especially in what they felt was a difficult time,

---

23. *La Internacional*, January 4, 15, 19, February 8, 1924; *Nuestra Palabra*, May 1, 1923; Cámara de Diputados, *Diario de sesiones*, IV, August 27, 1924, 805.

24. *La Organización Obrera, Boletín de Huelga*, May 5, 1924; *La Antorcha*, May 2, 1924.

25. *Boletín de la UIA*, January 15, 1924, 10–11; *Boletín de Servicios*, January 20, 1924, 34–39.

as they claimed to face dumping and increased foreign competition. The employer groups also stressed that the Socialist-sponsored legislation passed at the same time as 11.289, which called for study of a complete pension plan, was a good idea and ought to be supported. The employer groups realized the popularity of the idea of pensions, but what is unclear is whether supporting the other measure was intended to block any significant pension legislation or whether they realized the utility of such a law but had problems with 11.289. The former is more likely to be true. They objected to the costs of pensions, and they would lose control of their workers' social welfare. Many employers had long favored paternalistic policies.[26]

The complaints continued. The employers met with Alvear to express their dissatisfaction with the law. The UIA questioned the constitutionality of the law. It also raised objections to the vagueness of the regulations and that smaller establishments were exempt from participating and therefore had an advantage. It stressed that the supposed beneficiaries, the workers, were resisting. The AT claimed that a survey of workers and employees in both the capital and the interior indicated strong opposition to 11.289.[27]

The employers' commission called a meeting of its constituencies at the Bolsa de Comercio on April 28, 1924, because two days later the new regulations were to be implemented and it felt them to be inadequate. Also, the USA had scheduled a general strike for May 3. The meeting adopted a resolution calling on Alvear to postpone implementing the law or face chaos. A petition to the minister of hacienda was drawn up, but when a delegation met with him, he rejected it. The same day, Alvear met with representatives of an organization supporting 11.289. The following day, Alvear reconfirmed his minister's action. Another mass meeting of employers was held where feelings became so heated that a lockout was proposed in solidarity and sympathy with the workers. The organizers, who had not contemplated such a measure, called a recess and then pushed through a proposal for a lockout and giant rally for May 5.[28] The continuing protests of employers merged into a larger struggle.

26. *Boletín de la UIA*, February 15–April 15, 1924; Confederación Argentina del Comercio, de la Industria y de la Producción, *Estudios de problemas nacionales*, no. 20 (1923): 27–28, no. 23 (1924): 27; Rocchi, *Chimneys in the Desert*, esp. 165–70.
27. *Boletín de Servicios*, March–July 5, 1924, esp. March 20, 151–59, July 5, 313; *La Epoca*, March 9, April 11, 1924.
28. *Boletín de la UIA*, May 15, 1924, 31–34; *La Epoca*, April 29, 1924; *La Prensa*, April 29–May 3, 1924.

Unrest Against the Law

Growing worker unrest also drove employers to stiffen their resistance to the law. For example, when the UOL of the USA called a protest meeting for February 3, 1924, an estimated thirty thousand people marched through the streets of Buenos Aires in various columns to converge on the Plaza San Martín. Despite police efforts, individual unions agitated against the law.[29]

Implementation of the required salary deductions produced walkouts. Although strikers frequently did not belong to unions, they clearly had been influenced by the propaganda that swirled through working-class neighborhoods. In the Buenos Aires barrio of Villa Crespo, when announcements appeared on January 22 declaring that 5 percent was to be deducted from wages, some seven hundred workers, mostly women, walked out of the Italo-Americana spinning plant and met in the local headquarters of the Communist Party. In the next few days, the stoppage spread to other factories, and the Federación Obrera de la Industria Textil and the UOL scrambled to provide advice to these unorganized strikers. The police complicated this by banning open-air meetings. Strikes also occurred in the shoe industry. The USA claimed that by January 26 some 7,000 workers had walked out. According to the DNT, the stoppages involved twenty-nine plants and 5,549 workers, almost half of them women. The wave of unrest ended when Alvear postponed implementation of the law.

Worker resistance did not occur only in Buenos Aires. On April 13 in Mendoza, when management tried to deduct 5 percent from their wages, the printers for the newspapers *Los Andes* and *La Libertad* struck. The following day winery workers walked out for the same reason, and trolley workers threatened to follow suit if their wages were touched. The management of the latter backed down, but other industries had walkouts.[30] Heated opposition to the law appeared in such centers in the interior as Tucumán and Rosario.[31]

---

29. See, for example, *Bandera Proletaria*, February 9, 1924; *La Internacional*, January 1, 1924.

30. *La Internacional*, January 23–24, 1924; *Bandera Proletaria*, January 26, February 2, 1924; DNT, *Boletín*, November 1924, 1453; *La Prensa*, April 14–21, 1924. The government stated that the Buenos Aires strikes started on January 19 and lasted on average eight days.

31. *La Prensa*, April 26–May 1, 1924; *La Epoca*, April 1924; *Bandera Proletaria*, May 3, 1924.

The General Strike/Lockout

According to the Communists, the Central Committee of the USA yielded to pressure and in early April called for a strike but failed to set a date. The USA congress approved the strike call. The general strike was to be indefinite and begin on May 3. Anarchists and others seconded the call.

Workers began leaving their jobs prior to May 3. In the capital, for example, cooks and pastry chefs walked out. The DNT reported that on May 2 in Buenos Aires over two thousand workers struck numerous employers, including construction sites and shoe and textile plants. In the Province of Buenos Aires, six hundred workers at the Mihanovich shipyard in La Plata struck, and in Lomas de Zamora, bakers, chauffeurs, and tile makers walked out. A report in *La Prensa* indicated that in Mendoza the strike was complete. Only people driving their own vehicles had transportation, and roving groups of strikers forced businesses to close, including the central market, in part by smashing windows. The local labor organization in Rosario called for the strike to start on the second and it reached large proportions. Streetcars circulated but only with armed guards; by afternoon the city looked like it did on holidays. Government services, however, continued to function.[32]

Elsewhere the general strike began in earnest on May 3. The strike was more effective in the provinces than in the capital. The attitude of many employers, however, makes it difficult to judge the intensity of the stoppage. Was it a real strike or a movement partially encouraged by employers? Although employers did not encourage such activities as the window breaking in Mendoza, they did play a role in the stopping of work. The Anti-Personalist daily *La Acción* accused the AT of directly and indirectly stimulating the strike. Under questioning by a committee of the Chamber of Deputies in July 1924, Minister of Hacienda Víctor A. Molina claimed that the employers essentially controlled the campaign against the law, with workers playing a secondary role: "The violent speeches and even the revolutionary ones came from the bosses. Many times I have heard them say that they would arm their workers and they would go the government house."[33] These claims were, at least partially, intended to deflect the idea of popular unhappiness.

32. *La Internacional*, April 1924; *La Epoca*, April 1924; *Bandera Proletaria*, April 12, 26, 1924; Marotta, *El movimiento sindical argentino*, 3:136–37; *La Acción*, May 2, 3, 1924; *La Vanguardia*, May 2/3, 1924; *La Prensa*, May 3, 1924.

33. *La Acción*, May 3, 1924; Cámara de Diputados, *Diario de sesiones*, IV, August 27, 1924, 766; I, June 23, 1924, 583.

The stoppage on the third was uneven. In Buenos Aires, although some businesses were forced to close and the strike intensified during the day, a clear judgment on its impact is difficult because it was Saturday and traditionally many businesses stayed open only half the day. The Socialist Party paper, *La Vanguardia*, estimated that eighty thousand workers struck, but the transportation system functioned almost normally. Strike activity was spotty in the Province of Buenos Aires, with some areas seeing significant stoppages and others almost none. In Mendoza the strike continued to be intense and rumors of violence in the countryside swept through the city; wineries and all industries closed. In Rosario conditions remained the same as the previous day. The UIA claimed that the strike paralyzed most activities in the country and that, although quiet reigned in the capital, violence marked some interior regions.[34]

The employer organizations had set Monday for the lockout and demonstration, making it impossible to judge what was strike and what was lockout. According to the provincial police of Buenos Aires, most of the stoppages in that province occurred with the connivance of both workers and employers. In the capital, most stores and businesses closed. The port functioned with nonunion labor but not as well as normal. Violence increased, and there were attacks on trolleys. In the Province of Buenos Aires the stoppage intensified greatly. Most of the industries along the Riachuelo River, which divided the southern sector of the capital from the province, ceased functioning, with the exception of the meatpacking plants. The giant meat plants in La Plata owned by Armour and Swift, however, which together employed almost ten thousand workers, shut down. In Campana and Mar del Plata oil refineries closed. In Tucumán the strike took on surprising strength, and that afternoon the streetcars stopped running and the carriage drivers struck. Arrests and violence were frequent throughout the nation.

The employers' demonstration took place in the Plaza Colón, directly behind the government house, the Casa Rosada. A delegation met for an hour with Alvear. He told it what he had essentially earlier told a delegation from the USA, that when pressure was lifted and normality restored, he would act in the best interest of the nation. At the subsequent meeting of employer groups to discuss the encounter, Joaquín Anchorena, the head of the delegation, announced this and added that businesses should open

---

34. The information on the strike is drawn from May in *La Prensa; La Acción; La Epoca; Bandera Proletaria; La Vanguardia; La Internacional; Boletín La Antorcha; Boletín de la UIA*, May 1924, 31–36.

the next day. Many disagreed with this stance but were somewhat appeased by a motion passed by acclamation, calling on businesses not to pay into the pension funds. An interesting feature of the rally, and a good indication of the confused nature of the protest, was the presence of many workers. According to *La Prensa*, at the end of the demonstration some three hundred people, mostly members of the Anarchist drivers union, formed a rowdy column that marched up the Avenida de Mayo shouting slogans against the national authorities and merchants who remained open. Mounted policemen finally disbursed them and thirty-five were detained. This was not the only such group.

During the next two days, the strike grew in some regions and broke down in others. In Rosario some workers, particularly the unorganized, went back. So did the Armour and Swift workers. The strike intensified, however, in the small cities of Buenos Aires province and in Tucumán, where it became violent. On the seventh of May, the Central Committee of the USA called for a return to work on the following day in those industries where employers did not deduct wages for the pension funds. It did not make its reasoning clear, but its members seemed to have been motivated by the diminishing support for the strike in some localities and the problems that maritime workers were having sustaining the stoppage because of a rupture with the shipboard officers. Also, there appears to have been an unofficial agreement to release prisoners after the strike ceased. Shortly after the strike ended, the government postponed once again the implementation of the law. The UIA called on its members not to make deductions from workers' wages. The prisoners were freed, and work resumed in the same disorderly fashion that the strike had begun.

How successful was the general strike/lockout? Work did not uniformly cease, as it had during some past stoppages. In part this was due to the cause of the strike/lockout. Key groups were not directly affected, because they already had pension systems. These sectors, especially trolley and railroad workers, could have had a major impact, as their participation would have prevented many from getting to work. The support given by employers created confusion in an ideological world in which employers and workers were seen by many as having innately different interests. Also, considerable sympathy existed for pension plans among portions of the working population and among many employers, making support for a shutdown problematic at best. There were problems with the strategy as well. Why start on a Saturday? Why May 3 and not on the workers' holiday, May Day? In addition, there was friction between Anarchists and Syndicalists.[35] Still, the stoppage had an impact in wide areas of the country and, according to the DNT, some two hundred thousand workers struck in the capital.[36] The law was never fully implemented, but the strike had even wider repercussions.

The UIA called for a consistent and thoughtful approach to labor legislation and stated a preference for no legislation to what it thought was bad legislation: "The UIA demands from congress more attention to the problems of our workers. It demands harmonious laws, basic principles that fix the norms of work and of capital. It does not desire absurd rules that complicate the situation without advantages for anyone, an impressive example being law 11.289. Instead of that we prefer inertia."[37]

The labor movement, particularly the Syndicalists, the orientation closest to the Radicals, emerged severely weakened. The deterioration, which had begun with the defeat of the general strike in mid-1921, intensified.[38] The Syndicalists' problems could be attributed in small part to the Alvear administration no longer seeing them as a useful ally. They had worked too hard to disrupt what the administration saw as worthwhile legislation. Most of the problems occurred as a direct result of the strike/lockout. In Rosario, the retail clerks had struck for five days before going back to work. Their union had lost its power and employers ceased closing their shops on Saturday afternoon. The union could do nothing.[39] The conflicting interests of organized workers on the waterfront came to the fore because of disagreements about the pension plan. The shaky alliance between officers and crews on Argentine flag vessels that had allowed unions to maintain some control of the port of Buenos Aires shattered over pensions. Officers badly wanted a pension plan, but the dominant faction among the crew joined the rest of the labor movement in opposing it. Organized labor on shipboard never recovered.[40] Not just Syndicalist organizations were weakened. The printers' union, Federación Gráfica Bonaerense, one of the stronger unions in the country, suffered because of the general strike. Editorial Atlántida, the publisher of such popular magazines as *Para Ti* and *Billiken*, punished workers who had participated in the strike, and the

35. In addition to the sources above, see *Acción Obrera*, June 1924; *La Organización Obrera*, Boletín de Huelga, May 5, 1925.
36. DNT, *Boletín*, November 1924, 1455.
37. *Boletín de la UIA*, May 15, 1924, 21.
38. See Chapter 5.
39. Roberto Marrone, *Apuntes para la historia de un gremio (empleados de comercio de Rosario)* (Rosario: Tipografía Llordén SRL, 1974), 94.
40. See Chapter 6.

union replied with a work stoppage. The publisher replaced the strikers, and the union resorted to a long and ineffectual boycott.[41]

The strike/lockout intensified the squabbling between Communists and Syndicalists. Even before the general strike, the USA was sharply divided.[42] The strike's conclusion heightened the conflict. Almost immediately, Communist sources attacked the Syndicalist-controlled Central Committee, saying that the Committee should not have ended the strike when it did, that the strike should have been called for May Day, that the organizing had been poor, and that the Committee should not have sent a letter to the president. Although nothing is to be gained by examining the quarrel in detail, it reached the point of the Central Committee cutting off contact with the Communist-controlled UOL and then resigning. The USA then had to elect a new directive body.[43] The USA never fully recuperated from these quarrels. It is not clear whether the disagreements over the tactics used in fighting law 11.289 were an excuse for quarrels or a cause.

Continued Support and Opposition to 11.289

The May general strike and lockout did not prevent the government or the Radicals from continuing to support law 11.289, as did various organizations. Still, opposition stopped full implementation. Unrest cropped up in scattered industries when employers subtracted sums from workers' wages as required by the law. For example, when the Wilson meatpacking plant deducted the 5 percent from their wages, workers walked out, with some using weapons to keep others from working. The USA called a twenty-four-hour general strike for August 27, 1924, which it considered a great success. According to the DNT, some fifty thousand workers struck in Buenos Aires. The UOL called another such strike in September 1925. In Buenos Aires in 1925, 11.289 caused a quarter of the strikes. Employers continued their protests, reiterating their position that this was a bad law and studies needed to be made about implementing better pension laws.

---

41. See, for example, *El Obrero Gráfico*, August–November 1924, April 1926; *La Vanguardia*, May 10, 1924; *Nueva Era* (Avellaneda), July 5, 1924; *Bandera Proletaria*, August 16, December 6, 1924.

42. *Bandera Proletaria*, March 31, 1923, February 1 (really March 1), March 8, 1924; *La Internacional*, March 6, April 17–23, 1924; *El Obrero Municipal*, March–May 1924; Marotta, *El movimiento sindical argentino*, 3:125–51.

43. *La Internacional*, May 10, 17, June 7, 1924; *Bandera Proletaria*, June 7–October 25, 1924; *Acción Obrera*, March 1925; *El Constructor Naval*, August 1925.

On June 4, 1925, fifty thousand people attended a demonstration against 11.289 called by employer organizations.[44]

From the beginning, there were attempts in congress either to save the legislation by modifying it or to kill it outright. The debates remained heated. The Anti-Personalist Radicals did not persevere as long as did the Personalists, who never abandoned their support for the law. In early 1926 the Anti-Personalist deputies left the chamber instead of defending the measure (though by helping to deny a quorum they were defending the law). By September they had officially abandoned their support, leaving only the Personalist Radicals to defend it, and the law was indefinitely suspended by a vote of congress. For a party without a programmatic approach, this continued endorsement indicates that they perceived political benefits from their continued support.[45] As late as June 1930 *La Epoca*, after calling Yrigoyen "the father of the Argentine workers," goes on to praise the message that he had sent to congress that led to 11.289 and lamented its suspension.[46] In the minds of others, the AT for example, the bill had been badly crafted and had just become a cause of constant agitation.[47]

Conclusion

The 1920s were not a good time to try to craft widespread social legislation. Despite rhetoric about the welfare of the workers, the economic elites were unwilling to increase their costs. They worked hard to block the implementation of 11.289 and, despite words to the contrary, did not appear to have

---

44. *Bandera Proletaria*, August 11–30, 1924, April 11, December 5, 1925; DNT, *Crónica Mensual*, February 1925, 1530, July 1925, 1602–5, July 1926, 1822–24; *Boletín de la UIA*, June 1925, 27–33; *La Prensa*, May 30, 1924, October 10, 1925; *La Nación*, January 24, 1925; *La Internacional*, October 10–11, October 30–November 2, 1925; *La Argentina*, June 4, 1925; *El Constructor Naval*, June 1925; *Nuestra Palabra*, June 1925; *El Obrero Gráfico*, May 1925, April 1926; *Nueva Era* (Avellaneda), December 6, 1924, October 31, 1925; Cámara de Diputados, *Diario de sesiones*, VI (1925), January 13, 1926, 373; Aníbal Jáuregui, "El despegue de los industriales argentinos," in *Argentina en la paz de dos guerras, 1914–1945*, ed. Waldo Ansaldi et al. (Buenos Aires: Editorial Biblos, 1993), 189; *Boletín de Servicios*, May 20–July 5, 1925.

45. The level of political debate, both at the beginning and the end of the discussions about the pension plan, was extremely low and seemed to focus more on political benefits than the law. This is further evidence of the essentially political motivations. The debates on the law continued through the sessions of 1924, 1925, and 1926. The law was finally put to rest in September 1926. See Cámara de Diputados, *Diario de sesiones*, V, September 16, 1926, 712–14.

46. *La Epoca*, June 23, 1930.

47. *Boletín de Servicios*, September 20, 1926, 410.

favored better-crafted schemes. Unions also vigorously opposed the legislation for practical (largely the Socialists), political, and ideological reasons. The consequences were large. The USA was severely weakened and descended into sectarianism of the most extreme type. One reason may have been the problems created with the government. The Alvear administration implied that union opposition to 11.289 was political (in other words favoring the Personalists).[48] Key unions, especially the FOM, never recovered.

The failure of the project demonstrates the difficulties of establishing a full-scale social welfare program in Argentina. Little organized support existed, which made it politically difficult. Politicians could not count on support from either unions or the organizations of the economic elite. The Radicals had learned a painful lesson. In addition, as the decade progressed, congress became a less viable body, frequently unable to pass even routine legislation, as it became consumed by partisan wrangling. The Radical attempt to create a pension system that would tie workers to the social and political system had failed. Such policies could not be used to enlarge the party's popular base. Labor legislation in the 1920s was piecemeal; only politically crucial sectors received pensions.[49] The relationship between government and the working class remained dependent on personal connections.

This episode gives us a window to examine the strengths and weaknesses of Radical politics. Although intending to benefit the working class and to obtain labor peace and thereby build political support, the Radicals never consulted with their purported union allies, nor heeded their opposition. The relationship was too instrumental, based solely on shared mutual interests rather than an ongoing interaction. Similarly, the Radicals failed to make a major attempt to line up support among the business elite.

The failure of the Radicals of either faction to secure large-scale effective social welfare or labor legislation did not have immediately important deleterious political effects. By the 1920s, no effective opposition existed outside the capital to take advantage of the Radicals' problems, and the 1928 presidential election was largely between wings of the party. The Radicals had effective hegemony over the political landscape. In the capital this failure may have helped chip away at Radical support and helped the Socialists and the Independent Socialists. The two branches of the Socialist Party, however, could not by themselves produce any legislation.

48. See, for example, *La Acción*, April 22, 1924.
49. For dates, see Ramicone, *Apuntes para la historia*, 66.

The Radicals did have a sense of politics. The only explanation for the continued support of 11.289 is that the Radicals read public perception as not being against the legislation. Given the lack of polling, it is impossible to tell what the popular classes believed. If one were to compare the Radicals' record in Buenos Aires with that of the labor movement as a whole during the 1920s, the Radicals had more success appealing to the popular classes than did the unions. The Radicals continued to build a popular following, but they failed to institutionalize support from either employers or the popular classes. They also failed to leave a legacy of solid social legislation.

5

YRIGOYEN AND THE LIMITATIONS OF *OBRERISMO*, 1916–1922

When Yrigoyen assumed office in October 1916, his victory in the electoral college had been uncomfortably close, and he felt a need to widen his popular base. In part, this represented a politician's typical lust for votes, but it also reflected the Radicals' perception of themselves as the true representative of Argentine popular will.[1] In addition, the Socialists had strong support in the city of Buenos Aires and appeared to present a real challenge to Radical dominance.

A principal political target for Yrigoyen were the native-born popular classes, including the sons of immigrants. The symbolic acceptance of workers as citizens was critical. It enabled Yrigoyen to stand with the people against—in many cases—foreign-owned business. Yrigoyen's use of Syndicalist unions as a bridge to the working class was a critical element in his strategy for building a wider political base, part of *obrerismo*. The unions enabled Yrigoyen to achieve a personal connection to the popular classes. Although this foreshadows the tactics used by Juan Perón in the 1940s, it differed in that Yrigoyen never tried to formalize the relationship or extend it to all workers. He preferred informal relationships, as did the Syndicalists, making them an ideal target. The Syndicalists understood that given the harsh realities of labor relations, unions, which obtained government neutrality or better yet favor, did much better than those that did not. From Yrigoyen's perspective the Syndicalists had several advantages. They could offer an entree to the popular class; they welcomed the

---

1. See Chapter 2 for examples.

informal relationship that the Radicals desired because anything else would have challenged their basic ideology. Given their apoliticism, Syndicalists were also free to vote Radical. In addition, they were extremely antagonistic to the Socialists, and their growth would prevent the expansion of the Radicals' primary competition in the capital.

It is important to remember that even though unions in this era were small, they tended to influence large numbers of workers. Why did not more workers join? Salaries were low and therefore dues were a burden; moreover, no system of dues checkoff existed. Members faced retaliation from employers and little immediate benefits existed for joining. Despite the small number of members, however, strikes were frequently large and many attended demonstrations. Clearly unions had influence far beyond their limited membership.

Prior to mid-1921, a crucial tactic of Yrigoyen was supporting or at least tolerating the strike activity of certain unions. Support for strikes is tricky. Strike waves cannot be controlled and labor unrest tends to snowball; this was especially so because of the elation created among many workers by the Bolshevik Revolution and the ensuing political and labor turmoil in both Europe and the Americas. Many among the elites and the middle classes feared the revolution's impact, at least as much as some were excited by it. All this took place in a new political landscape in which the rules were unclear. Despite the ultimate rejection of this tactic, Yrigoyen achieved important relationships that had political ramifications as late as his second term.

Yrigoyen's approach to strikes was never systematic. Moved by political considerations as well as a general belief in public welfare, Yrigoyen operated on a case-by-case basis. He preferred to intervene personally or through trusted aides, especially the police chief of Buenos Aires. He intervened in a favorable manner in industries in which strikes would be visible even to those not directly involved and when a considerable number of workers were Argentine citizens or the political ramifications were large for other reasons. Yrigoyen favored Syndicalist union leaders and displayed hostility to those who had ties to political organizations that were rivals of the Radicals. As Ernesto Garguin has pointed out, however, he was willing to help La Fraternidad, the railroad engineers' union, despite the prominent role that the Socialists played in that union.[2] He did so

2. Ernesto Garguin, "Mediaciones corporativas entre estado y sindicatos, Argentina (1916–1930)" (paper delivered at the Latin American Studies Association Congress, 1998), 20–21.

largely because the leadership subordinated politics to what they perceived as the union's interest.

Yrigoyen made his approach to labor a fundamental element of his attempt to widen his political base. He did not immediately abandon this tactic even after it became a serious liability among certain sectors of the population. It continued after the Tragic Week. Even after Yrigoyen found such policies to be unsustainable in mid-1921, he continued to explore ways to build relationships with the working class through unions. Yrigoyen's willingness to treat workers as important citizens played a key role in expanding his popularity. Workers could feel that the Radicals considered them important, and many gave their loyalty in return.

The Port

The first major attempt to create a bridge to the working class occurred in the port of Buenos Aires. The workers on the waterfront were not heavily Argentine. In 1914, according to Socialist leader Angel M. Giménez, only some 23 percent of Argentine maritime personnel were citizens, but those 3,139 citizens were still a significant number. A more recent study by Geoffroy de Laforcade indicates a much heavier presence of Argentines, at least on a seasonal basis; he also found that regulations forced many sailors to become naturalized citizens and therefore potential voters.[3]

The center of the maritime world of Buenos Aires was the neighborhood of La Boca, which contained a heavy concentration of industries connected with the waterfront, such as dock work, shipbuilding, and repairs, and was home to many sailors. Much of the community depended on waterfront prosperity, even the small shopkeepers, so that what happened in that arena rippled through others. La Boca early became a Socialist Party stronghold, and the Radicals felt that it needed to be wrested away.[4]

Since the turn of the twentieth century, unions had been forming in the port of Buenos Aires. In 1910 what became the strongest union in the port, the Federación Obrera Marítima (FOM), was founded with the inten-

3. Dora Barrancos, "Vita materiale e battaglia ideologica nel quartiere della Boca (1880–1930)," in Identità degli italiani in Argentina, ed. Gianfausto Rosoli (Rome: Edizioni Studium, 1993), 197; Geoffroy de Laforcade, "Port Cities, Trade Unions, and the Merchant Marine" (paper delivered at the Latin American Studies Association Congress, 1994), 6–7.

4. Barrancos, "Vita materiale"; Laforcade, "Port Cities"; Jeremy Adelman, "State and Labour in Argentina: The Port Workers of Buenos Aires, 1910–21," Journal of Latin American Studies 25, no. 1 (February 1993): 86–87; Walter, Politics and Urban Growth, esp. 63, 65.

tion of representing all the subordinate shipboard personnel, both on large ships and on the supporting port craft, tugs, launches, and so forth. The FOM became a true federation with each work specialty (sailors, waiters, cooks, etc.) organized separately; each had different interests in work rules and had separate wage scales. The specialties tended to pull in different directions. Almost from the beginning, the glue that held the organization together was Francisco J. García, "El Gallego." Despite his nickname, he was Argentine-born. He was a dedicated Syndicalist with great talents as an organizer, and he rapidly became the heart and soul of the federation.

The Radical government took a special interest in the FOM. Why this attention to the FOM? In addition to its base being the politically important La Boca, the FOM could shut off trade with the outside world through control of the personnel of tugs and lighters. Most overseas trade left on foreign vessels. FOM members also manned the boats that the upriver provinces, Corrientes and Entre Ríos, and the territories of Misiones and Patagonia depended on for connection to the outside world. This is the type of argument that Charles Bergquist has made about the crucial role of export industries in the development of labor, though his emphasis for Argentina was different. The government could view the FOM favorably because Syndicalists dominated it. Moreover, as Jeremy Adelman has pointed out, a key segment of the waterfront district lay directly behind the Casa Rosada and close to the ministries, making it difficult to ignore large-scale unrest.[5]

Within days of Yrigoyen's assumption of office, the FOM had prepared a detailed set of demands, hoping to reverse deteriorating working conditions and salaries. Although the union accepted an offer of mediation from the Departamento Nacional del Trabajo (DNT), the employers refused it. The workers struck on November 30 and severely limited port activity. A split in the attitudes of the bureaucratic structures was apparent from the beginning. The DNT clearly sympathized with the union, and the naval prefecture—which controlled the port—backed the employers; it made distribution of propaganda difficult and helped the shippers in other ways. This lack of bureaucratic unity in the port is characteristic of the entire Radical period. The DNT personnel, because of the nature of their jobs, tended to be sympathetic to labor, while the conservative navy controlled

---

5. Charles Bergquist, *Labor in Latin America* (Stanford, Calif.: Stanford University Press, 1986); Adelman, "State and Labour," 80. For Garcia, see Trocoso, *Fundadores del gremialismo obrero/1*, 77–96.

the prefecture. Civilians lacked either the desire or the ability to fully control the navy.

The offices of those with power were open to the FOM, which first met with the minister of the interior, the most important cabinet minister, and later with Yrigoyen himself. This readiness to meet with union leaders was unprecedented and the administration's response to the employers' refusal to accept mediation was to pledge neutrality.[6] The prefecture then removed its personnel who were manning some support craft and refused to permit ships to sail without crews that met all the extensive government regulations. In other words, it did not allow the recruitment of strikebreakers.

On December 20, facing a noncooperative government and unable to move their vessels, the shippers asked for mediation by the president, and the FOM readily went along. Yrigoyen handed over the arbitration to his chief of police, Julio Moreno. After a long debate, the strikers voted 967 to 461 to return to work while awaiting the decision. This marked an important step for the Syndicalists, accepting an increased role for the government.

According to union calculations, the arbitration decision gave the workers between 75 and 90–95 percent of what they asked.[7] Why? The strike was conspicuous and involved some six thousand workers; it was early in the regime and therefore likely to set a pattern. In addition, the union behaved in what from the government's perspective was an acceptable fashion. It had been willing to accept government involvement and while violence had occurred, it had not been a primary tactic.

The FOM did not go unchallenged. The Mihanovich lines, the most important firm in the river trade, formed a company union under the control of Juan Colmeiro. He had been expelled from a previous sailor's union as a police agent and had been a policeman. By March 1917 the shipping companies were disputing the interpretations of the arbitration award and

---

6. Earlier governments had been open to dealing with workers. See Adelman, "State and Labour," 82–83.

7. Ibid., 84–88; Geoffroy de Laforcade, "Ideas, Action, and Experience in the Labor Process: Argentine Seamen and Revolutionary Syndicalism" (paper delivered at the Tenth Annual Latin American Labor History Conference, 1993), 14–17; Alfredo Palacios, *El nuevo derecho* (Buenos Aires: Claridad, 1934), 194–98; Alfredo Fernández, *El movimiento obrero en la Argentina* (Buenos Aires: Plus Ultra, 1937), no. 4 y 5, 205–11; José Tomás Sojo and Manuel V. Ordóñoz, "Historia y organización de la Federación Obrera Marítima," *Revista de la Facultad de Derecho y Ciencias Sociales* (January–March 1924): 169–74; DNT, *Boletín*, January 1918, 5, 45–46, 179–85, March 1918, v–59, February 1919, 31–50, April 1919, 30–35; *La Unión del Marino*, November 1916.

the FOM was turning to the head of the naval prefecture for help. An attempt by Mihanovich to employ workers belonging to the new union sparked violence, and on March 20, 1917, the FOM struck the company. The first day five FOM members were wounded. The government sent troops, who prevented the circulation of any propaganda in the port. The FOM with the backing of the FORA IX threatened a general strike. Through the police chief, Yrigoyen informed the FOM that he wanted a meeting. García and the FORA IX met with Yrigoyen and convinced him to withdraw the troops rather than face an expanded stoppage. Yrigoyen had given the union a green light to use force and Colmeiro was shot and killed as he left his house. On two occasions, the FOM besieged the company union headquarters for days and did not permit strikebreakers to leave until they pledged to abandon their activities.

The company seriously miscalculated by lowering the salaries of those shipboard officers whose vessels could not sail. They struck and for the first time created a community of interest among all shipboard ranks. This unity proved to be crucial in the short period of the FOM's success. Although it was relatively easy to replace the less skilled subordinate ranks, it was almost impossible to do so with the officers, who needed years of training. Mihanovich attempted to increase the pressure on the government by trying to convince other shipping lines to lock out their workers starting April 3, but most companies refused to join. The contending parties finally agreed to mediation by the head of the division of social order of the capital police. An agreement was signed on April 22, which among other things dissolved the company union and permitted all to return to their jobs without reprisals.[8] The union's victory had come with the cooperation of the government.

The impact of the FOM's victories was immense. Not only had it won, but it appeared to have the backing of the state. The DNT claimed that the FOM's victories had a large impact on the Syndicalist confederation, the FORA IX, which had 70 member organizations in 1916 and 199 the following year. In addition, monthly dues payers jumped from 3,292 to 11,994. The FOM's willingness to aid other unions quickly made it the most important union in the country, arguably exerting more influence on the nature of the labor movement than any other union in the history of Argentina.

8. Laforcade, "Ideas, Action, and Experience," 13–17; Fernández, *El movimiento obrero*, no. 6, 253; DNT, *Boletín*, March 1918, 61–72, February 1919, 50–64; Marotta, *El movimiento sindical argentino*, 2:205–6; Sojo and Ordóñoz, "Historia y organización," 173–75; *La Epoca*, March 20–April 19, 1917.

According to the DNT, "By virtue of its solidarity so permanently, widely and wisely carried out, the FOM has become in this manner something like the head organization of national workers' organizations of advanced tendencies, which in moments of struggle look for its moral and material aid."[9]

The FOM continually acted in solidarity with officers and other waterfront crafts; it also provided support to a wide variety of workers, from millers and railroaders to packinghouse workers. The FOM's envoys played a critical role in organizing some of the most oppressed workers in Argentina, those who labored on the northeastern quebracho and maté plantations. Most shipboard activities were unionized and locals existed in ports from Bahía Blanca northward.[10]

Railroads

The relationship between the railroaders and the government helps make understandable the administration's dealings with the port. Together they give us a good idea of what the regime hoped to achieve. Like the maritime workers, the railroaders could strangle the country economically. Until the 1930s, roads were notoriously bad and therefore disruption of rail traffic cut off not only the vital export/import trade but also most internal trade. In addition, railroad workers fit into electoral calculations even more than port workers. There were many more of them, 112,175 in 1916 and 148,717 in 1930.[11] Although distributed around the country, most lived in three crucial districts, the capital, Santa Fe, and Buenos Aires province. Like shipboard workers, many railroaders had the ability to move around and spread the idea of unions and revolution. Railroad unionization faced a problem similar to that on the waterfront, rivalries based on the nature of the job. Railroads had engineers, workers engaged in running the train, shop workers, track maintenance workers, and so forth. Engineers considered themselves superior to the rest of the railroaders, but the differences aboard ship were much greater because shipboard officers had legal com-

    9. DNT, Boletín, February 1919, 64. See also April 1919, 31.
    10. For a summary, see DNT, Boletín, February 1919; Angel Borda, *Perfil de un libertario* (Buenos Aires: Editorial Reconstruir, 1987), 19–23; Marotta, *El movimiento sindical argentino*, 2:251–52.
    11. Ministerio de Obras Públicas, Dirección General de Ferrocarriles, *Estadística de los ferrocarriles en explotación*, año 1916, 330; and año 1930, 318.

mand of the vessel. The railroad companies were largely foreign-owned and unpopular.

Railroaders developed a sense of occupational community. They identified with one another: "Members of occupational communities are affected by their work in such a way that their non-work lives are permeated by their work relationships, interests and values. . . . Members of occupational communities build their lives on their work; their work friends are their friends outside work and their leisure interests and activities are work-based."[12] The reasons for the existence of such identification among railroaders are unclear, but it existed not only in Argentina but also in the United States and Britain. Status questions, importance of the industry, concentration of shop workers, and irregular schedules all may partially explain its presence. The sense of community helps account for the strength that rail unions developed, because it gave unions the power to exclude workers from the community.[13]

Even more than with the port, we can see the motivations of Yrigoyen: he wanted to consolidate political support through personal ties. But also we can see the limits of tolerance. When the rail unions failed to halt the avalanche of strikes in 1918 and 1919, Yrigoyen lost patience. The engineers had a tradition of unionization dating back to the founding of La Fraternidad in 1887. La Fraternidad's focus on improving salaries and working conditions, discipline, and centralized control ultimately shaped the entire railroad union movement. This was not initially obvious because La Fraternidad's failures led to the unionization of other sectors.

In 1912 La Fraternidad may have been the largest union in the country, but a strike called in January revealed a glaring weakness. Although elements of the government helped the union negotiate with the companies, and continued to do so while the strike lasted, La Fraternidad failed to shut down the rail system. The state permitted the companies to employ strikebreakers, but as important, of the approximately eleven thousand railroaders who struck, eight thousand worked as engineers or firemen. The vast majority of the others did not belong to unions and continued working. This left La Fraternidad vulnerable. After fifty-two days an agreement was reached, but many strike leaders did not get their jobs back. A chief goal of La Fraternidad became to help organize the other railroaders.[14]

12. Graeme Salaman, *Community and Occupation: An Exploration of Work/Leisure Relationships* (London: Cambridge University Press, 1974), 19.
13. Horowitz, "Occupational Community," 55–81.
14. Juan Suriano, "Estado y conflicto social: El caso de la huelga de maquinistas ferrovi-

The Federación de Obreros Ferroviarios (FOF) was founded shortly before the 1912 strike but had played an insignificant part.[15] It did not fit well with La Fraternidad. Dominated by Syndicalists (unlike La Fraternidad, in which Socialists played a crucial role), the FOF had a decentralized structure with much power going to the locals, reflecting ideology and the dispersed nature of the rail system. Decentralization tended to lead to constant regional strikes because leaders lacked the tools to restrain locals.

After Yrigoyen's election, the two unions began to position themselves. The FOF merged with a smaller rival and signed a solidarity pact with La Fraternidad. Shortly after Yrigoyen assumed office, a delegation from La Fraternidad met with Minister of Public Works Pablo Torello, who, according to the Radical daily, *La Epoca,* assured them that the workers could have faith that Yrigoyen would pay attention to their complaints. Despite another meeting, nothing happened to support the railroaders' demands, although a high government official did attend La Fraternidad's annual assembly.[16] When a delegation from the FOF met with Torello on January 17, 1917, to complain about bad working conditions, it was told that the government could not defend the workers, but the government would see that laws and regulations were enforced. The FOF was also told to have patience, because a railroad strike would ruin the country and create difficulties for the government. In May another delegation met with Yrigoyen to ask for freedom (which they received) for Avelino Zapico, a union member convicted of murder, and while there, they complained about the late payments received by State Railroad workers. Yrigoyen promised to fix this.[17] Clearly, the administration was sending out signals of a willingness to cooperate.

The two unions planned to shut down the rail system during the harvest season in late 1917. Wildcat strikes, however, disrupted these plans. These

---

arios de 1912," *Boletín del Instituto de Historia Argentina y Americana "Dr. E. Ravignani,"* 3rd ser., no. 4 (segundo semestre de 1991): 91–115; Marcelino Buyán, *Una avanzada obrera* (Buenos Aires: La Vanguardia, 1933), 9–10, 28–29; Juan B. Chiti and Francisco Agnelli, *Cincuentenario de "La Fraternidad"* (Buenos Aires: Revshino Hnos., 1937), 22–25, 457; Heidi Goldberg, "Railroad Unionization in Argentina, 1912–1929: The Limitations of Working Class Alliance" (Ph.D. diss., Yale University, 1979), 41–52; Ruth Thompson, "The Engineer Drivers' and Firemen's Strike of 1912" (unpublished paper); Fernández, *El movimiento obrero,* no. 4 y 5, 184–87; William Rögind, *Historia del Ferrocarril Sud* (Buenos Aires: Establecimiento Gráfico Argentino, 1937), 481–83.

15. It was also called the Federación de Obreros Ferrocarrilera.

16. *El Obrero Ferroviario,* June, August 1916; Goldberg, "Railroad Unionization," 149; Goodwin, *Los ferrocarriles británicos,* 70–71; Jorge Larroca and Armando Vidal, *Rieles de lucha: Centenario de La Fraternidad* (Buenos Aires: La Fraternidad, 1987), 54–55.

17. *El Obrero Ferroviario,* February, June 1917.

began in the problem-plagued Central Argentino workshops in and around Rosario, when the company further limited the workweek. Accompanied by a good deal of violence, the stoppage spread up and down the rail line, completely snarling traffic. The strikers escaped the control of the unions. Still, both the police chief of Rosario, a political appointee of the governor of Santa Fe, and the troops sent reluctantly by Yrigoyen were remarkably restrained. The strike was finally settled after considerable pressure was placed on the company by the government, and Torello played a key role. La Fraternidad openly applauded the government's actions.[18] The Radicals were clearly attempting to attract worker support. *La Epoca* defended the lack of protection provided to the company by proclaiming, "Never would the present government belittle the honor of its army by entrusting it with a mission of assassination." Despite the strike being dominated by Anarchists (some have accused the Rosario Anarchists of having agreements with the Radicals), the strikers' commission thanked Rosario's police chief and the army colonel who commanded the troops for their behavior.[19] A key motivation, besides a general opening to labor, was the fractured condition of the Radical Party in Santa Fe and Yrigoyen's desire to build his strength there.

During and directly after this stoppage, wildcat strikes erupted on several lines, including a very similar stoppage at the State Railroads' workshops at Tafí Viejo, Tucumán. Afraid of losing control, the two rail unions moved ahead their planned strike. Tensions already existed between the two sets of leaders, which were caused by different reactions to the government's efforts to help settle strikes and the attempts by Torello and the Radical Party to prevent a strike. In September the unions began a strike that lasted twenty-five days and stopped rail traffic nationwide. Solidarity strikes, including one by port workers, and a threat of a general strike began to shut down the entire economy. The agrarian and business elites pressured the government but were at times treated with disdain. A delegation from elite organizations needed to wait more than a week before being able to see Yrigoyen. Violence was pervasive and troops were again

18. *El Obrero Ferroviario*, September 1916, July, August, 1917; Rock, *Politics in Argentina*, 139–43; Goodwin, *Los ferrocarriles británicos*, 69–101; Goldberg, "Railroad Unionization," 151–62; Manuel F. Fernández, *La Unión Ferroviaria a través del tiempo: Veinticinco años al servicio de un ideal* (Buenos Aires: Unión Ferroviaria, 1948), 83–87; Fernández, *El movimiento obrero*, no. 4 y 5, 217–20; Matthew B. Karush, "Workers or Citizens: The Construction of Political Identities in Democratic Argentina, Rosario, 1912–1930" (Ph.D. diss., University of Chicago, 1997), 187–91; Rögind, *Historia del Ferrocarril Sud*, 563–64; Ruth Thompson, "The Making of the Confraternidad Ferroviaria" (unpublished paper); Silvana Palermo, "Railways and the Making of Modern Argentina," chapter 6; Larroca and Vidal, *Rieles de lucha*, 57.

19. Goodwin, *Los ferrocarriles británicos*, 93; Karush, "Workers or Citizens," 190n9.

deployed, but this time they did not hesitate in trying to protect property. The FOF displayed a reluctance to negotiate with the government. The key leader of the FOF, Francisco Rosanova, was ill and had been temporarily replaced by another Syndicalist, Bautista V. Mansilla, who seemed less pragmatic. The union alliance splintered. The FOF refused to negotiate with government help, while La Fraternidad did, some of it in secret, winning concessions on work rules, as well as considerable pay raises. The companies had begun to restore service using strikebreakers until the government forced an agreement with the FOF, which reluctantly then urged a return to work. Most railroaders received little aside from vague promises contained in a government provisional regulation of work. Mansilla created a great scandal by claiming that he ordered a return to work only in homage to Yrigoyen, an odd statement for any Syndicalist, but especially for one who had resisted giving the government a role in negotiations. Mansilla was later accused of being a Radical Party operative.[20]

The alliance between La Fraternidad and the FOF had definitively broken. The FOF continued to strike and give recognition to worker initiatives. Because of the large number of railroad strikes, thirty-one in 1918, seventy-three in 1919, and twenty-one in 1920—many of which were crushing defeats—it is not surprising that the government offered little assistance, though it continued to meet with union delegations.[21] The FOF was also wracked by internal disputes, making it difficult to deal with. The government had little to gain from continuing to support this constant upheaval.

Negative Reactions

Not all unions received the benevolence of the Radical regime. A prime example was the attempt by the municipal workers of Buenos Aires to

20. For Mansilla, see Ruth Thompson, "Trade Union Organisations: Some Forgotten Aspects," in *Essays in Argentine Labour History, 1870–1930*, ed. Jeremy Adelman (London: Macmillan, 1992), 164. *El Obrero Ferroviario*, August 1917; *La Epoca*, September 13–October 29, 1917; *La Prensa*, September 13–October 29, 1917; Palermo, "Railways and the Making of Modern Argentina," chapter 6; Rock, *Politics in Argentina*, 143–50; Hora, *The Landowners of the Argentine Pampas*, 150; Mónica Gordillo, *El movimiento obrero ferroviario desde el interior del país (1916–1922)* (Buenos Aires: Centro Editor de América Latina, 1988), 73–83; Larroca and Vidal, *Rieles de lucha*, 61–75; Goodwin, *Los ferrocarriles británicos*, 103–48; Goldberg, "Railroad Unionization," 172–85; Thompson, "The Making of the Confraternidad"; Marotta, *El movimiento sindical argentino*, 2:208–10; Fernández, *La Unión Ferroviaria*, 85–89; Fernández, *El movimiento obrero*, no. 4 y 5, 228–53.

21. DNT, *Crónica Mensual*, January 1922, 790–91; *El Obrero Ferroviario*, July 1918–December 1920, esp. December 1918; Fernández, *La Unión Ferroviaria*, 90–106; Goodwin, *Los ferrocarriles británicos*, 134–80; *La Prensa* and *La Epoca*, 1918–20.

improve their conditions. They labored in a conspicuous industry, but the government was the employer. As important, their union was Socialist-dominated, and the Radicals wanted a freer hand to appoint the party faithful to the city administration. The city's workforce was sizeable, about twelve thousand in 1914.[22]

Workers' conditions remained miserable. The sixty-five or seventy pesos or less per month that unskilled workers received had been reduced by 5 percent by the Conservative administration because of budgetary problems. Workers often received their pay late. Suspensions and fines were levied outside of regulations. Foremen frequently abused workers, forcing them to pay bribes. The rising cost of living further intensified tensions. The UOM was founded in January 1916 with close ties to the Socialist Party. A series of strikes occurred later that year. The union had its greatest strength among the sanitation workers, many of whom were Spanish. These were the least skilled portion of the workforce, but those who could have the most immediate impact. By leaving the city festooned in garbage, a third strike forced major concessions from the still-Conservative-run municipality: the abolition of fines, the eight-hour day, the firing of an oppressive foreman, and the rehiring of those fired during the earlier strikes. The Conservatives' motivation, besides attempting to make the city run smoothly, was their desire to use the Socialists to block the rising influence of the Radicals.

Cooperation ceased when Yrigoyen came to power, for which the Radicals blamed the Socialists, and the UOM blamed the new government. In all probability, the fault lay with the Radicals, who were motivated by two basic desires: to replace existing workers with their clientele, and to weaken a growing Socialist beachhead (the union had some six thousand dues-paying members by the end of 1916). In an atmosphere worsened by talk of further salary cuts and of the firing of recent hires, supposedly produced by Conservative clientelism, the *intendente* provoked a strike in 1917 by refusing to meet with union delegations, by paying salaries late, and by firing and suspending union delegates. The strike was effective but was met with the hiring of strikebreakers, mass arrests, and simulated executions. The extent of the violence caused the Spanish consul to intervene and plead for his co-nationals, a highly unusual step. The Radicals blamed the Socialists for the strike. The *intendente* refused to deal with the UOM, and only a general strike threat by the FORA IX forced a face-saving

---

22. Municipalidad de la Capital, *Anuario estadístico 1914*, 316.

gesture. The city promised to respect the gains made in past strikes, but it agreed to take back only those who had not been replaced. Between five and seven thousand workers lost their jobs. The city did place some of the fired workers in public works projects at low salaries and promised to reincorporate the others. The union continued to charge that only those who had the recommendations of Radical congressmen or presidents of local Radical committees got their jobs back. Ultimately, union pressure and other factors restored many to their jobs, but the Radicals did get an opportunity to place large numbers of their own in municipal employment.[23]

In 1917–18 the government hesitated prior to helping the meatpacking companies crush strikes. Those who have studied these strikes have disagreed about whether to assign the repression to pressures from agrarian elites, to foreign influence, or to the lack of positive impact that supporting these workers could have had. Many were foreign-born, though a significant percentage were Argentines. The strikes were perceived as dominated by Anarchists, and numerous other strikes were occurring simultaneously. Still, the government did try to negotiate an end to the stoppages, and at least for a time, La Epoca blamed the companies' refusal to negotiate for its failure.[24] What is important from our perspective is the government's selectivity. It was inconsistent about which strikes it supported.

The government's positive intervention occurred not only in strategic industries. When millers struck the Molinos Río de la Plata, owned by the multinational grain exporter Bunge and Born, they received backing from carters and the FOM. Threat of a general strike hung in the air and union delegations met with officials of the DNT and with Yrigoyen himself, both of whom offered to mediate the strike. The company's refusal to cooperate made things more complex, but the union eventually triumphed.[25]

23. Fundación Simón Rodríguez, Francisco Pérez Leirós collection, Box 2, periodo previo al peronismo, Unión Obreros Municipales, "Huelgas año 1916"; *El Obrero Municipal*, January, March, August 1917, March 1920, January 1923, August 1927, October 16, 1928, August 16, 1930; *La Confederación*, July 1926; *La Epoca*, March 2–April 12, 1917; Martín S. Casaretto, *Historia del movimiento obrero argentino* (Buenos Aires: José Vescovo, 1946), 1:179–81; Rock, *Politics in Argentina*, 131–44; Walter, *Politics and Urban Growth*, 46; Domingo Varone, *La memoria obrera* (Buenos Aires: Editorial Cartago, 1989), 30–31.

24. *La Epoca*, November 28, 1917–February 27, 1918; Peter H. Smith, *Politics and Beef in Argentina: Patterns of Conflict and Change* (New York: Columbia University Press, 1969), 71–73; Rock, *Politics in Argentina*, 288–98; Bergquist, *Labor in Latin America*, 121–33; Mirta Zaida Lobato, *La vida en las fábricas: Trabajo, protesta, y política en una comunidad obrera, Berisso (1904–1970)* (Buenos Aires: Prometeo Libros/Entrepasados, 2001), 105–95. The latter gives the best and most detailed account.

25. María Ester Rapalo and María Victoria Grillo, "La organización de los obreros molineros y la confrontación con la empresa Molinos Río de la Plata (1917–1918)," *Estudios Soci-*

The Tragic Week

In January 1919 a crisis erupted that shows the weaknesses of the first Radical model of labor relations, yet the government did not alter its policies. Although the Tragic Week is one of the more studied events of the Radical period, it remains wrapped in enigmas.

On December 2, 1918, an Anarchist-led strike began against the metallurgical firm Vasena. The company tried to crush the movement, arming strikebreakers and what were essentially private police. They probably obtained permission to carry guns through the good offices of the company's lawyer, Leopoldo Melo, a Radical senator from the capital. Melo's bad relationship with Yrigoyen, however, may have caused the government to temporarily withdraw police protection from Vasena. Other sources deny that an uneven amount of police protection occurred.

On January 7 the police intervened in a shootout between strikers and company men by opening fire, killing four and wounding forty. Most of those struck by bullets were bystanders. The police hail of gunfire was in apparent retaliation for the killing of a police officer during earlier strike violence. The situation quickly deteriorated. A general strike began, driven more by workers than their organizations, and spread into the interior. The funeral of those killed by the police was marked by large-scale violence from all parties. Troops moved into the city under the orders of General Luis F. Dellepiane, without first seeking approval from Yrigoyen, and labor violence ceased relatively quickly. The government negotiated an end to the general strike. Gangs composed of men from the middle and upper classes, however, attacked the Catalan and Jewish communities, and institutions of the Left and of unions. The government tolerated or perhaps sponsored the violence. The Tragic Week's death toll numbered in the hundreds.[26]

Why did the Radical Party respond in this fashion? Social tensions had risen quickly, sparked by economic problems, and strains inspired by the Bolshevik Revolution combined with the strike wave surging across the country. In 1917 the capital had 138 strikes with 136,062 participants and

---

ales 10, no. 18 (primer semestre de 2000): 137–60, esp. 152–57; *La Epoca,* July 2–July 23, 1918.

26. Edgardo J. Bilsky, *La semana trágica* (Buenos Aires: Centro Editor de América Latina, 1984); Julio Godio, *La semana trágica de enero de 1919* (Buenos Aires: Hyspamérica, 1985); Marotta, *El movimiento sindical argentino,* 2:241–48; Rock, *Politics in Argentina,* 157–79; Deutsch, *Counterrevolution in Argentina,* 73–79; Beatriz Seibel, *Crónicas de la semana trágica* (Buenos Aires: Corregidor, 1999).

the following year 196 stoppages with 133,042 strikers. Moreover, the percentage of strikes lost by the workers shrank.²⁷ There are no statistics for the rest of the country, but an examination of newspapers shows that strike activity may have been even more intense. Faced with a spasm of violence, the government lost its nerve, permitting the army, the police, and members of the elite and middle classes to lash out at those perceived as threatening. Once order returned, the government went back to its old strategy with labor but faced a more complex political landscape.

After the Tragic Week

Elites formed the Liga Patriótica, a far-right pressure group that exalted patriotism and mobilized to break strikes. This intensified the violence around labor unrest, making the Radicals' position more difficult. The Liga's leader, Manuel Carlés, however, always had good relations with crucial elements of the Radical Party. Before 1919 he had served as an intervenor of a province for Yrigoyen and served in the same capacity for Alvear. Many important Radicals belonged to the Liga.²⁸

As early as mid-1918, portions of the commercial, industrial, and rural elites—both local and foreign—formed the Asociación del Trabajo (AT) with the express intent of changing the administration's labor policies. It focused on labor problems in the port, though it had influence elsewhere as well. As we shall see, it did not just act as a lobby.²⁹

Despite the repression in January, labor unrest intensified. In 1919 the capital had 367 strikes, with 71 percent of the 308,967 strikers participating in at least partially successful movements. The following year labor unrest eased somewhat with 206 strikes and some 134,000 strikers, and victories came less often. Simultaneously, the FORA IX grew from 306 member organizations and 35,726 monthly dues payers in 1918 to 734 organizations with 68,138 dues payers in 1920.³⁰

27. Municipalidad de la Capital, *Anuario estadístico 1915–1923*, 269.
28. Caterina, *La Liga Patriótica*; Deutsch, *Counterrevolution in Argentina*.
29. Schvarzer, *Empresarios del pasado*, 54–57; Jáuregui, "El despegue de los industriales argentinos," 171–74; María Silvia Ospital, *Inmigración y nacionalismo: La Liga Patriótica y la Asociación del Trabajo (1910–1930)* (Buenos Aires: Centro Editor de América Latina, 1994); Deutsch, *Counterrevolution in Argentina*, 64–65; Rock, *Politics in Argentina*, 154–55. For the AT's leaders and the openness of its strikebreaking, see its journal, *Boletín de Servicios*.
30. Municipalidad de la Capital, *Anuario estadístico 1915–1923*, 269; Palacios, *El nuevo derecho*, 189–90; *Revista de Ciencia Económica*, August 1927, 973.

The crisis created by the Tragic Week was profound, but it produced less change than many commentators have presumed. Despite intense pressure from crucial sectors of society, many of whom were Radical Party members, Yrigoyen continued to selectively aid strikes for an additional two and a half years. Government policies were never consistent. For example, in September 1919 the police began issuing certificates of good conduct to those who needed it for employment purposes, thus helping employers identify "troublemakers."[31]

The most obvious example of the continuation of Yrigoyen's policies was his maintenance of support for the FOM. In December 1918 the FOM had presented an ultimatum to the shippers, which contained demands on wages and working conditions, but the real issue was union recognition. The employers resisted the DNT's attempts to mediate. A strike began on January 7, 1919, simultaneous with the violent upheavals of the Tragic Week. The sticking point was the FOM's use of boycotts. According to David Rock, an agreement was worked out with the help of the government in which the union forswore the use of boycotts, but the government wanted the agreement to be secret and it fell apart. The union denied any agreement on boycotts. A settlement was finally made with the help of the prefect of the port, and the workers returned on February 1. The crew of the *Suiza* refused to allow boycotted flour to be loaded, however, and two days later, at the urging of the AT, two major shipping associations began a lockout. The port was tied up. British ships boycotted it, and U.S. authorities advised their shipping companies of the conditions. *La Epoca* made it very clear that the administration was unhappy with the attitude of the shippers. A settlement was reached in March and April only because the government took over the selection of labor for the ships, using its own lists. The staffing process was the so-called officialization, and its start occasioned the presence in the port of the ministers of the navy, finance, and public works. Like most decrees by Yrigoyen, it was vague. It was not clear who would benefit, but the quick acceptance by the workers and the reluctance of the employers hint at the type of promises made. The government used its control of staffing to enforce a union shop. Only those who belonged to the union would be hired. This was a sizeable victory for the FOM. Not only did the workers gain a union shop, but also the agreement made in January stood and they received pay for February.

There had been considerable foreign pressure to end the strike on

---

31. Rodríguez, *Historia de policía federal*, 7:52.

terms favorable to the companies, and the continual disruptions were costly. Some contemporary commentators, such as the U.S. military attaché, believed that the off-year elections in March 1919 in Buenos Aires had played a crucial role in Radical actions. The Radical candidate for senator won a narrow victory over a Socialist. During the simultaneous elections for two seats in the Chamber of Deputies, a Socialist came in first, but a Radical claimed the other seat.[32] Given the events of January, this was not a bad outcome for the Radicals, especially because the Radicals did not fare badly in La Boca.

In addition, the FOM presented itself as representing true Argentines against the foreigners. Despite frequent claims that unions never made nationalistic appeals in the period before Perón, the FOM appropriated the language of nationalism to reply to those who saw union activists as foreign agitators. The FOM referred to the Norwegian-born head of the AT, Pedro Christophersen, as a frightening foreign agitator. It claimed that "foreigners dominate here as in a conquered country" because of the servility of the native elite and that the exploiting "mafia" is almost all composed of foreigners.[33] Many of the strikes that the Radicals supported were against foreign-owned businesses.

A similar government intervention occurred in the telephone industry. On February 2, 1919, telephone workers in Buenos Aires formed the Federación Argentina de Telefonistas and presented a request for improvements in salaries and union recognition. The British-owned telephone company, which had a reputation for bad service and high profits, responded by firing sixty workers, including the union's secretary general. The ensuing strike began on March 12 and lasted until the end of the month. *La Epoca* appeared sympathetic and did mention prominently the union's rejection of involvement by the Socialists. The government intervened actively. Worker delegations met with the minister of interior and the police chief, and the latter got Yrigoyen involved. The president met several times with strike leaders and helped arrange a settlement. According to a later union source, the workers received most of what they wanted.

32. *Boletín de la Unión del Marino*, February 19–April 12, 1919; Adelman, "State and Labour," 90–93; *La Epoca*, esp. March 5, 12, 17, 18, April 1, 2, 1919; March 18, 1920; U.S. Diplomatic Dispatch, Buenos Aires, no. 835.5045/90, March 12, 1919; Sojo and Ordóñez, "Historia y organización," 177–79; Marotta, *El movimiento sindical argentino*, 2:251–53; Rock, *Politics in Argentina*, 184–90; U.S. Military Intelligence Reports, Buenos Aires, 1605, February 22, 1919, 1622, March 5, 1919, 1643, March 16, 1919, 1685, April 19, 1919; Ministerio del Interior, *Las fuerzas armadas restituyen*, 1:380–81.

33. *Boletín de la Unión del Marino*, March 18, 20, 1919.

Government support, however, did not guarantee long-term success. The union called another strike in September when two workers were fired, including the head of the organization. The workers failed to respond, and the strike and the union collapsed.[34]

In December 1920 workers at the West Indian Oil Company refinery in Campana struck, and workers at another refinery soon joined them. Within days, Buenos Aires had a shortage of gasoline. Taxi drivers began to charge passengers double. On December 31, the chauffeurs' union voted 957 to 907 to strike in solidarity. Despite the meager approval margin and threats from the Liga Patriótica, the strike was effective. No taxis were available, and few private cars circulated. Gasoline sellers also joined the stoppage. Both the *intendente* of the city of Buenos Aires, José Luis Cantilo, and the police chief, Elpidio González, worked to mediate the strikes at Campana's West Indian refinery and the connected ones in the capital, receiving delegations and successfully negotiating. Despite a series of problems, cars were again on the streets by January 13. An editorial in *La Epoca* expressed happiness that a settlement had occurred without bloodshed and felt that this "revealed in the working class a state of mind of absolute confidence in the tutelary action of the government."[35]

A key example of Yrigoyen's determination to continue his fruitful interaction with labor is the FOM's new struggle with the Mihanovich lines. In February 1920 disputes peaked over union solidarity with shipyard workers and the size and union status of crews. The FOM began a series of boycotts, and the company locked out the workers. Paraguayan onboard personnel walked out in sympathy. Hoping to restore service, congress passed a law permitting the government to run the ships; but the Yrigoyen administration made no move to do so, despite severe economic dislocation in the upriver provinces. During the long stoppage, workers depended on loans from the union and on the solidarity of the community. The minister of public works and the Buenos Aires police chief conducted negotiations. Finally, in mid-March 1921, under the government's aegis, the company and the union reached an agreement that met almost all the FOM's demands.[36]

34. *La Epoca*, March 22, July 1, 1918, March 12–28, September 16, 17, 1919; *La Prensa*, March 13–29, 1919; FOET, *Luchas y conquistas: Las organizaciones telefónicas en el país* (Buenos Aires, 1944), 8–18.

35. Quote from *La Epoca*, January 10, 1921. *La Epoca*, December 11, 15, 1920, January 2–12, 1921; *La Prensa*, January 1–14, 1921; *Review of the River Plate*, December 10, 1920–January 14, 1921. For another example of mediation by González, see *La Epoca*, February 13, 1921.

36. *Boletín de la Unión del Marino*, March 6, 1920–March 9, 1921; *Boletín Oficial del*

The government's pro-union stance became even clearer during a dispute over the interpretation of the agreement. In the shipyards where strikebreakers had worked during the stoppage, would the strikers receive seniority for the time they were out, ensuring them more seniority than the strikebreakers? The government decided that they would, and also said that workers who had lost jobs would receive positions with the state.[37] The government not only favored the workers but, by failing to restart river traffic, had caused itself political problems in the upriver provinces.

Compromises

The unwillingness of the FOF to control the constant stoppages on the rail lines made it an unappealing interlocutor. Exports, travel, and commuting were disrupted, making the government increasingly unpopular with wide sectors of the population. Even the Socialist Party's longtime leader Juan B. Justo expressed unhappiness with the constant turmoil: "But we never could have believed . . . that railroad strikes would be transformed into a custom. The railroads are the most indispensable of the public services for the work and life of the working people in general. A railroad strike is not a simple question of a craft, but a conflict that affects the entire working masses."[38]

Yrigoyen adopted a policy of aiding railroaders operating in a more centralized union structure. His strategy developed because the FOF created problems and La Fraternidad offered an alternative model. The latter attempted to keep its members under control. It used strikes sparingly and tended to stay aloof from other unions. Only after the railroaders re-

---

Sindicato Unión de Cocineros, Mozos y anexos de a Bordo, January 1, 1922; *La Unión del Marino*, November 1919–February 1921; Fortunato Marinelli, *Por el derecho obrero: Resumen histórico de la gran huelga marítima (febrero 12 de 1920–marzo 10 de 1921)* (Buenos Aires, 1921); *La Prensa*, February 3, 1920–March 18, 1921, esp. February 3, 7, 10–14, 1920, January 1, March 2, 8, 1921; *La Epoca*, esp. September 18, 21, October 11, 13, November 4, 1920; *Review of the River Plate*, February 1920–March 1921, esp. November 12, 1920, March 11, 18, 1921; Milda Rivarola, *Obreros, utopías y revoluciones: Formación de las clases trabajadores en el Paraguay liberal* (Asunción: CDE, 1993), 205–19; Cámara de Diputados, *Diario de sesiones*, VI (1920), March 10, 1921, 752–56; *The Standard*, March 13, 1920, enclosure in U.S. Diplomatic Dispatch, Buenos Aires, no. 835.5045/179, March 13, 1920; U.S. Diplomatic Dispatch, Buenos Aires, no. 835.5045/187, March 3, 1921; U.S. Diplomatic Dispatch, Asunción, no. 835.5045/190, April 11, 1921.

37. *Review of the River Plate*, April 8, 1921, 863–65, April 15, 1921, 929; DNT, *Crónica mensual*, August 1921, 719–20.

38. Marotta, *El movimiento sindical argentino*, 2:217, 214–22.

sponded to defeats of the preceding years by reorganizing would Yrigoyen attempt a new approach.

In September 1919 an agreement had been worked out to reorganize the rail unions, and in June 1920 railroad workers created La Confraternidad, composed of La Fraternidad and two unions representing the other rail workers. The new unions modeled themselves after La Fraternidad. The reorganization was probably encouraged when in mid-1919 Yrigoyen appointed to the newly created railroad pension board two members of La Fraternidad and a member of the Asociación Ferroviaria Nacional, who had a personal connection to the president. In the union movement, the Asociación was considered a company organization. The other railroad unions complained about the appointment until elections to the board were held under Alvear.

The reorganization proved almost immediately successful and the number of union members increased rapidly. La Confraternidad pushed for agreements with the companies at a propitious moment. The companies were trying to obtain government approval to increase freight rates, giving the administration a great deal of leverage. The first agreement was signed in the presence of the minister of public works in September 1920 and covered workers potentially belonging to La Fraternidad. It established job categories, salary scales based on seniority, grievance committees, and even gave advantages to the workers' families. Children received free rail passes to go to school and preference in hiring.

The unions hoped to win similar agreements for other sectors but remained stymied by the companies' refusal to negotiate. In order to force the issue, in January 1921 La Confraternidad planned to work-to-regulation, but that was postponed until February. Work-to-regulation was a slowdown that used the large number of government and company rules, which railroaders carried out to the point of absurdity: making sure orders were in writing, doing only and exactly what the rules called for. The railroaders allowed others to use violence. With trains running far behind schedule, disgruntled commuters frequently rioted. Before the work-to-regulation began, a union delegation visited Yrigoyen, who promised to intervene with the companies to work out a solution. Torello issued a decree establishing mixed commissions of workers and companies presided over by the minister. The unions were given a role in selecting the delegates. During the next several months, seven agreements were drawn up covering different specialties, which marked an important first step in establishing uniform working conditions and salaries in the industry. Certain major sectors still lacked contracts.[39] In addition, it required several years of hard work before the agreements were carried out. Unrest still continued to disrupt service.[40] The government's actions had a political impact. As early as 1919 a railroad union newspaper could claim that the minister of public works was the first one appointed without the approval of the railroad companies.[41]

Parallel to the developing relationship of the railroad unions with the national administration was that of the UOM with the municipal government. In the wake of its 1917 defeat, the union had practically disappeared, averaging 197 dues payers in 1918. In the ensuing years, it called a series of partial strikes, during several of which the *intendente* intervened to settle the conflicts in the workers' favor. Ironically, in a number of cases this was the same *intendente* who had broken the earlier strike. The UOM became an accepted part of the municipal structure. As early as 1919, three members of the city council's budget committee attended a union meeting accompanied by a representative of the *intendente*. The executive branch of the municipality began to cordially receive delegations from the union and at times acceded to its wishes. The reason for this change in attitude cannot be exactly pinpointed, but it derived from pressure emanating from the recently created elected city council, combined with the increased tensions resulting from the Tragic Week. In addition, by 1919 a considerable number of municipal workers were Radical clients and concessions improved their conditions.[42]

---

39. *El Obrero Ferroviario*, esp. November 1916, March 1917, July 1, September 1, October 1, 1919, May 16, July 16, October 1, 1920, January 16–February 16, April 1, December 16, 1921; Cámara de Diputados, *Diarios de sesiones*, 11, June 4, 1923, 589–90; DNT, *Crónica mensual*, September 1920, 529–36; *La Confraternidad*, January 31–July 1921; *La Epoca*, esp. August 6, September 4, 1920, February 5, 11, March 2, April 1, 17, 19, 1921; *Review of the River Plate*, January 28–February 11, 1921; *Boletín de Servicios*, February 20, 1921, 3–5, 32–34; Casaretto, *Historia del movimiento obrero*, 2:5; Fernández, *La Unión Ferroviaria*, 131–33; Goodwin, *Los ferrocarriles británicos*, 181–218; Goldberg, "Railroad Unionization,"194–214. For work-to-regulation, see, for example, *La Confraternidad*, January 31, 1921; *La Vanguardia*, April 25, 1926.

40. For examples, see *Review of the River Plate*, November 4, 1921–January 27, 1922.

41. *El Obrero Ferroviario*, June 1, 1919, as quoted in Torcuato Di Tella, "Perón and the Unions: In Search of the Roots" (unpublished paper, 2001), 5. While the railroaders always had nice things to say about Yrigoyen's minister of public works, Pablo Torello, they were sometimes less kind to Yrigoyen. See the manifesto of La Fraternidad in *El Obrero Ferroviario*, March 16, 1923.

42. *El Obrero Municipal*, January, September, December 1919, March 1920, January, February, July, August 1921, February, July, October, November 1922, January 1926, January 1, July 1, 1930; *Bandera Proletaria*, November 7, 1922; Concejo Deliberante, *Actas*, October 14, 1924, 1353–54.

1921

By 1921 Yrigoyen faced a series of challenges that caused him to alter his policy of supporting strikes. The constant labor unrest took a toll on his popularity and on the fragile economy. A perceived political challenge from within the governing party also contributed. Within the Radical Party, strife had always simmered about the extent of Yrigoyen's control. A split occurred with the governor of the electorally critical Province of Buenos Aires, José Camilo Crotto. Crotto had been a personal friend of Yrigoyen but had taken independent stands on labor unrest and other issues. From early in his term, elements in the Radical Party savagely attacked him. When rumors spread that the national government would take over the province, Crotto gathered police and prison guards near the capital and increased his stock of arms and ammunition. After several months the crisis peaked in May 1921, just before Crotto resigned. At the same time, workers and shippers faced off in the port of Buenos Aires. According to a later report, "An individual visiting the president in May 1921 asked Yrigoyen if he was unduly worried about a serious port strike in Buenos Aires. The president allegedly responded: 'No! but [I am concerned] about that pig Crotto!'" That Yrigoyen worried more about Crotto than the port is doubtful, but in all likelihood the coincidence of these two challenges made him uneasy.[43]

Pressures also came from outside the political system. The Liga Patriótica's brigades frequently conducted armed demonstrations and worked to break unions. This led to violence because participants in both union and political activity commonly carried revolvers. Even legalistically minded unions felt threatened and prepared to defend themselves.[44] The Liga incited violence and appeared to be a serious contender for political power.

---

43. For quotation, Walter, *The Province of Buenos Aires*, 60, quoting U.S. Diplomatic Dispatch, Buenos Aires, no. 835.00/373, August 31, 1921; see also 55–60; *La Epoca*, September 18, 1919; *El Telégrafo*, May 17, 1921; *Review of the River Plate*, May 13, 1921, 1187, May 20, 1921, 1253–55; U.S. Military Intelligence Reports, Buenos Aires, 128, May 23, 1921; Donato Chaquesien, *Los partidos porteños en la vía pública* (Buenos Aires: Talleres Gráficos Araujo, 1919), 56–57; Martha Ruffini de Grané, "Un aspecto de la relación Yrigoyen-Crotto: Agro política en la provincia de Buenos Aires," in *Estudios de historia rural* (Buenos Aires: Facultad de Humanidades y Ciencias de la Educación, 1993), 3:33–58; Archivo General de la Nación, Ministerio del Interior, 1921, Legajo 16, no. 5246. For the importance of the port over other issues, see *El Telégrafo*, May 24, 1921.

44. *La Confraternidad*, February 28, 1921. For the Liga, see Deutsch, *Counterrevolution in Argentina;* Caterina, *La Liga Patriótica*.

An incident in 1921 in the city of Gualeguaychú, Entre Ríos province, exemplifies the Liga's violent tendencies. Workers had planned their traditional May Day celebration for the central plaza. The Liga intended to demonstrate the same day to honor Justo José de Urquiza, a nineteenth-century president from Entre Ríos. After consulting with provincial authorities, the worried local police chief made futile plans to keep the demonstrations separate. Armed Liga members entered the plaza anyway and became upset at the sight of the workers' red flags. The police chief persuaded the workers to take down the flags, but this failed to calm the situation. An unknown gunman fired a shot, and a general shootout followed. At least six people died and twenty-eight were wounded. The governor, the police chief, and *La Epoca* blamed the Liga for the violence. Futilely, the authorities asked for troops to protect the police station and union headquarters from the Liga. The Liga exacerbated the violent tendencies of the society; both politics and labor strife frequently produced armed clashes. Even rumors of military rebellion circulated.[45]

Added to these strains was the constant labor turmoil, which had begun to take a heavy economic and psychological toll. Numerous strikes marked the first half of 1921. In the city of Buenos Aires workers struck 70 times— fewer strikes than in the immediately preceding years, but larger ones, averaging more than 1,810 workers per stoppage. At no time in the strike wave of 1916–20 had the average exceeded 1,000.[46] During the same six months, workers outside the capital struck at least 103 times, and this is likely a gross underestimation.[47]

In the first half of 1921, general strikes rocked five cities besides the capital. Although some failed miserably, the two strikes in Campana completely shut down this industrial city in northeastern Buenos Aires province, a hotbed of labor militancy that saw major strikes in oil refineries, paper plants, and the Las Palmas meatpacking facility. When general strikes were called to support those strikers, traffic ceased. The only cars

---

45. *La Confraternidad*, March, April 1921; *La Epoca*, May 2–3, 1921; *La Prensa*, February 11, May 2, 3, 13, 1921; *Review of the River Plate*, May 6, 1921, 1119; Archivo General de la Nación, Ministerio del Interior, 1921, Legajo 16, no. 5440; U.S. Military Intelligence Report, Buenos Aires, 128, May 23, 1921; Deutsch, *Counterrevolution in Argentina*, 129–40.

46. DNT, *Crónica Mensual*, May 1922, 861–64.

47. These figures were taken from *La Prensa*; undoubtedly some were missed. A study of *La Organización Obrera* for this period indicates that *La Prensa* covered only a portion of the strikes. During the first three months of 1921, the Department of Labor of Buenos Aires province counted thirty-one strikes. *La Epoca*, April 8, 1921.

on the road belonged to doctors, and they had to fly white flags. During the second general strike, not enough workers showed up to operate the generators, and the city plunged into darkness.[48]

General strikes connected partly to politics occurred in the country's second- and third-largest cities. Since 1912 Rosario had been a center of labor agitation, connected at least partially to factions of the Radical Party attempting to rally popular support. In 1921 politics contributed to the mix. Although the Radicals had governed the Province of Santa Fe since the opening up of the political system, the dominant party on the city council in Rosario was the Progressive Democratic Party. The governor, however, appointed the *intendente*. At the beginning of the year, the *intendente* went on leave, ostensibly for health reasons but apparently because he had quarreled with allies of the governor. The acting *intendente*, a Progressive Democrat named Fernando Schlesinger, believed strongly in cutting costs. His budget lowered some salaries and dismissed some temporary workers. The city was already several months behind in paying salaries.

On January 18 the municipal workers struck, but the stoppage was effective only among street sweepers and trash collectors. Rosario still had many horses, however, so the lack of street sweeping in midsummer presented a grave health hazard. The city administration organized strikebreakers, but the strikers limited their effectiveness by responding with violence. Schlesinger received no help from the governor in restoring peace, and a new *intendente* was not appointed. The AT charged that the strike was not solved because of political problems. Support for the municipal workers slowly grew. Carters, carriage and taxi drivers, news vendors, and streetcar personnel walked out, and so did slaughterhouse workers and bakers, causing shortages of meat and bread. Streetcars circulated only with armed guards and on restricted schedules. Finally, on February 4, the local Anarchists' organization called a general strike to aid the municipal workers. Police with carbines patrolled the streets, and many businesses closed after midday. The strike continued to spread, reaching the giant railroad shops near Rosario and the port. Food grew scarce, in part because local farmers and milk vendors did not want to enter the city. The strike

48. *Review of the River Plate*, April 1, 1921, 809, May 13, 1921, 1185–87, May 20, 1921, 1262; *La Prensa*, May 12–14, 1921. For general background, see *La Prensa*, December 1920–May 1921, esp. January 17, February 13, March 1, 18, 1921. On general strikes in Tandil and Tucumán, see *La Prensa*, March 17, April 8–10, 1921; *Review of the River Plate*, April 15, 1921, 937; U.S. Diplomatic Dispatch, Buenos Aires, no. 835.5045/193, May 28, 1921, 2–3; Hugo Nario, *Los picapedreros* (Tandil: Ediciones del Manantial, 1997), 100–103. The strike in Tandil was solved with government intervention.

was resolved on February 12, but only after a new, more accommodating *intendente* was appointed. He quickly met with the municipal union, made concessions, and even offered to pay 50 percent of the wages lost during the strike.[49]

In Córdoba, labor unrest reached the intensity of 1919, especially on the Central Córdoba Railroad. The Conservative provincial government responded with police raids on meetings, closures of union halls, and arrests of union leaders. On February 23 the leader of the provincial labor federation sent a telegram to the minister of the interior in Buenos Aires asking for the takeover of the province. This was not a far-fetched idea because local Radicals had a similar desire. In March, faced with continuing police pressure and spreading strikes, the local labor federation declared a general strike with the public aim of securing the release of prisoners and the opening of union headquarters. It really hoped to obtain help from the national government. Several key unions, however, refused to join the stoppage or, like the printers, limited the time of their participation. The lack of support plus continued pressure from the police doomed the strike, though it spread beyond the city of Córdoba. After forty-eight hours it was called off. The Radical Party displayed sympathy but did not make the dramatic move of taking over the province. An editorial in the party mouthpiece, *La Epoca*, declared, "The attitude of the Córdoba workers (even if it is not justified) has an explanation."[50]

Elsewhere, a series of highly visible strikes further undercut the image of the Radical government. In Buenos Aires, the theater season was interrupted when the Federación de Gentes de Teatro struck over whether impresarios could stage works by local authors, who did not belong to the Sociedad Argentina de Autores. The striking actors made extraordinary efforts to continue the stoppage, including paying the salaries of low-paid workers. Chorus girls used hat pins to defend themselves from mounted

---

49. *La Prensa*, January 3–February 14, 1921; *La Epoca*, January 18–February 14, 1921; *Review of the River Plate*, January 21–February 18, 1921; *Boletín de Servicios*, February 20, 1921. For an overview of Rosario politics, see Karush, *Workers or Citizens*.

50. *La Epoca*, March 3, 1921. The size and scope of the strike varied according to the source. See also *La Epoca*, February 21–March 7, 1921, esp. February 25, March 4–7; *La Organización Obrera*, February 26, March 5, 1921; *La Prensa*, March 1–6, 1921; *Review of the River Plate*, February 25–March 11, 1921, May 26, 1922, 1281; *Revista Argentina de Ciencias Políticas*, April 12–May 12, 1921, 106–7; Ministerio del Interior, *Memoria 1921-22*, 90–117; Ofelia Pianetto, "The Labour Movement and the Historical Conjuncture: Córdoba, 1917–1921," in *Essays in Argentine Labour History, 1870–1930*, ed. Jeremy Adelman (London: Macmillan, 1992), 153–54. Radical papers were frequently much less kind to general strikes, especially if the authorities were Radicals. See *La República*, April 9–11, 1921.

policemen. The actors had difficulty maintaining the strike because they let plays by foreign authors continue and because of the competitive nature of the industry. After several weeks the strike faded away, despite efforts by the chief of police to mediate.[51]

More embarrassing to the regime was an elementary school teachers' strike in the wealthy Province of Santa Fe. The predominantly female teachers were not well paid; in addition, since 1918 the province had owed them fourteen months' salary. *La Prensa*, which rarely saw a strike it liked, expressed sympathy for the teachers, who were demanding not only their back pay but a system of tenure and established working conditions. The latter remained the stumbling block, and after more than a month the strike collapsed; teachers who did not return to work lost their jobs.[52] This strike displayed a level of incompetence among the governing Radicals, who failed to meet payrolls and alienated a group that should have been a prime party constituency. As we have seen in Chapter 3, many teachers received their appointments as political rewards, and the party turned its back on them.

Rural unrest menaced the government even more because many of the threatened properties belonged to local elites or were controlled by British interests. The best-known example of rural labor upheaval is the strikes and boycotts that wracked Patagonia from 1920 to 1922, which were immortalized by the film *La Patagonia rebelde* (1974). Many of the region's sheep estancias were British-owned, while North American interests controlled the packing plants. British and U.S. diplomatic representatives applied pressure for strong action, adding their weight to local protests. Although the repression began earlier, it was after November 1921 that the slaughter of strikers started, leading to at least fifteen hundred deaths.[53]

In northern Santa Fe province a British-owned company, La Forestal, controlled vast tracts of quebracho trees, from which tannin was made. Since 1919, labor unrest there had been almost continuous and extremely violent. In January 1921 the company possessed more tannin than it could

---

51. Teodoro Klein, *Una historia de luchas: La Asociación Argentina de Actores* (Buenos Aires: Ediciones Asociación Argentina de Actores, 1988), 16–21; *La Epoca*, May 12–24, 1921; *La Prensa*, May 13–June 2, 1921.

52. *La Prensa*, January 8, May 2–July 20, 1921; *La Epoca*, May 5–June 30, 1921.

53. For an overview, see Osvaldo Bayer, *Los vengadores de la Patagonia trágica*, 4 vols. (vols. 1–3, Buenos Aires: Galerna, 1972–74; vol. 4, Wuppertal: Peter Horner Verlag, 1978). For a good short synopsis, see Deutsch, *Counterrevolution in Argentina*, 144–51. For an interesting view of the employers' side, see *Review of the River Plate*, December 10, 1920–December 1921. For fear that ran through the employer class, see Archivo General de la Nación, Ministerio del Interior, 1921, Legajo 2, esp. no. 705, 706.

sell. It began closing operations and driving workers off the estate. Pitched battles erupted between the workers and company police, backed by provincial police. Workers throughout the province struck in sympathy. The company succeeded in driving out the workers and for a time closed all its operations before slowly reopening them with full control over hiring. The cost of its victory was high in human terms, though the actual number of deaths remains unclear.[54] Similar upheavals occurred in the British-based Las Palmas Company, whose land lay west of La Forestal.[55]

Patagonia and the quebracho region were peripheral areas, far from Buenos Aires and economically of secondary importance. Strikes in the cereal zones of the pampas more directly threatened the strategies of the elites and the government. Cereals were Argentina's largest export, and elites owned much of that land. The harvest seasons of 1919–20 and 1920–21 saw major labor unrest. The Liga Patriótica worked vigorously to break strikes, but it seems that the police had more impact. Numerous armed clashes erupted between police and strikers, and there were fatalities on both sides.

The strikers tended to be the men who loaded bags of grain at the railroad stations and carters who transported the grain from the farm. Many carters owned their equipment and were therefore small-scale capitalists. Harvest workers frequently joined the strikes as well. The pampas strikes became the kind of all-out combat that can exist only in small communities, involving the burning of fodder, boycotts of businesses, and lockouts. A wave of fear crossed the countryside. Proprietors and tenant farmers were badly outnumbered, and they frequently begged the police for protection. The *Review of the River Plate* reported rumors of rural worker uprisings and added, "Such a happening would surprise nobody considering the absolute lack of control that exists today all over the country."[56]

54. Gastón Gori, *La Forestal: La tragedia del quebracho colorado* (Buenos Aires: Editoriales Platina/Stilcograf, 1965), esp. 123–48; *Review of the River Plate*, December 3, 1920–December 30, 1921; *La Epoca*, January 30–February 8, 1921; *La Prensa*, February 3–15, 1921; Borda, *Perfil*, 18–32.

55. *Review of the River Plate*, May 13, 1921; Deutsch, *Counterrevolution in Argentina*, 123–27; José García Pulido, *El gran Chaco y su imperio Las Palmas*, 2nd ed. (Resistencia: Casa García, 1977).

56. *Review of the River Plate*, February 4, 1921, 324. For general information, see *Review of the River Plate*, esp. December 10, December 31, 1920, April 8, 1921; *La Prensa*, esp. January 7, 13–17, 23, February 9, 10, 18, 27, March 13–19, 1921; Arturo Marcos Lozza, *Tiempo de las huelgas* (Buenos Aires: Editorial Anteo, 1985), 203; G. Cuadrado Hernández, "La rebelión de los braceros," *Todo es Historia*, October 1982, 78–96; *Revista Argentina de Ciencias Políticas*, December 12, 1920–January 12, 1921, 243–44; Solberg, *The Prairies and the Pampas*, 167–70; Waldo Ansaldi, ed., *Conflictos obrero-rurales pampeanos (1900–1937)*, 3 vols. (Buenos Aires: Centro Editor de América Latina, 1993).

What finally made the government change its support of strikes was the constant conflict on the Buenos Aires waterfront. How long could the Yrigoyen government appear to have lost control of the port? In April 1921 the FOM wielded enough power to force the captain of a river steamer to put off a passenger who, the union crew believed, had been sent by the Liga Patriótica.[57] An opposition congressman, Julio Costa, could refer to the Buenos Aires port "where there is a 'soviet' of which the vice president is the president of the republic and the president a Mr. García [secretary general of the FOM]." The stoppages were constant and threatened trade and relations with other countries.[58]

Employers on the waterfront wanted to loosen the workers' grip, but first they needed a change in government attitudes. This happened because of a jurisdictional dispute between unions. Four longshoremen's unions merged to become the Sociedad de Resistencia Obreros del Puerto de la Capital and attempted to impose a similar unity on the two carters' unions that served the port. In mid-April 1921 the longshoremen's union began a boycott of all carters who did not belong to the Sociedad de Resistencia de Conductores de Carros.[59]

The users of the port reacted vociferously but also recognized that this was the moment they had been waiting for. The AT and the port users' employer organizations protested to the government and set a deadline of May 9, by which they would employ "free" (nonunion) labor to load and unload ships. That day the government sealed the port while unionized workers met. The government claimed that a strike had closed the port. A strike vote took place, but it was the government that shut the port to cargo traffic while looking for a solution that would favor organized workers. The FOM did not strike, and its members operated the tugboats so that passenger traffic could continue. The employers' association brought in workers from the provinces, housing them at the exposition grounds of the oligarchical Sociedad Rural, where the annual rural exhibition was held.[60]

The government intended to take over the hiring of port workers—so-

57. *La Prensa*, April 6, 1921.
58. Cámara de Diputados, *Diario de sesiones*, VI (1920), February 23, 1921, 390. See also Horowitz, "Argentina's Failed General Strike of 1921," 71–73.
59. *Boletín de Servicios*, May 5, 1921; U.S. Diplomatic Dispatch, Buenos Aires, no. 835.5045/205, January 31, 1922, enclosure no. 1, "Labor Unions in Argentina"; *Review of the River Plate*, May 13, 1921, 1183–85, May 20, 1921, 1251–53; Shipley, "On the Outside Looking In," 298–99; Adelman, "State and Labour," 94–95.
60. *Boletín de Servicios*, May 20, 1921; *La Union del Marino*, May 1, 1921; *La Epoca*, May 6–9, 1921; *La Prensa*, April 23, May 4, 10, 1921; *Review of the River Plate*, May 6, 1921, 1121, May 13, 1921, 1181–85.

called officialization—as it already had for shipboard personnel. It would then favor the unions. The government obviously wished to settle the conflict, especially after longshoremen in other ports began walking out in solidarity. It faced, however, two major stumbling blocks: the irresolvable conflict between the two carters' unions, and an ultimatum from the representatives of the shipping lines presented on May 18. If the officialization plan went into effect, the shipping agents would ask their companies to boycott Argentina. It also faced pressure from the major powers, Britain, the United States, and France.

The government clearly wanted to resolve the port crisis on terms favorable to the workers. The pro-Yrigoyen daily *La República* continually stressed the desire for social justice. The jurisdictional dispute made this difficult. Faced with this and the general tensions, the government embraced the employers' position.

On May 21, in characteristic fashion, the government issued an announcement that in two days the port would reopen but left unclear whether employers or unions would be favored. The AT did not know how to interpret the government's actions, but a delegation was assured by the minister of hacienda that the government would permit all workers physically able to work to do so. The port opened on May 23, but hardly any traffic moved despite the two-week shutdown. The shippers waited for the results of a meeting that day. When operations resumed the following day, the government did not permit the unions to control the situation. Violence erupted as the nonunion labor of the AT attempted to work the docks. Both sides exchanged gunfire. Each suffered one death and numerous wounded.[61]

The port closed again on May 25 and 26 for holidays, but by May 27 the mood had changed dramatically. The militant chauffeurs' union had called a twenty-four-hour stoppage for Independence Day, May 25, affecting both taxis and private cars. The strike declaration claimed that while the bourgeoisie cried, "Liberty, liberty"—words from the national anthem—liberty for workers was a farce. The AT had created a league of car owners, and strikebreakers were soon on the streets, organized by some of the cream

---

61. *La República*, May 7, 10, 22, 1921; *Boletín de Servicios*, June 5, 1921; *La Unión del Marino*, June 1921; Document 71, R. Clausse, July 28, 1921, in María Estela de Lépori Pithod, ed., *Selección de informes franceses sobre Argentina, 1897–1930* (Mendoza: Universidad Nacional de Cuyo, Facultad de Filosofía y Letras, 1998), 159–62; *La Prensa*, March 23, May 18, 25–28, 1921; *La Epoca*, May 19, 21, 23, 24, 1921; *Review of the River Plate*, May 20, 1921, 1249–53, May 27, 1921, 1317–19.

of society. On the morning of May 25, revolvers in hand, a group of men belonging to the Liga Patriótica forced their way into the chauffeurs' headquarters and made the workers kneel and salute the flag. That evening Liga members again attacked the headquarters, killing two workers and wounding several others. They also attempted to burn down the building. The police responded by arresting both attackers and attacked but soon began to hunt down strikers and sympathizers. Not surprisingly, the chauffeurs extended the strike. When the May 28 edition of *La Prensa* went to press, the police had picked up 250 people. More than 100 were chauffeurs; the rest were union leaders and leftists. The police also closed other union headquarters.[62]

The police repression continued to expand, and the two leading union confederations joined with the chauffeurs' union to demand that prisoners be freed and union offices be reopened.[63] Many outside the labor movement believed that the chauffeurs had insulted the nation. Injured patriotism combined with the showdown at the port and the general turmoil forced the government to reevaluate its relationship with labor. The government continued to receive union delegations but conceded nothing.

At the same time, the situation at the port worsened from the unions' perspective. Heavily armed security forces guarded the port. Travelers to Montevideo had to pass between a double file of cavalrymen armed with lances. Still, unionized dockworkers continued to labor, except when they encountered nonunion workers; then they withdrew, leaving the docks open to their competitors. The FOM, while continuing to boycott nonunion labor, made no move to shut the port. Only on May 29 did the dockworkers strike. On May 30 the FOM voted to strike the following day. As important, the Anarchist union confederation voted for a general strike. The police, however, raided the Communist Party's press where the strike call was being printed and seized the manifesto. The FORA IX had been meeting with the police chief, Elipidio González, demanding the release of prisoners and the return to normal union activity and reminding him that Yrigoyen had told them that prior to calling a general strike they should go see him to have their problems solved. With police permission, on the

---

62. *Review of the River Plate*, December 31, 1920–January 14, 1921, June 3, 1921, 1377; *La Prensa*, March 23, May 18, 25–28, 1921; *Nueva Era* (Avellaneda), May 28, 1921; *La Epoca*, May 26, 27, 1921; *La Organización Obrera*, May 1, 1922, suplemento extraordinario no. 2, 36; Deutsch, *Counterrevolution in Argentina*, 117–19.

63. *La Organización Obrera*, May 1, 1922, suplemento extraordinario no. 2, 38; *La Prensa*, May 29, 1921; *New York Times*, May 29, 1921.

evening of the thirtieth the FORA IX met with representatives of Anarchist and independent unions; but the police raided the meeting anyway and arrested 180 attendees. Only two members of the hierarchy escaped to announce a general strike. According to Elipidio González, a general strike had become inevitable and the police had acted on the orders of a judge. The strike call was greatly hindered by the shutting down of the presses of both the Communist Party and the principal Anarchist organ, La Protesta.[64]

Despite a joint strike committee composed of both major confederations—the committee lasted only four days—the strike was uneven. Syndicalists and Anarchists wasted energy in a needless rivalry, and the former, until the last moment, seemed reluctant to break relations with the Radicals by calling a general strike. Although many workers in greater Buenos Aires did walk out, crucial sectors did not cooperate. The trolley workers for the main company in Buenos Aires remained at their posts except for a half-day stoppage by shop workers. The railroad unions went to the government seeking promises that union offices would be reopened and prisoners freed; reassurances satisfied them. Even the shipboard officers, allied to the FOM, refused to participate. In the interior of the country, union organizations called for walkouts but did so in a staggered fashion, in some cases after the strike was already essentially lost. The cooperation between the two confederations collapsed. Unions began sending their members back to work, including the FOM and then finally the longshoremen. The unions had lost, and lost badly. On June 7, among the 1,863 unskilled men working on the docks, 1,631 were nonunion. The municipality began vetting the licenses of taxi drivers.[65]

More than from repression, the strike seems to have failed because of poor timing and key unions' reluctance to break with Yrigoyen. Workers were tired after four years of almost constant agitation, and the economic

64. La Prensa, May 27–31, 1921; La Epoca, May 31, 1921; El Telégrafo, May 28–30, 1921; La Organización Obrera, suplemento extraordinario no. 2, 38–43; Marotta, El movimiento sindical argentino, 2:38–41; Cámara de Diputados, Diario de sesiones, 1, June 1, 1921, 135–50; El País (Montevideo), June 1, 1921 enclosed in Archivo General de la Nación, Ministerio del Interior, 1921, Legajo 21, no. 7318; and Legajo 22, no. 7859; Concejo Deliberante, Actas, May 31, 1921, 936–50, June 6, 1921, 959–62.

65. La Epoca, May 31–June 8, 1921; La Prensa, May 31–June 12, 1921; El Telégrafo, May 31–June 6, 1921; La Unión del Marino, July 1921; New York Times, June 3, 1921; London Times, June 3, 1921; Review of the River Plate, June 3, 1921, 1377–85, June 10, 1921, 1441–45, July 15, 1921, 178; La Organización Obrera, May 1, 1922, suplemento extraordinario no. 2, 36–51; La Antorcha, June 17, 1921; La Confederación, May 1921; Times of Argentina, June 6, 1921, enclosed in U.S. Diplomatic Dispatch, Buenos Aires, no. 835.5045/196, June 6, 1921; DNT, Crónica Mensual, May 1922, 862; Marotta, El movimiento sindical argentino, 3:41–45, Adelman, "State and Labour," 98–99.

downturn of 1920–21 undoubtedly made many workers fearful. The strike wave, which swept over much of the world starting in 1917, petered out in many countries just about the time that it did in Argentina. The government, facing presidential elections in 1922 and tough economic times, wanted to make sure that exports were not disrupted by labor unrest.[66]

After 1921

Labor relations changed quickly after the general strike collapsed. In Buenos Aires during the second half of 1921, only 13,064 workers walked out in sixteen strikes. In February 1922, the *Review of the River Plate* expressed contentment at the quietness of the labor scene. Slightly later, the U.S. consul gleefully reported the lack of disturbances in the port.[67] The new models for the government were the relationships with the railroad unions and the UOM. While during Yrigoyen's remaining time in office this type of relationship was not explored very far, what was sought was a relationship in which both sides could gain and labor peace was not disrupted.

In the run-up to the presidential election in April 1922, the Yrigoyen administration made a number of gestures to the railroaders with the hope of winning their support. Shop workers were promised eight days of annual leave. All railroad workers were supposed to have gained this in 1917, but the shop workers had not. Also, the personnel of the State Railroads based in the capital received a 20 percent raise if they made less than 200 pesos a month or a 10 percent raise if they made between 201 and 300 pesos.[68]

Despite the massacre in Patagonia, the Tragic Week of January 1919, and the collapse of the general strike in 1921, Yrigoyen had become extraordinarily popular with certain sectors of the populace. In two studies of voting in the capital, the working-class vote for the Radical Party increased during the presidential term; the only setback occurred in the election directly after the Tragic Week.[69] According to *La Epoca*, at a

66. Anglo-South American Bank Ltd., *Cabled Reports from Branches*, April 20, 1921, 5; *Review of the River Plate*, July 8, 1921, 61; *Revista de Economía Argentina*, August 1921, 154–55, April–May 1923, 354–55; Shipley, "On the Outside Looking In," 348; Arthur M. Ross and Paul Hartman, *Changing Patterns of Industrial Conflict* (New York: Wiley, 1960), 194.

67. DNT, *Crónica Mensual*, May 1922, 864; *Review of the River Plate*, February 10, 1922, 337; U.S. Diplomatic Dispatch, Buenos Aires, no. 835.5045/207, April 4, 1922.

68. *La Epoca*, February 12, March 10, 1922.

69. Richard J. Walter, "Elections in the City of Buenos Aires During the First Yrigoyen Administration: Social Class and Political Preferences," *Hispanic American Historical Review* 58, no. 4 (November 1978): 610; Canton and Jorrat, *Elecciones en la ciudad, 1892–2001*, 2:215.

demonstration at the end of his first term, thousands of men "of humble condition" cried, "We are the workers," "We want to embrace the Father of the People," "Long live the apostle of liberty!"[70]

Conclusion

Despite the violence and the ultimate collapse of the strike wave, in the years from 1917 to 1921 Yrigoyen created a strong relationship with a group of union leaders. More important, his support of strikes and unions helped seal a special bond between many in the popular sector and Yrigoyen. In a public and open way, in a manner that had not happened previously, he had supported them against the elites. This public recognition of their importance was not something that many would easily forget, despite the many inconsistencies of Yrigoyen's policies.

70. *La Epoca*, October 13, 1922.

ALVEAR AND THE ATTEMPTED ESTABLISHMENT OF AN INSTITUTIONALIZED RELATIONSHIP WITH LABOR, 1922–1928

The Alvear administration is usually viewed as much more conservative than that of Yrigoyen. This assumption is largely based on the charges made by his contemporary opponents. His administration has been little studied. For example, Félix Luna in his biography of Alvear spends just twelve pages out of over three hundred on his presidency.[1] Some aspects of Alvear's labor policies resembled those of Yrigoyen, and where they differed, they were not always more conservative. The Anti-Personalists seemed motivated more by opposition to Yrigoyen's control of the party than by policy disagreements. They remained Radicals and shared with their rivals a major motivating force, a constant search for votes.

Neither the Anti-Personalists nor the Personalists had clearly defined ideas about labor. The Alvear administration did appear more comfortable with large, centralized unions that worked well with the government. The idea was to assist in the creation of organizations that would trade labor peace for material improvements for their members. The unions would also hopefully serve as a bridge to the working class and help obtain votes. The administration's efforts, while failing to obtain votes for the Anti-Personalists, served as a model for at least a generation.

As we have seen, the other major attempt to influence the working class under Alvear was the enactment of the pension law, 11.289. The Alvear administration's approach to labor was less personal than that of the two

---

1. Luna, *Alvear*.

Yrigoyen governments. Although cabinet members and Alvear met with union delegations, the administration preferred to use bureaucratic channels. The impact of the routinization of negotiations can be seen in the uproar created in 1929 and 1930 when Yrigoyen returned to personal intervention in labor conflicts.[2]

One stereotype of the Alvear government does hold true. Individual cabinet members had a major impact. Little coordination of policy within the government existed. The government's attitude toward the railroad unions turned more favorable in early 1925 when Roberto M. Ortiz became minister of public works. Other ministers, such as Naval Minister Admiral Manuel Domecq García, took a decided antilabor stance on the waterfront at the same time that government allies attempted to build support among port workers. The lack of coordination made the Anti-Personalists' search for support almost impossible.

Railroads

A key area where we can see the Anti-Personalist interest in labor is the railroad industry. Starting in 1925, the government played a crucial role in helping the Unión Ferroviaria (UF) become a powerful union. The willingness of the Anti-Personalists to do this should not be surprising. As Paul Goodwin has shown, the Alvear administration was willing to be tougher on the British rail companies in setting freight rates than was the second Yrigoyen administration.[3] Helping a union such as what the UF became— one that helped keep the peace on the rail network and that had the potential to help make the administration popular among sectors of the working class—was an obvious if somewhat daring strategy.

The UF tried to steer clear of politics, which meant that it could cooperate with almost any government that was willing to cooperate with it. When numerous committees of railroaders were created to rally support for the reelection of Yrigoyen, the executive committees of La Fraternidad and the UF felt compelled to issue a joint statement calling for political neutrality.[4] During the 1920s, the UF's executive board was split between Syndicalists and Socialists. For most of the leadership, the union was more important than ideology. Antonio Tramonti, the secretary-general during

---

2. *La Prensa*, July 8, August 4, 23, 1929.
3. Goodwin, *Los ferrocarriles británicos*, 270–85.
4. *La Epoca*, July 16, 1927–March 12, 1928; *La Confederación*, December 1927.

the 1920s, was a Syndicalist who quarreled with the Syndicalist-dominated confederation, the USA. During a negotiating session with the railroads, Tramonti said, "The other day Dr. Videla referred to a French Socialist who, he said, was more advanced than we are. I replied that we are not Socialists, and if some are, we do not take it into account."[5]

This attitude—plus its determination to stick to the matters directly at hand—made the UF an attractive interlocutor not only for the government but also for the companies. During the same negotiations with the railroads, a company representative said, "With you one can talk, because you have the ability to do so and you could, as I have said in private to Becerra, occupy a bench in the Chamber [of Deputies] with more merit than many. You possess a faculty that is worth a lot, that of attention, in the sense of focusing, which is already the beginning of comprehension and you treat matters with resounding sobriety, although in my judgment wrongly."[6] What the rail unions offered the companies was what it offered the government: relative peace in return for concessions.

Even if, as is often argued, the Alvearistas represented the more elite wing of the Radical Party, it is not at all obvious that they would favor the railroad companies. Rural elites had long-standing complaints against the companies on issues such as freight rates and availability of cars. Moreover, throughout much of the period, the Argentine representatives of the companies were Conservatives and not from either branch of Radicals.[7]

The opportunity to create this new relationship came out of further reorganization of the railroad unions. The loose structure created by the formation of La Confraternidad had not provided enough discipline and centralization for many union leaders. In 1922 these men, over the objections of many and playing rather fast and loose with their own rules, created the UF by combining the two unions not representing the engineers and firemen. They modeled the new union on La Fraternidad. La Confraternidad, the umbrella organization, continued to exist.

The UF's centralized structure faced serious challenges during the next

5. Comisión especial de representantes de empresas y obreros ferroviarios, *Revisión de escalafones, convenios y reglamentos* (Buenos Aires: Guillermo Kraft, 1930), 159. For quarrels with the Syndicalists, see *Bandera Proletaria* for the entire period.
6. Comisión especial de representantes de empresas y obreros ferroviarios, *Revisión de escalafones*, 176. Bernardo Becerra was elected to the Chamber of Deputies in 1931 on the Conservative Party list in the Province of Buenos Aires. For the incident, see Horowitz, *Argentine Unions*, 139.
7. See Goodwin, *Los ferrocarriles británicos*, esp. 273, for the importance of having a Radical lawyer.

few years. Most accounts have shown the union's victory as inevitable, but that is projecting its future on its beginnings. Many traditional railroad leaders opposed centralism, and in 1922 they remained strong enough to control the union convention. They needed to be circumvented by a special referendum of the locals. Centralization faced the determined opposition of the nascent Communists and, more important, of the Syndicalists who controlled the USA, the new labor confederation. The confederation used its resources to combat centralization.[8]

The UF needed to produce results quickly or its opponents would crush it. In the short run, union leaders who appear more confrontational have an advantage because they seem to be standing up for their members. Although disciplined approaches may in the long run be much more successful, the immediate advantages tend to be fewer.

When the Alvear administration took office in October 1922, it indicated that it would cooperate with La Confraternidad. Minister of Public Works Eufrasio B. Loza met with a delegation from the UF. Shortly thereafter, the administration took on an issue that had simmered since 1917, the rail companies' unwillingness, despite government decrees, to give shop workers annual paid vacations and sick leave. The government established an arbitration tribunal. Despite previous uses of such boards, the companies refused to cooperate, saying that the government had no right to force the use of arbitration. Faced with potential court delays and after the direct intervention of Alvear, who appeared friendly to the union, the administration pushed the companies into direct negotiations with their workers. They won sick leaves but not paid vacations.[9]

A key goal of the founders of the UF was the achievement of *personería jurídica* (legal status). This would give the union the same legal status as, for example, a club, but it made contracts legally binding. La Fraternidad had *personería jurídica* and many UF leaders thought receiving it would be an important step. The UF was indicating an acceptance of the political/juridical system, because organizations with legal status had to follow cer-

---

8. *La Confraternidad*, March–November 1922; *Unión Sindical*, April 8–July 29, 1922; *Bandera Proletaria*, September 28–October 29, 1922, January 14, March 24, 1923; *Copiadores de Cartas de USA*, letters from April to August 1922; Fernández, *La Unión Ferroviaria*, 127–48; Goldberg, "Railroad Unionization," 194–238; *El Obrero Ferroviario*, February 1, 1922–February 1, 1923.

9. *El Obrero Ferroviario*, March 16, April 1, October 16, December 16, 1922–February 1, 1923, August 16, 1923; *La Confraternidad*, January, February 1923; DNT, *Crónica Mensual*, January 1923, 983–88; Goodwin, *Los ferrocarriles británicos*, 223–26, 230–32; Ministerio del Interior, *Crónica Informativa*, December 1926, 89.

tain norms. The opponents of a centralized union vociferously attacked this goal. On the other hand, the government must have found it reassuring, because it granted *personería jurídica* relatively quickly and this was not a given. A rival organization, the Asociación Ferroviaria Nacional, frequently seen as a company union, was turned down when it applied.[10]

In 1923 and 1924 the unions in La Confraternidad made little progress, although the administration continued to deal with them. The government assisted in solving grievances with the companies and, after a long delay, salaries were set for telegraphers and the contract of the workers who could belong to La Fraternidad was updated.[11] The government's attitude can be summed up by the 1923 report of the police division responsible for public order: "The entity [UF], perhaps the only one, that one can adjudge [to have made] certain progress in their organization, owing in great part to the methods employed until now in their negotiations for improvements, which in some case they have obtained."[12]

Loza's resignation as minister of public works and his replacement by Ortiz in early 1925 changed the relationship between the railroaders and the government. Loza is believed to have been the only member of Alvear's original cabinet loyal to Yrigoyen. He resigned, supposedly for health reasons, amid a controversy within the cabinet over the potential intervention of the Province of Buenos Aires, which would have altered the political landscape dramatically in favor of the Anti-Personalists. Alvear eventually blocked the intervention. Loza also faced a scandal about the condition of the State Railroads. According to Marcelino Buyán, secretary general of La Confraternidad and a member of the Socialist Party, Loza had a reason for not favoring the UF. He was a good friend of the lawyer of the Asociación Ferroviaria Nacional, the rival of the UF. Ortiz, a dedicated Anti-Personalist, was not the first choice for the position, but, as he demonstrated during his presidency in the 1930s, he was a politician of considerable ability. The

---

10. Unión Ferroviaria, *Memoria y balance de la Comisión Directiva, 1922/23* (Buenos Aires: Talleres Gráficos de Federación Gráfica Bonaerense, 1924), 6 (hereafter UF, *Memoria y balance*, year); *Boletín de Servicios*, February 5, 1921, 3; *La Unión del Marino*, July, September 1922; Fernández, *La Unión Ferroviaria*, 163–64; Goldberg, "Railroad Unionization," 245–57; *Bandera Proletaria*, January 14, 1923; *El Obrero Ferroviario*, October 16, 1922, June 1–16, 1923. For role of *personería jurídica*, see Line Schjolden, "Suing for Justice: Labor and the Courts in Argentina, 1900–1943" (Ph.D. diss., University of California, Berkeley, 2002), 230–34.

11. *El Obrero Ferroviario*, June 16, July 16, August 16, November 1, December 1, 16, 1923; February 16, 1924.

12. Policía de la Capital Federal, *Memoria, antecedentes, datos estadísticos y crónica de actos públicos, correspondiente al año 1923* (Buenos Aires, 1924), 75.

administration now had a minister of public works eager to expand the political base of the Anti-Personalists.[13]

The UF won a series of victories with government assistance in 1925 and 1926. Why these years? Already the UF had become a powerful force willing to work with both government and companies. The railroads were in a position to make concessions, averaging profits of 5 percent between 1921 and 1928 and paying sizeable dividends after 1924.[14] Most important, the Anti-Personalists needed popular support if they were going to be competitive in the presidential elections in 1928. Just as they had under Yrigoyen, the railroaders became a key target.

La Confraternidad had been agitating almost since the creation of the railroad pension board for better representation. Yrigoyen had made the initial appointments and, although he had appointed two members of La Fraternidad, the union had subsequently disavowed its two members. The other worker representative had ties to the Asociación Ferroviaria Nacional. La Confraternidad accused the Asociación of blocking changes in representation, under both Yrigoyen and Alvear. The 1923 reform of the railroad pension plan called for elections to the board within three months of enactment, but they did not occur until April 1925. La Confraternidad blamed the Asociación Ferroviaria Nacional and the administration. The latter claimed that bureaucratic problems caused the delay.[15]

In the elections, La Confraternidad demonstrated that it had become the dominant organization among the railroaders. In what was the only open contest of strength, La Confraternidad's candidates obtained almost three-quarters of the vote and won on all the major railroads. The rival organization led by Syndicalists and Communists had called for abstention, but the turnout was high.[16] The government and the companies could hardly fail to recognize such a dramatic assertion of hegemony.

The UF had long complained of the companies' failure to raise salaries, lamenting that in 1921 then–Minister of Public Works Pablo Torello had said that the railroaders deserved a raise but that the economic condition

13. Molina, "Presidencia de Marcelo T. de Alvear," 278, 296–97; Goodwin, *Los ferrocarriles británicos*, 223; *El Obrero Ferroviario*, June 16, 1923; *La Prensa*, January 8–February 7, 1925.

14. Winthrop R. Wright, *British-Owned Railways in Argentina: Their Effect on the Growth of Economic Nationalism, 1854–1948* (Austin: University of Texas Press, 1974), 127.

15. *El Obrero Ferroviario*, March 16, June 1923, July 16, 1924; Ministerio del Interior, *Crónica Informativa*, December 1926, 129–41; Cámara de Diputados, *Diario de sesiones*, II, June 4, 1923, 585–93, I, June 25, 1924, 745–47, II, July 3, 1924, 281–312.

16. *Nueva Era* (Avellaneda), June 13, 1925; *El Obrero Ferroviario*, February 16, March 16, June 1, 1925.

of the companies did not permit it. In 1924 after it had become abundantly clear that the companies' economic situation had improved, the UF pressed for raises and a meeting with the president.[17]

In 1925, although willing to revise the existing agreements, the companies refused to negotiate directly with the union, saying that they would only talk with their own workers. When this made selecting negotiators difficult, Ortiz intervened and arranged elections to pick negotiators, which the UF easily dominated. The rewritten contracts vastly improved conditions.[18]

In 1926, if Luis M. Rodríguez's account is to be believed, with the aid of the government, the UF won recognition from the companies as the workers' representative. Rodríguez sat on the governing board of the UF from 1927 through 1936 and in the 1930s was a Radical and a key leader of the UF's Syndicalist faction.[19] Rodríguez claimed that Ortiz advised the UF leaders to see Alvear if they wanted to obtain union recognition. Alvear then told them, "Boys, I cannot intervene directly. I cannot invent decrees nor do anything to compel them, but if you rock the boat of the English a little, in a certain way I am obliged to intervene."[20]

Whether the UF's work-to-regulation that began in April 1926 was intended solely to win wage increases for the railroaders, who lacked contracts, or had a wider aim, as Rodríguez claimed, cannot be definitively known, but the latter is more than likely. As usually happened with this form of protest, it tied up rail service but allowed workers to draw salaries, and it did not totally cut off traffic and therefore challenge the government. Still, during the first day a livestock train arrived seven hours late. The government participated in all the negotiations, and the key one occurred with the Pacífico line. After it appeared that the company had agreed to accept the UF as the official representative of the blue-collar workers, another issue arose that prolonged the work-to-regulation: would the union be recognized as representing white-collar workers? Ortiz's direct intervention resolved the standoff. The union ended its protest in return for significant wage increases and recognition of the UF as the representative of blue-collar workers. The right to officially represent white-collar employ-

17. Ministerio del Interior, *Crónica Informativa*, December 1926, 96; *La Acción*, January 22, 1925; *La Prensa*, March 26, August, October 2, 1925; and see below.
18. *El Obrero Ferroviario*, July 1, 1924, February 1, 1925–January 1, 1926; UF, *Memoria y balance, 1925*, 5–13; Fernández, *La Unión Ferroviaria*, 152, 168.
19. Fernández, *La Unión Ferroviaria*, 152; Horowitz, *Argentine Unions*, 157–60.
20. Luis M. Rodríguez, Instituto Di Tella Oral History Program, 17.

ees was temporarily shelved. With the help of direct government involvement, the other lines quickly made agreements based on that of the Pacífico.[21]

The Anti-Personalist daily *La Acción*, in contrasting what it claimed was the violence produced by the political goals of labor agitation during the Yrigoyen years, proclaimed that the current administration "determined to maintain order in all the activities of the country has heard and resolved satisfactorily the problems raised as causes of the work-to-regulation."[22] Even the UF later acknowledged the government's crucial role.[23] The 1925 and 1926 agreements set conditions and wages (with some exceptions) that endured until the rise of Perón in the 1940s.[24]

The companies' acceptance of the UF as the workers' bargaining agent was critical. It froze out competing unions and permitted the UF to deal directly with the railroads. It also granted the UF a privileged position on the grievance committees that had been created.

Ortiz and Alvear both involved themselves with smaller issues. For example, when the Pacífico line suspended shop workers for only working the eight-hour day that the government railroad board had decreed, instead of the ten hours demanded by the company, they both intervened to see that the punishments were lifted.[25]

The pre-presidential-election period of 1927 and 1928 was politically dangerous for both the rail unions and the Alvear administration. Up and down the rail lines, organizations composed of rail workers backed Yrigoyen's candidacy. It is difficult to judge their true size and influence, but issue after issue of *La Epoca* published information about new groups and the rallies they held. The number of workers involved must have been considerable, because in many cases numerous names appeared in the announcements, although these would have been padded.[26]

Clearly, Yrigoyen had widespread, organized support. Although winning over some union leaders, Ortiz's efforts failed to win fervent support

21. *El Obrero Ferroviario*, May 1–July 1, September 1, 16, 1926; *La Vanguardia*, April 23–May 6, 1926; *La Argentina*, April 23–May 6, 1926; *Boletín de Servicios*, May 5, 1926, 197–98; Ministerio del Interior, *Crónica Informativa*, December 1926, 95–118; Fernández, *La Unión Ferroviaria*, 168–76; Goodwin, *Los ferrocarriles británicos*, 241–47; Félix Luna, *Ortiz: Reportaje a la Argentina opulenta* (Buenos Aires: Sudamericana, 1978), 96.
22. *La Acción*, February 23, 1927.
23. Fernández, *La Unión Ferroviaria*, 172.
24. *El Obrero Ferroviario*, October 16, 1942.
25. *El Obrero Ferroviario*, September 16, 1925.
26. *La Epoca*, May 1927–March 31, 1928; see for examples July 16–18, 25, 1927. See also *La Acción*, January 28, 1928; *La Vanguardia*, December 16, 1927.

among the rank and file. Yrigoyen's actions in 1917 and his overall ability to generate popular support counted for more. This posed political dangers for the union leaders, who in any case felt threatened by the developing parallel organizations.[27] Any such group potentially created an alternative base of power, capable of challenging the union or at least the leadership. The Anti-Personalists saw this activity as a threat to their goal of winning elections. The railroad unions felt compelled to publicly proclaim that they were politically neutral and that this was the best policy.[28]

According to Félix Luna, Ortiz tried to neutralize the growing support for Yrigoyen with the help of the union leaders. Facing the threat of another work-to-regulation, the government helped La Fraternidad secure a new agreement with changes in work rules and salary increases. Again with the aid of the government, the UF secured a number of successes on local issues. Its campaign for a general wage increase, however, got underway after the presidential elections. With Yrigoyen's overwhelming victory, the Alvear administration lacked the strength and the will to be of much help.[29]

The impact of Ortiz and the Alvear administration is demonstrated by the nice things that both factions, which developed in the late 1920s within the UF, had to say about the administration. José Domenech, who led the "Socialist faction," said that "the cabinet of Alvear was good, speaking in general. They were good people. The truth is that Alvear, according to my recollection, was the person that most respected the constitution and demonstrated that he was completely a gentleman in the good sense of the word." Luis M. Rodríguez claimed that Ortiz "said that he was our friend." As shown above, he also gave Ortiz and Alvear credit for helping the union achieve recognition from the companies. It should not be surprising that Ortiz, when he became president in the 1930s, helped establish an alternate rail union with the goal of creating political support, using connections made during the 1920s.[30]

---

27. *La Internacional*, July 23, 1927 (the Communist paper), saw Syndicalists with ties to the Radicals as behind some of this.
28. *Confederación*, December 1927; *El Obrero Ferroviario*, September 1, October 1, November 16, December 16, 1927.
29. Luna, *Ortiz*, 96–97; *El Obrero Ferroviario*, March 16, September 1–November 1, 1927, April 16, May 16, 1928; Fernández, *La Unión Ferroviaria*, 176, 178; *La Prensa*, August 24–26, 1927, May 16–June 14, 1928; *La Acción*, August 26, October 20, 1927; *La Epoca*, August 27, October 21, 1927; Goodwin, *Los ferrocarriles británicos*, 251–58.
30. José Domenech, Instituto Di Tella Oral History Program, 65; see also 25–26; Luis M. Rodríguez, Instituto Di Tella Oral History Program, 17; Horowitz, *Argentine Unions*, 140–44, 157–63.

Even during Alvear's term, Ortiz and the rail unions expressed their mutual admiration publicly. For example, the UF's third annual congress voted to send a delegation to Ortiz to press for additional measures for the membership; but also, because he had "acted correctly in all moments in which he had to act, this congress resolves to designate a delegation to transmit these impressions."[31] Ortiz, when he spoke at the opening of the headquarters of the railroad pension board, expressed the view "that the collaboration of the companies and the workers in the fulfillment of the progress of the Argentine Nation, the former escaping the tendency to all encompassing capitalism and the latter the influence of demagoguery, suggests an eloquent example for other industries."[32]

Ortiz was not the only government official to laud the railroad organizations. A subinspector of the DNT, Luis Grüner, praised the UF in an official document and in an article in *El Obrero Ferroviario*. Minister of War and future president Agustín P. Justo sent a note to the UF commending the cooperation of its members during military maneuvers.[33]

What did the unions and regime gain in all this? The unions did well. The UF quickly became larger than any confederation of which it was not a member. It averaged 18,925 monthly dues payers in 1923 and 19,683 and 28,432 the following two years. It had 41,556 dues payers in 1926 and 55,355 in 1928, and the figure climbed in the following two years to 63,485 and 70,793. These are remarkable figures, given that the number of members was always considerably higher than the number of dues payers because no system of dues checkoff existed. In 1930 if one added the 13,515 members that La Fraternidad claimed to the dues payers of the UF, they represented 59 percent of those who paid into the railroad pension fund. Those paying into the pension system included numerous managers who were not permitted to join, as well as peripheral enterprises only tangentially connected to the railroads.[34] Wages and working conditions had im-

---

31. *El Obrero Ferroviaria*, June 16, 1926. The praise was tempered by criticism of the head of the office of control of railroad work.
32. *El Obrero Ferroviaria*, October 16, 1927.
33. Ministerio del Interior, *Crónica Informativa*, December 1927, 70–161; *El Obrero Ferroviario*, May 1, December 16, 1927.
34. The number of dues payers in the UF was calculated from the Unión Ferroviaria, *Memoria y balance*, 1922–23, 1925, 1926, 1928, 1930, and from Mario Bravo, *Capítulos de legislación obrera* (Buenos Aires: Imprenta A. García y Cía., 1927), 51. The figures from the *Memoria* and Bravo differ for 1923. I have used the official figures. For La Fraternidad, Chiti and Agnelli, *Cincuentenario de "La Fraternidad,"* 457. For payers to the pension fund, Ministerio de Obras Públicas, Caja Nacional de Pensiones de Empleados Ferroviarios, *Memoria correspondiente al año 1941* (Buenos Aires, 1942), 54.

proved dramatically. For example, a telegraph linesman earned 115 pesos a month in 1918 and 180 in 1930, while workshop artisans went from an average of 145 to 206.[35] Most wages were set during the Alvear era.

The Alvear administration had two principal motivations. It wanted to avoid the turmoil that marked the railroads between 1917 and 1921. Due to its centralized structure, the UF offered labor peace in return for concessions from the companies. The UF worked to isolate disturbances and impose order. It refused to protect railroaders who struck without first consulting the union. Discipline needed to be maintained.[36] The UF had recognized that one of the things that a union can offer an employer and the government is labor peace, but that is only possible if it can control its members.

The other motivation was politics. The Anti-Personalists were distancing themselves from the Personalists and therefore needed to build support, and the unions could act as a bridge to the railroaders. This was a form of *obrerismo*. It is impossible to know with certainty how the railroaders voted in 1928, but it is unlikely that large numbers did so for the Anti-Personalists. The majority probably voted for Yrigoyen. Labor leaders always claimed that railroaders tended to vote Radical.[37] The Anti-Personalists could not pry the political loyalty of the workers away from older attachments. The administration achieved its other goal because it coincided with that of many railroaders who had been scarred by the defeats and upheavals of the previous years. They too wanted a disciplined organization that was capable of disrupting rail traffic but preferred not to do so. The railroaders willingly accepted the government as an intercessor between the union and the companies. They traded some freedom of maneuver in return for government help.[38]

What we see under Alvear is the realization that a powerful union could be a major asset. It would be wrong to suppose that the initiative was all the government's. A sense of mutual self-interest developed between the

---

35. *Review of the River Plate*, March 21, 1930, 23.
36. Goldberg, "Railroad Unionization," 260–72; Horowitz, *Argentine Unions*.
37. Juan Rodríguez, Instituto Di Tella Oral History Program, 6–7; José Domenech, Instituto Di Tella Oral History Program, 166; Sebastián Marotta, interviewed by Robert J. Alexander, November 27, 1946.
38. According to Steve Fraser, *Labor Will Rule: Sidney Hillman and the Rise of American Labor* (New York: Free Press, 1991), U.S. labor leader Sidney Hillman made a similar decision in an extremely different industry, the garment industry. Hillman felt that due to the lack of skilled labor in his industry, conditions could only improve with government help and that he was willing to stifle strikes and accept some policies he did not like to get the policies he wanted.

rail unions and the administration. It would be giving the government too much credit to assert that in 1922–23 it had the vision to see what the relationship would become by 1928. The relationship developed incrementally, as both unions and the administration struggled to find their way.

On Shipboard

The Alvear administration, like its predecessor, wanted to win votes in La Boca by building relations with unions in the port. It tried to encourage the development of a shipboard union modeled after the UF that would limit the constant disruptions by maintaining discipline. The administration needed a strong union with which to work, but the FOM was riddled by internal conflict. Tensions between officers and crews intensified rather than diminished. As important, the government never had a consistent policy on the waterfront, which underlines the problem of Alvear's hands-off political style. Some Anti-Personalist politicians, such as Anastasi, took a special interest in building support among the port unions. Naval Minister Domecq García, however, provided political protection for the prefect of the port, Ricardo Hermelo, who was extremely unpopular with union workers and those interested in winning their support. Domecq García had been a key early member of the Liga Patriótica and remained one. In late 1921 he spoke to an organizational meeting of a union of shipboard personnel that the Liga was trying to form.[39]

In the wake of the 1921 defeat, the FOM confronted a series of problems, including tensions between officers and crews, and the loss of total control of shipping. It also faced internal ideological tensions and a rival organization sponsored by the Liga. Still, it recovered control of a significant portion of the vessels flying the Argentine flag.[40] Conditions, however, grew more complex. Almost from the beginning of the Alvear administration, the FOM expressed unhappiness with it, especially with the influence of the Liga Patriótica and of Domecq García. The union periodical even took the unusual step of criticizing the attendance of Alvear's wife at a Liga function.[41]

The idea of a pension plan helped splinter the FOM. On one side stood

---

39. Deutsch, *Counterrevolution in Argentina*, 76–85; Caterina, *La Liga Patriótica*, 31–35, 91; *La Unión del Marino*, November 1921.
40. *La Unión del Marino*, July 1921–November 1922.
41. *La Unión del Marino*, December 1922, March 1923.

Francisco García, some allies, and the Socialists; on the other were Communists and doctrinaire Syndicalists. The former appeared ambivalent on the question, at least publicly, but according to their enemies they supported it, while the latter groups opposed any pension scheme. According to an article authored by opponents of pensions that appeared in the August 1925 issue of *La Unión del Marino*, the Radical club "La Marina," composed chiefly of merchant marine officers, invited Anastasi to draw up a pension plan for the maritime industry to present to the Chamber of Deputies. The plan was published in the union paper, and García claimed that he was sure that the immense majority of members favored such legislation. This turned out not to be true, creating a struggle between the governing council and García that he won, but he softened at least his public position on pensions. According to his enemies, García continually violated the will of the membership on pensions.[42]

As we have seen, the 1923 pension plan included those in the maritime industry. The officers wanted to be included, and the FOM opposed the plan. Those around García seemed willing to accept pensions, particularly to maintain relations with the officers. With the government unwilling to protect a divided union that was attacking it, employers sought to destroy any vestiges of union control of the port.

Tensions had been building in the industry since the 1921 defeat; the union agitated against wage cuts and worsening working conditions. The FOM tried playing the nationalistic card. In a union meeting an FOM leader, Vicente Tadich, referred to the Liga as "simply an institution of foreigners to defend foreign interests." The meeting ended with cries of "Death to the Liga Anglo-Argentina la Asociación del Trabajo."[43] In January 1924 the FOM approved a set of demands to present to the employers. Long negotiations began with the threat of a strike continually there, but it was not a propitious time for a stoppage. The government hinted that a strike would be seen as political in nature and the disagreement over the pension plan presented a major obstacle, as García's comments at a meeting made clear. The union did not strike.[44]

---

42. *La Unión del Marino*, October 1922–February, September 1923, February, April, May 1924, August 1925.

43. *La Unión del Marino*, March 1923.

44. See especially *La Unión del Marino*, November 1923, February–April 1924; *La Epoca*, January 18–28, March 17–25, 1924; *La Acción*, January 20–29, 1924; *La Prensa*, March 21–26, April 1, 1924; *Boletín de Servicios*, April 5, 1924, 181–83; *La Internacional*, January 21–22, 1924. The administration's unease may be explained by the union's refusal to allow it to intervene in the FOM's favor. Geoffroy de Laforcade, "Ideas, Action and Experience," 27.

Questions about onboard discipline worsened tensions between officers and the FOM. In April 1924 the FOM asked the captain of the *Asturiano* to disembark a sailor who was not a union member. The captain refused, saying that the man had already signed the roll book and had done nothing wrong. The union asserted that he had never signed. The crew refused to sail, and the captain went to the government and had the entire forty-two-member crew arrested. The ship sailed with a nonunion crew; the officers embarked because of threats by the government. The FOM sent a three-man delegation to complain to Alvear about the port authorities.[45]

García and his allies were keenly aware of the difficult position of the FOM, trying to negotiate a new contract and facing sharp divisions over the pension plan. Their stand became that the pension plan needed to be opposed, but that they supported the idea of pensions. In other words, they avoided taking a clear stance. Nevertheless, García lost control of the union to Communists and doctrinaire Syndicalists who strongly opposed pensions.[46]

On May 3, 1924, the FOM joined the general strike against the pension plan, but the officers said that they would sail with nonunion crews. After three days, the officers reversed their decision upon realizing that this would break not only the FOM but also their own power. On May 8 when the FOM sent its people back to work, a number of shipping firms insisted on sailing with nonunion labor, most of whom lacked the necessary government papers. The port unions boycotted the vessels. Representatives of the officers and from the FOM met with Alvear (union sources fail to mention the FOM's presence). The delegates complained bitterly about the behavior of the naval minister. According to the FOM, Alvear criticized

---

45. *La Internacional*, April 16, 1924; *Bandera Proletaria*, April 26, 1924; *La Epoca*, April 15–16, 1924; *La Prensa*, April 15–17, 23, 1924; *La Acción*, April 24, 1924; *Boletín de Servicios*, April 20, 1924, 201–2; *La Unión del Marino*, May 1924. The details of the incident are obscure. The naval minister claimed that the crew member just owed one month's dues, 1.50 pesos, but the FOM claimed that during the previous trip the captain had sailed with eight crew members who should not have been permitted to sail. The captain had promised that on his next voyage all would be in condition to sail, but at the last moment he attempted to disembark a man in condition to sail and replace him with one of the eight. See especially Cámara de Diputados, *Diario de sesiones*, v, August 29, 1924, 81–83; *La Prensa*, April 16, 1924. The crew paid an extremely high price for this conflict: six months in jail. *Bandera Proletaria*, November 29, 1924.

46. *La Internacional*, January 20–22, April 16, June 27, November 22, 1924; *Bandera Proletaria*, January 26, April 25, November 24, 1924; *La Epoca*, April 24, 1924; *La Acción*, April 26, 1924; *El Obrero Ferroviario*, December 1, 1924; *La Unión del Marino*, May 1924; Marotta, *El movimiento obrero argentino*, 3:160–61; Cámara de Diputados, *Diario de sesiones*, I, June 23, 1924, esp. 443–46, 466–67, 475, 483–84, 501–2, 555; Ministerio del Interior, *Memoria 1924–25*, 571–72.

Domecq García and said that labor organizations were good for the economic well-being of the nation. He proposed establishing a mixed commission to settle the problems of the industry and gave instructions that naval personnel stay out of the conflict. He later had the head of customs, Captain Ricardo Hermelo, begin negotiations, but the shippers refused Hermelo's proposal. On May 13 the FOM declared a general strike in the port and shipping hardly moved. Almost immediately the government intervened, forcing off ships crew members who lacked proper credentials. There were not enough nonunion workers with the correct papers to man the ships, and the employers caved in. A compromise was reached. Captains chose the crews; so long as the alliance between captains and the FOM held, ships were union shops. When the *Bandera Proletaria* of May 17 went to press, only four tugs operated with nonunion crews.[47] The government had helped the FOM survive a difficult situation.

In mid-July captains who sailed to Patagonia handed over staffing of their vessels to the companies, ostensibly because of friction with crews over work rules, but more likely because of the collapse of the relationship with the FOM. The officers badly wanted the pension plan. The officers rejected efforts by the government to return the situation to that which had existed before. The authorities then began to favor the companies, which were permitted to staff their ships with nonunion workers, and FOM boycotts could not prevent their sailing. On August 24 in an attempt to reverse this loss of control, the FOM struck all maritime activity. The FOM probably had little choice, but it placed in jeopardy those sectors, the port, and the upriver trade, which it still controlled.

Some eleven thousand crew members and two thousand officers struck, but the government permitted the shippers to use unlicensed workers. After backing the FOM briefly, many officers had enough and went back to work. The strikers did meet with Alvear, but so did a group of "free workers" (nonunion), who were told, according to the AT, that the government would respect the liberty of work, code words for allowing nonunion labor. The port authorities favored the shippers to the extent that they expressed gratitude for the attitude of both the port prefect and Alvear himself. In a debate in congress Leopoldo Bard, a Personalist deputy from the capital, called the naval prefecture a recruiting agency for strikebreakers. The gov-

---

47. *Bandera Proletaria*, May 17, 1924; *La Unión del Marino*, June 1924; *Boletín de Sevicios*, May 20, 1924, 262–64; *La Vanguardia*, May 5–15, 1924; *La Acción*, May 9–15, 1924; *La Prensa*, May 3–17, 1924; *La Epoca*, May 3–14, 1924; Marotta, *El movimiento obrero argentino*, 3:66–67.

ernment took over the staffing of pilots in order to try to force them back to work. Despite efforts of parts of the union movement to support the FOM, it was crushed. In late October La Confraternidad intervened with the government and helped work out an arrangement that at least saved face; conditions and wages would remain the same, and captains would choose crews and would not discriminate against union members. This ended the strike.[48] The FOM lost control of the ships, however, and the Alvear administration had turned against it. A key factor was the dominance of leaders who rejected cooperation with the government. In addition, the FOM fiercely attacked the government-sponsored pension plan, making it difficult for the government to feel supportive.

The Anti-Personalists wanted order in the ports and they wanted votes. They could now back employer attempts to keep order without authentic unions. The AT had the resources and the desire to establish control of the port.[49] However, the government knew that the port had a tradition of labor militancy and that the likelihood of further unrest was extremely high. Such a strategy would win the gratitude of influential and wealthy groups, but the political benefits were limited. Elites did not control many votes and such a scheme offered few ways to obtain them. Was there a way to keep order and woo votes at the same time? The desire to do this was intensified by the split in the Radical Party.

The obvious model was the UF, but the problem was how to create such a union. Workers needed to be convinced that they would be well represented by a centralized union. In addition, early victories needed to be won so that the new form of organization could establish hegemony. This never occurred, in part because of struggles within the FOM, and in part because the Alvear administration lacked a clear policy.

In late 1924 both government authorities and the shipping companies placed increasing pressure on the FOM, making it difficult for the union to have an impact.[50] The Federal Council, which held together the various sections of the FOM, had ceased to exist, but by the beginning of 1925

---

48. *Bandera Proletaria*, July 12–December 6, 1924; *La Internacional*, August 16–November 7, 1924; *El Obrero Municipal*, September–November 1924; *El Obrero Gráfico*, August–September, October–November 1924; *La Confraternidad*, October 1924; *La Epoca*, July 8–October 24, 1924; *La Prensa*, July 8–October 24, 1924; Cámara de Diputados, *Diario de sesiones*, IV, August 27, 1924, 716–27, V, August 29, 1924, 80–145, esp. 129; Marotta, *El movimiento obrero argentino*, 3:179–81; *Boletín de Servicios*, August 20–November 5, 1924; *El Obrero Ferroviario*, September 1–December 1, 1924; Ministerio del Interior, *Crónica Informativa*, August 1927, 71–82.

49. See *Boletín del Servicios* for this period.

50. See, for example, *Bandera Proletaria*, February 28, 1925.

efforts were being made to reorganize the union. An emergency Committee of Relations was created, composed of representatives of all the locals in the capital with the exception of the *patrones* (launch coxswains) who long had had differences with the other crafts. When several months later they joined the Committee of Relations, the *patrones* insisted on García's return as the leader of the FOM. In a mass meeting on March 4, 1925, attended by an estimated four thousand, the FOM was reorganized and García elected secretary-general. This was crucial, because if anyone had legitimacy with the membership, it was García. He had withdrawn from the union because he felt that it needed a more disciplined and centralized approach.[51]

The new executive council took a series of actions that had the potential to alter its relations with the government. It issued an extensive communiqué that essentially called for the acceptance of the pension law as it then existed. A delegation met with Alvear, asking for the creation of a commission composed of representatives of shippers and the union to examine rules for the industry. The president expressed a willingness to meet the union's demands. According to the Communist Party paper, *La Internacional*, the delegation was purely *criolla*, that is, composed of native Argentines, and the selection had been made at the suggestion of two key Anti-Personalist Radicals, José Tamborini and Anastasi. Tamborini, then a deputy, was soon appointed minister of interior. On May 14 Alvear sent a message to congress calling for the creation of a mixed commission that would contain representatives elected by workers and by the companies with the tie-breaking vote held by the government. This board would act as an arbitrator in cases where agreements could not be reached, including on working conditions. If the AT is to be believed, Alvear seemed eager to please everyone and was also accommodating to the union's opponents, receiving a delegation of "free" workers.

The FOM's policy of conciliation with officers and the administration faced opposition from Communists and more militant Syndicalists; two key locals, sailors and stokers, rejected the new direction. The executive committee submitted its resignation to a mass meeting on May 22. After a heated discussion, it was accepted. The new committee stated that it would not accept arbitration. García resigned and the union took a belliger-

51. *Bandera Proletaria*, January 10, March 25, 1925; *La Argentina*, January 26, 1925; *La Acción*, March 5, 10, 1925. See also *La Internacional*, January 20–22, April 16, June 27, November 22, 1924; *El Obrero Ferroviario*, December 1, 1924, March 16, 1925; *Bandera Proletaria*, January 26, April 25, November 15, 1924.

ent stand but soon began to disintegrate.[52] The FOM abandoned its headquarters because it could not afford the rent. Even earlier, in April 1924, the FOM had lacked the money to pay its dues to the USA.[53]

Any hope of establishing a firm relationship with the FOM had failed, but the administration had options. In a 1927 report, Luis N. Grüner of the DNT wrote about a new organization, the Unión Obrera Marítima (UOMAR): "Presently, the industry is reconstituting its union files and the most intelligent and perspicuous of these workers are building a new type of union organization that will exclude from its breast all the tendencies that until now have disturbed its free evolution as an entity representing the maritime workers. The Confraternidad Ferroviaria inspires and serves as an example for those who struggle for the renovation of the values of the maritime unions."[54]

The UOMAR grew out of a Junta Reorganizadora founded in mid-1925. A number of the key leaders had been active in the FOM. It had the support of a committee that had been created to back the establishment of a pension system and the organizations of officers. The driving force was the *patrones*, who had always seen themselves as similar to the officers. It also had the support of the Socialists, who were in the midst of an ideological struggle with the Syndicalists, which was shortly going to lead to the establishment of a Socialist-dominated union confederation. In addition, the new union had the backing of La Confraternidad.[55]

UOMAR tried to model itself on the rail organization. According to the first number of the new organization's periodical, "We say without ambiguity that to reorganize the union on a serious and stable base, it has to be done in the same form as the railroaders. . . . The railroaders have passed through all our difficulties, due to that in earlier periods they were orga-

---

52. See, for examples, *Bandera Proletaria*, November 15, 1924, January 10, March 21, July 18, 1925; *El Obrero Municipal*, April 1925; *El Obrero Ferroviario*, May 16, 1925; *La Prensa*, April 1, 1925; *La Argentina*, May 11, 23, June 6, 1925; *Boletín de Servicios*, May 5, 1925, 205; *La Internacional*, November 22, 1924, May 12, 20–22, 1925; *La Epoca*, February 1, 1925; Cámara de Senadores, *Diario de sesiones*, 1, May 15, 1925, 72–79; *Almanaque del Trabajo para el año 1929* (Buenos Aires: Partido Socialista Independiente, 1928), 274–75; Casaretto, *Historia del movimiento obrero*, 2:29–32; Marotta, *El movimiento obrero argentino*, 3:182.

53. Ministerio del Interior, *Crónica Informativa*, August 1927, 85; Marotta, *El movimiento obrero argentino*, 3:206.

54. Ministerio del Interior, *Crónica Informativa*, August 1927, 61.

55. Ibid., 85–86; Casaretto, *Historia del movimiento obrero*, 2:30–33; *La Argentina*, June 18–July 25, 1925; *La Unión del Marino*, August, September, 1925; *Bandera Proletaria*, July 25, August 15, September 26, October 31, 1925; *La Internacional*, July 28, September 27, 1925; *El Obrero Ferroviario*, October 16, 1925.

nized in the same manner as the sailors. The defeats suffered were for them an education that they intelligently profited from. Consequently, they have the present system of organization." La Confraternidad was prepared to adjudicate differences between officers and crews.[56]

The government began to favor the UOMAR. Accusations were leveled that when activists made propaganda in the port area, they were stopped and asked to which organization they belonged. If they replied the FOM, they were arrested. The courts provided no protection, because when the activists were released, they were picked up again later. The government also chose a member of the newer group to be a labor representative to the International Labor Organization meeting in Geneva, a public signal of government approval.[57]

According to the Communists, the government played a much more complex game. It supported a committee intended to create unity among the different elements of the shipboard personnel. A key member of the committee, Fortunato Marinelli—a longtime maritime activist—was labor editor of the Anti-Personalist paper *La Argentina*, which also backed unity. The port prefect, Hermelo, created an Anti-Personalist committee in La Boca. Hermelo tried to reshape the unions in the port by favoring some factions over others and was feted by the shippers.[58] Clearly the government lacked a defined project.

Did the political situation change in La Boca because of labor policies? We cannot be sure why people voted the way they did, but a major change seemed to be taking place. In the city council elections in late 1926 in the fourth ward, which included La Boca, a traditional stronghold of the Socialists, the Personalists won 3,909 votes, the Anti-Personalists 3,635, and the Socialists only 3,157. In almost identical words, Communist and Socialist sources claimed that the Anti-Personalist totals were due to the influence of Anastasi with the shipboard personnel and to an organization

---

56. Reprinted in Ministerio del Interior, *Crónica informativa*, August 1927, 85; and see also 86.

57. *La Internacional*, September 29, October 1, 11, November 29, December 10, 1925, January 14, 1926; *Bandera Proletaria*, October 10, 17, 31, December 5, 12, 1925; *El Obrero Gráfico*, December 1925; Ministerio del Interior, *Memoria 1925–26*, 454; *La Argentina*, July 11, 1925, August 2, 1926; *La Unión del Marino*, August 1925. The position of the government was not consistent. See, for example, *La Internacional*, March 27, May 5, 1926.

58. *La Internacional*, September 29, 1925, January 14, 20, July 20, August 15, 1926; *La Prensa*, September 25, 1925; *Bandera Proletaria*, October 10, 17, 1925, January 23, July 24, September 11, 1926; *La Argentina*, October 1, 11, 18, December 14, 1925, January 12–26, February 1, 4, March 28, May 1–6, July 13–16, August 2, 8, 12, 14, 1926.

of state employees run by Juan Popovich, a former central committee member of the USA who had represented the shipbuilders' union.[59]

The confused nature of the Anti-Personalist policies was further demonstrated in December 1926 and January 1927 when a strike broke out over work rules in the shipyards of the Mihanovich Lines. Although the strike lingered until mid-May, according to the DNT by the end of January the strikers had been replaced, with 530 out of 548 losing their jobs. The Anti-Personalist response was mixed. Hermelo used the Admiral Brown Library in La Boca, which claimed to be an Anti-Personalist organization, as a site for recruiting strikebreakers. This was denounced by Reinaldo Elena, an Anti-Personalist leader in La Boca, saying that "in the battles between capital and labor, the committees and the authorities of the Radicals maintain neutrality and disavow in a categorical manner all acts that lead to separation from its principles."[60] In denouncing Hermelo's activities, Elena did not mention his name, probably because Alvear could have replaced Hermelo.

The confusion intensified when a bomb went off in Hermelo's house. The police closed the headquarters of the FOM and of the shipyard workers, as well as arresting some sixty workers, including union leaders. The Anti-Personalist daily, La Acción, condemned the police actions. The final end of the shipyard strike was arranged with Hermelo's help.[61]

Political pressures on workers in the port increased. Creditable accusations were made that port workers had to enroll for jobs through Hermelo's Admiral Brown Library. The Independent Socialists claimed that Hermelo hoped to use his vote-getting ability to be made either naval minister or a senator.[62] It also appears that harassment of the UOMAR had begun.[63]

As the 1928 presidential elections approached, all elements jockeyed for position and charges flew. Hermelo organized workers for company unions. The Socialist ties to the UOMAR become clearer and the Personal-

---

59. La Internacional, December 4, 1926; La Chispa (Rosario), December 27, 1926; Marotta, El movimiento obrero argentino, 3:86.

60. La Acción, January 19, 1927.

61. See La Acción, January 20, 28, 1927. For the strike and the bombing, see Bandera Proletaria, December 25, 1926, January 15–29, February 12, March 12, May 28, 1927; La Internacional, January 29, February 5, March 12, 1927; La Acción, January 19, 26–29, February 8, 1927; La Vanguardia, December 21–30, 1926, May 7, 20, 1927; Ministerio del Interior, Crónica Informativa, January 1927, 69; DNT, Crónica mensual, July 1927, 2067; Marotta, El movimiento obrero argentino, 3:252–53.

62. La Internacional, April 30, 1927; Libertad, September 1, 1927.

63. La Acción, January 22, February 1, 1927.

ists tried to use support for the FOM to attract votes. In the meantime a reshuffling of the shipboard unions occurred. A Committee for Unity had existed for some time, trying to achieve a merger between the two rival organizations. When the Committee proposed negotiations among the three parties (the officers, the FOM, and the UOMAR), the officers agreed, but only if García would play a key role. The FOM also accepted, but the UOMAR refused, claiming that it was the only legitimate organization. The officers then reorganized and swung their support to the FOM. A new Council of Relations headed by García was created to coordinate issues between the officers and the FOM. The UOMAR was left isolated.[64]

The Anti-Personalists still pursued votes along the waterfront, and Hermelo gave jobs though his political operations and helped Mihanovich organize a series of company unions for its personnel. Accusations were made that to get a job with Mihanovich a worker needed to affiliate with the Admiral Brown Library. Another political committee was called the Subcommittee Ricardo Hermelo. Hermelo freely used his police powers to repress rival organizations. The company unions operated in apparent close cooperation with a committee of merchant marine personnel that supported the Anti-Personalist presidential ticket of Leopoldo Melo-Vicente Gallo. A major rift still existed between some Anti-Personalists and Hermelo.[65]

Veiled accusations were made that García worked for the Personalists, which were of course denied.[66] The FOM and allied unions started a major campaign against Hermelo and the conditions that existed in the port of Buenos Aires. Protesting Hermelo's attempts to control hiring on the waterfront, in late 1927 dockworkers and other land-based port workers called two twenty-four-hour strikes. The Council, composed of officers and the FOM, even charged Hermelo with extorting money from organizations in the port. No doubt some of the charges were true, but the timing, the

---

64. Casaretto, *Historia del movimiento obrero*, 2:32–33; *La Epoca*, June 8, 1927; Ministerio del Interior, *Crónica Informativa*, August, 1927, 91–95; *Bandera Proletaria*, July 9, October 8, 29, November 26, 1927; Consejo de Relaciones Marítimas, *Actas*, 1–5, September 15–October 22, 1927; *Confederación*, July 1927; *La Internacional*, October 1, November 19, 1927; *Libertad*, September 10, 15, October 1, 4, 1927; *La Acción*, March 19, April 29, June 30, July 17, September 6–October 4, 1927.

65. *Bandera Proletaria*, October 15, December 3, 1927, January 7, March 31, 1928; *Libertad*, Mar, 7, 14, 1928; *La Internacional*, December 24, 1927; *La Epoca*, September 17, 20, December 30, 1927; *La Vanguardia*, December 1, 29, 30, 1927; *La Acción*, November 17, 1927.

66. Consejo de Relaciones Marítimas, *Actas*, 6, October 29, 1927; *La Prensa*, January 3, 4, 1928; *La Epoca*, January 7, 1928; *Bandera Proletaria*, January 14, 1928.

drumbeat of publicity, and the echoing of the charges by *La Epoca* gives the impression of a campaign to undermine Hermelo before the elections.[67]

Shorn of its support from the officers and with some of its key leaders deserting, the UOMAR became increasingly tied to the Socialist party. José Palmeiro, its leader, had no historical connection to the waterfront but had been active in La Fraternidad—though expelled—and had been a Socialist city councilman in the industrial suburb of Avellaneda. The union's connections to the railroad unions remained strong, but it increasingly was tied to Mihanovich and became a company union.[68]

Despite the tensions between the FOM and Hermelo, the union met with figures in the administration, including Alvear himself, though not as frequently as desired and not with great success.[69] Still, it grew and its Rosario local reemerged. The FOM created a dental clinic for its members in Buenos Aires.[70]

The Anti-Personalists had failed to create the kind of labor union that they desired, but were they any more successful politically? The congressional elections of April 1928, which occurred concurrently with the presidential elections, demonstrate the Anti-Personalists' complete failure. In the fourth ward, which included La Boca, the Anti-Personalists received just 16 percent of the vote, barely above the 11.2 percent of their citywide average. Usually a Socialist bastion, that party received only 21 percent of the vote, though it was their second-best showing. The Personalist Radicals won 43.5 percent of the vote.[71] Efforts to win votes on the waterfront had been a failure, except perhaps through the FOM.

The struggle for influence in the port did not end with the election. Hermelo's attitude changed with Yrigoyen's victory, and he appeared more willing to cooperate with the FOM. Problems arose with Mihanovich, however, over lowered salaries and pressure to force officers and crew to affiliate with company unions. The FOM had great expectations for the new administration and a strike broke out days before the inauguration.[72] The action was timed for the change in power.

67. See *La Epoca*, September 17, 1927–March 8, 1928, esp. October 24, December 30, 1927; *La Internacional*, December 31, 1927; *Bandera Proletaria*, February 4, March 10–24, 1928; *Libertad*, February 27, March 3, 22, May 18, 1928; Consejo de Relaciones Marítimas, *Actas*, 17–18, March 17–April 1, 1928; DNT, *Crónica mensual*, January 1928, 2276–77.

68. Casaretto, *Historia del movimiento obrero*, 2:33–35; *Libertad*, March 22, April 8–17, May 4, 1928; *Bandera Proletaria*, November 5, 1927, April 14, June 2, 9, September 22, 1928.

69. Consejo de Relaciones Marítimas, *Actas*, 9, 12, 19, November 24, December 31, 1927, April 30, 1928; *Bandera Proletaria*, December 3, 1927, January 7, 1928.

70. *Libertad*, April 4, 15, 1928; *Bandera Proletaria*, August 11, 1928.

71. For the election results, see Walter, *The Socialist Party*, 215.

72. *Libertad*, April 4, May 31, June 5, 21, 1928; *Bandera Proletaria*, June 2, 9, 24, July 21,

Creation of New Unions

Closely connected to the search for voters in the port area and the desire to have a union movement that the administration could work with was the formation of the Asociación Trabajadores del Estado, an organization that still exists. It was founded in early 1925. For three months congress had not provided money to pay workers of the Ministry of Public Works employed in the port, and a group had successfully protested. They soon formed a union, principally based in the central shop of the Ministry of Public Works; the union had its greatest strength in the area around the port. From the beginning, its leaders met with the ministers of hacienda and public works, and the workers were quickly granted sick days and vacations. In an unusual move, the union publicly thanked Minister of Public Works Ortiz. The union succeeded in establishing locals upriver from Buenos Aires, where the Ministry of Public Works had significant numbers of workers. It received favorable publicity in the progovernment newspaper, *La Argentina,* whose labor editor was Marinelli.

The union's ties to the government can be seen in some of its leaders who received state jobs with the expectation that they would form a union that would bring political benefits. It is difficult to believe that they would have obtained such posts for any other reason. After the defeats of 1924, a number of Syndicalist leaders needed employment. A key early leader was Popovitch, the already-mentioned former leader of the shipyard workers. Another was Miguel Altrudi, who had been active in the furniture makers' union and had sat on a central committee of the USA. Altrudi had been looking for a government job since at least mid-1926, when a Socialist member of the city council had requested that he be hired by the city government. A third, Augusto Sparnochia, had been active in one of the waterfront unions.[73] The Alvear administration was looking for votes and, as we have seen, may have acquired some in La Boca in 1926.

28, September 22, 29, 1928; *La Internacional,* August 25, 1928; *La Unión del Marino,* May, June 1928; Consejo de Relaciones Marítimas, *Actas,* 19–22, 24–25, 32–33, April 30–September 8, 1928.

73. *La Argentina,* September 21, October 1, 30, November 25, 1925, January 18, July 12, 15, 1926; *La Acción,* November 1, 7, 1927; *Crítica,* February 23, 1929; *Unión Sindical,* April 8, 22, 1922; *Bandera Proletaria,* August 17, 1927; Marotta, *El movimiento obrero argentino,* 3:86, 150; Andrés Cabona, "Un homenaje y una reivindicación," in *Vida, obra y trascendencia de Sebastián Marotta* (Buenos Aires: Editorial Palomino, 1971), 153; http://www.torcuatoditella .com/ [no longer available] (July 10, 2004); Colección Emilio Ravignani, Serie 2, Caja 6, 260. Altrudi joined the state workers' union in 1928 and it is unclear whether it was before Yrigoyen assumed the presidency. I do not know when Sparnochia joined the union.

Its hopes to reshape the union movement can be seen more clearly among the municipal workers of the city of Buenos Aires. Several Syndicalist leaders received positions with the city and rapidly formed their own union after their attempt to have influence in the UOM failed. In addition to the reasons given for helping form the state workers' organization, the Socialists controlled the UOM.

The first evidence that the Anti-Personalist Radicals were appointing prominent Syndicalist labor leaders to the municipal workforce surfaced at a meeting of the UOM in February 1926, in which the debate centered around whether the union ought to withdraw from the USA and join a new Socialist-controlled confederation. Several new UOM members, who played a prominent role during the debate, turned out to be recent appointees to the municipal workforce and to have held important posts in the labor movement. Accounts vary as to what exactly happened at the meeting, but the Socialists retained control. Charges and countercharges began to fly. A new union was created in mid-1927, which eventually became the Asociación Trabajadores de la Comuna (ATC).

In 1924 and 1925 (and to a lesser extent later), a series of prominent Syndicalist union leaders received jobs from the city, many of whom, at least according to the Socialists, had rather dubious reputations. Several had ties to unions based in La Boca. The Socialists claimed that the Syndicalists had made agreements with Anti-Personalist caudillos to establish a new "apolitical" union in return for jobs with the city. The Socialists also leveled accusations that the Syndicalist leaders did not really work, or at least did not work on a regular basis. According to the UOM, in 1930 the ATC's secretary general had worked for the city for three years but half of that time had been spent on medical disability.[74]

The charges that surfaced, even though they may not all be true, do show what the Alvear administration wanted to do. They also permit us to know who these leaders were and why they needed jobs with the city. Many had belonged to unions that had suffered major defeats. The most interesting case is that of José R. Luz or Maximo Rita (there was disagreement over what exactly his name was and why he used different variations). Luz received a job with the city in July 1925, and he joined the UOM in January 1926, eight days before the controversial meeting mentioned above, in which he played a prominent role. According to his own account,

74. *El Obrero Municipal*, October 1925, March, April, October 1926, May, July 1927, June 1, 1930; *Bandera Proletaria*, February 13, 1926; *La Vanguardia*, May 8, 1927; *La Internacional*, December 4, 1926; *La Acción*, April 23, June 17, 1927.

he had worked for eighteen years for various unions of Syndicalist tendencies, many of them based in La Boca, including the FOM and the shipbuilders' union. In 1923 he was expelled from the UOL of Buenos Aires, the regional federation of unions, for accepting money from the organization for days he did not work. He claimed that a misunderstanding had caused him to take the money, but his opponents were less charitable.[75]

Another leader, Américo Biondi, had been active in the shipbuilders' federation, joining the union in 1906. Apparently, he was close to bosses in La Boca and to Alberto Barceló, the Conservative boss of the nearby industrial suburb of Avellaneda. Biondi supported the antipolitical position of his union. He argued against his union petitioning the government to pardon a union leader, Atilio Biondi, imprisoned for defying a government ban on publishing Anarchist materials; with the help of the bosses of La Boca, however, he convinced Yrigoyen to sign a pardon. He labored with his union against the pension law of 1923, but he was seen in the working-class neighborhood of Maciel campaigning for the law. He joined the municipal administration on June 6, 1924, as a pension law inspector with a monthly salary of 250 pesos. He was laid off in December, undoubtedly because the law was never fully implemented, but the following month he received another municipal job paying 220 pesos a month.[76]

Alejandro Protti had been a major player in both the shipbuilders' union and the FOM. He had attended national labor confederation conventions, sat on the central committee of the Syndicalist confederation, and had been secretary of the UOL. He received his city job through a recommendation of a powerful political boss who was a personal friend. By 1928 he was a foreman at the trash incinerator, and twelve workers accused him of using his post to help the ATC. He could not, however, become a citizen: several times the police refused to grant him a certificate of good conduct because of his role in distributing antimilitary propaganda.[77]

Other people who held key posts in the ATC had long union histories and been appointed to city jobs roughly simultaneously. Sebastián Ferrer had been active in the Anarchist union federation, the FORA V, and then was the secretary-general of the USA, before joining the municipal work-

75. *Bandera Proletaria*, September 21, 1929; *El Obrero Municipal*, September–October 1926, March, May 1927; *La Vanguardia*, May 8, 1927; *La Unión del Marino*, July 1923.
76. *El Obrero Municipal*, March–July 1927. See also Bilsky, *La semana trágica*, 102–3.
77. *La Confederación*, December 1927; *El Obrero Municipal*, July 1927, June 16, August 16, November 1, 1928; Marotta, *El movimiento obrero argentino*, 3:132, 150, 173; Policía Federal Argentina, Archivo General, Orden Social, *Extractos y diligencia*, July 26, 1928–June 26, 1929, no. 3073, 18, *Copiadores de notas*, June 26, 1929–October 7, 1930, no. 1230, 55.

force and the ATC. Pedro Milesi had attended the last congress of the FORA IX and been secretary general of the metalworkers' union. He left the latter with some dispute over money still pending. Milesi had ties to Syndicalism but had joined the Communist Party and quickly been expelled. The party later charged that he was a police agent. Angel López had sat on the central committee of the USA. Manuel Monzón had been active in a railroad workers' organization in Entre Ríos and been a key figure in a provincial labor confederation that had collapsed during a strike.[78] Others who received appointments had similar backgrounds, and it taxes credulity that the party bosses who made the recommendations and those who actually made the appointments did not know what they were doing. They wanted to create a sympathetic union among the municipal workers. In dealing with municipal authorities, the ATC did behave in a fashion similar to the UOM.[79]

The ATC had bet on the wrong horse, and the Personalists' victory in 1928 put the ATC in an awkward position. According to the UOM, the ATC tried to make accommodations with the victors. If the accusations made by their Socialist-dominated rival are accurate—they offered improvements in conditions to those who joined their union—then they must have achieved a modus vivendi with the Personalist Radicals.[80]

The Anti-Personalists tried to create friendly unions and ones that could help them acquire votes, especially in La Boca. They offered too little and faced serious competition, especially from the Socialists and from the personal popularity of Yrigoyen.

Conclusion

Like its predecessor, the Alvear administration attempted to attract support from the popular classes through contacts with the labor movement. It too had a policy of *obrerismo*. The administration was partially successful in helping transform the labor movement by helping to create unions that offered better conditions in return for discipline. It aided in the building

---

78. *El Obrero Municipal*, July, August, December 1927; *Bandera Proletaria*, December 6, 20, 1924; *Libertad*, June 23, 1928; Marotta, *El movimiento obrero argentino*, 3:52, 68, 132, 144, 150, 173, 185; Cabona, "Un homenaje y una reivindicación," 153; Partido Comunista de la Argentina, *Esbozo*, 52. For leaders of the ATC, see, for example, *Bandera Proletaria*, March 2, 1929, March 15, 1930.

79. *Libertad*, April 9, 1928; *Bandera Proletaria*, November 17, 1928.

80. *El Obrero Municipal*, November 16, 1928, April 1, October 16, December 16, 1929, January 16, 1930.

of a powerful rail union, but it is unlikely that it gained a large number of votes by doing so. The creation of state and municipal employees unions did not have wide repercussions. They were small and could offer little. The Anti-Personalists did not win a great deal of popularity. In the 1926 and 1928 congressional elections in Buenos Aires there was a strengthening positive correlation between workers and votes for the Personalist Radicals.[81]

The situation on the waterfront makes clear the administration's problems. In 1925 the Communist Party daily claimed that the administration was divided into two camps: those that openly opposed the workers and those—like the then new head of the Anti-Personalist apparatus in the capital, Anastasi—who were antiworker but interested in gaining workers' votes. The antiworker claim about Anastasi is disingenuous, but the rest makes sense. Hermelo and Domecq García were antiunion. Anastasi did have good contacts with a large number of Syndicalists and he had served as lawyer for the FOM. He also claimed to follow an *obrerista* policy. Tamborini when he was minister of interior had a hand in this strategy.[82] Yet Alvear never made his government go in one direction or the other.

The activities of an Ortiz or an Anastasi did not outweigh a Hermelo or the generally awkward policies of the Alvear administration. The presence of many Liga members in the government, and the support for the pension plan, all helped undermine the government's position with unions and workers. The administration's labor policies, however, cannot be simply labeled conservative, as its aid to the UF indicates.

81. Canton and Jorrat, *Elecciones en la ciudad*, 2:215.
82. *La Internacional*, May 16, 22, August 13, 1925, January 16, 1926, April 9, 1927; *La Argentina*, March 23–April 4, 1926.

YRIGOYEN AND THE FAILURE TO REESTABLISH
OBRERISMO, 1928–1930

Contradictory moods gripped the public in October 1928, when Yrigoyen took office for the second time, after having been reelected by a wide margin. Many feared and loathed the thought of Yrigoyen once again in the presidential palace. Rumors of coups existed and Alvear's minister of war, Agustín Justo, felt compelled to deny his role in such a plot.[1] On the other hand, in the simultaneous presidential and congressional elections, the Personalist Radicals had swept every ward in the city of Buenos Aires. In the more competitive congressional elections, the Personalists had won comfortable pluralities in all the worker-dominated wards.[2] *Obrerismo* had had an impact.

There was hope (and fear) that Yrigoyen would return to the policies of the early years of his first administration by aiding striking workers. These expectations partially came to pass. During the first days of the new administration, *La Epoca* gave support to workers. For example, during a conflict in the workshop of the Central Argentino railroad in Pérez, just outside of Rosario, which the minister of public works was attempting to solve, the paper commented, "As is known, this conflict is caused by the company not having complied with the contracts signed with the rail workers in regard to the building, repairing and assembling of rail cars."[3]

Yrigoyen's response to expectations raised by his return to the Casa

---

1. Potash, *The Army and Politics in Argentina*, 19.
2. Darío Canton, *Materiales para el estudio de la sociología política en la Argentina* (Buenos Aires: Editorial del Instituto, 1968), 2:103; Walter, *The Socialist Party*, 215.
3. *La Epoca*, October 19, 1928.

Rosada was somewhat muddled. He hoped to build on his past relationships with the labor movement, but this was made difficult by a series of obstacles. He was suspicious of the UF because of its centralized structure and the Socialists in key positions. Other parts of the labor movement were badly divided, making cooperation with them difficult. Yrigoyen also wanted better relations with the British and rapidly faced serious political problems, partly produced by the onset of the Depression. In addition, he lacked the energy of previous years.

Labor's Initial Response to the Yrigoyen Administration

Many workers believed that Yrigoyen would be sympathetic and thus used the opportunity presented by his return to the Casa Rosada. After the election of Yrigoyen, a union emerged in the telephone industry for the first time since 1919, what became the Federación Obreros y Empleados Telefónicos (FOET). Despite early connections to the Socialist-dominated Federación Empleados de Comerio, Syndicalists controlled the new organization. Luis Gay, a dominant leader almost from the beginning, claimed that he was not a Radical at that time but that he had always been sympathetic to the Radicals. His father had been a Radical, and through his connections, Gay got his first job, a post with the legislature of the Province of Buenos Aires.[4] The new union had several other advantages. The U.S.-based International Telephone and Telegraph was about to purchase the British-owned telephone company, and Yrigoyen preferred British capital to North American capital. The company also wanted to secure higher rates from the government.[5]

When the FOET pressed for a contract, *La Epoca* sympathized and Yrigoyen and Minister of Interior Elipidio González met regularly with the union and the company. They helped negotiate a contract that not only raised wages but established paid vacations, sick pay, and set job classifications. In addition, the company recognized the union's grievance committee. This was a major triumph for the union and would have been

---

4. FOET, *Luchas y conquistas*, 22–29; *Boletín de Servicios*, August 20, 1928, 363–65; September 5, 1928, 393; *Confederación*, August/September 1928; Luis Gay, author interview, October 17, 1975.

5. Ricardo T. Mulleady, *Breve historia de la telefonía argentina (1886–1956)* (Buenos Aires: Guillermo Kraft, 1956), 27; Max Winkler, *Investments of United States Capital in Latin America*, 2nd ed. (Port Washington, N.Y.: Kennikat, 1971), 69–70; *La Epoca*, November 28, 1928. The union did meet with the minister of interior under Alvear. *Confederación*, August/September 1928.

impossible without government intervention. The union was pleased, but so was the company. Not only did the company state its satisfaction publicly, but according to the U.S. chargé d'affaires ad interim, "The attitude of the Minister of Interior towards the company was . . . most satisfactory."[6]

The increased threat of labor unrest fed the fear of a return to the turmoil that engulfed the country in the years after 1916. At a meeting of the Liga Patriótica, its longtime leader Manuel Carlés proposed that given the agitation that gripped the working class and given what had happened when Yrigoyen had been president previously, the brigades should adopt their martial organization of 1919 and 1920 in order "to find themselves in condition to defend the people against the aggression of villainous groups, disguised as strikers, I mean assaults, murders and crimes of all types." The meeting approved the proposal.[7]

In reality the situation was more complex. The strike rate in 1928 in the city of Buenos Aires increased considerably over preceding years but did not intensify after Yrigoyen assumed office; stoppages did seem to become more frequent in the provinces. Strikes were small; in 1928 and 1929, the number of strikers averaged 208 and 250 per stoppage compared to 659 in 1927. The results of the strikes were not encouraging for labor.[8] The telephone workers' ability to meet with Yrigoyen or González was not unusual; frequently they met with more than one group of workers per day.[9] The success of the FOET, however, did remain unusual.

The Port and Rosario as Indications of Limits of Tolerance

The telephone company's willingness to negotiate made a government-brokered settlement possible, but employers frequently remained intransi-

6. *La Epoca*, November 5, 1928–March 4, 1929, esp. November 6, 1928, January 5, 7, February 28, 1929; *La Prensa*, November 9, 1928–March 6, 1929, esp. November 9, 1928, January 8, March 1, 5, 1929; Ministerio del Interior, *Memoria 1928–29*, 143–45; FOET, *Luchas y conquistas*, 35–36, 206–29; Luis Gay, Instituto Di Tella Oral History Program, 2–7; and author interview, October 17, 1975; U.S. Diplomatic Dispatch, Buenos Aires, no. 835.504/53, March 12, 1929.

7. *La Prensa*, October 18, 1928.

8. DNT, *Crónica Mensual*, July 1928, 2427–34, January 1929, 2621–28, August 1929, 2898–906; DNT, División de Estadística, *Estadística de las huelgas*, 18, 20. The statistics gathered for strike activity by the police are quite different, and, if correct, the number of strikers in 1927 was actually much higher than in subsequent years. Policía de Buenos Aires, *Memoria, antecedentes y datos estadística correspondiente al año 1928* (Buenos Aires: Imprenta y encuadernación de la Policía, 1928), 186. See, for example, *La Prensa*, October 12, 1928; *La Epoca*, December 6, 1928; and below.

9. *La Epoca*, January 5, 7, February 28, 1929; *La Prensa*, January 8, 1929.

gent. The economic situation still was good, but that did not last. Yrigoyen's voting base appeared secure, meaning that he did not need to continually enlarge it. He remained unwilling to tolerate serious disruption of public order or the economy, making union gains difficult when management dug in their heels.

The key, early test of Yrigoyen's labor policies was the port of Buenos Aires, which had retained its symbolic role earned during the first presidency. Moreover, the perception existed that the FOM had ties to the Radical Party; if the position of labor was to change, FOM was the obvious candidate to begin the process. In addition, with the possible exception of the railroaders, no other workers could so easily place the government in a difficult position.

Many maritime workers saw Yrigoyen's election as an opportunity to regain a dominant position. Tensions had been running high between the Council of Relations (the coordinating body of the FOM and the organized officers) and the Mihanovich line. The issues were clear. The company had not fulfilled the agreements that it had made in 1924, as even *La Prensa* acknowledged.[10] Also crucial were the pressure, especially on the officers, to join company unions and the difficulty posed to union activity. The council believed that Hermelo had worked to weaken the union and that a change in administration would favor them. Because the existing arrangements in the port had been intended to favor the Anti-Personalists, the Personalists would want to reverse the situation.

The Council of Relations had readied itself for the change of administration. It made agreements with maritime unions in Uruguay and Paraguay, many of whose members also worked for Mihanovich. A set of demands was presented that called for the fulfillment of the 1924 agreements and for Mihanovich to recognize the right to unionize and to establish a union shop.

The company precipitated a crisis just prior to Yrigoyen assuming office by firing the captain of the *Bruselas* and, when he was backed by his crew, using force to throw them off the ship. In internal discussions, Francisco García argued that the strike should be postponed, saying that it should occur only when the union wanted it to happen and not when the company found it convenient. García failed to brake the rush to strike, which began just six days before the change in administration. Although the FOM received cooperation from its counterparts in the other countries, most offi-

---

10. October 28, 1928.

cers did not disembark. This permitted Mihanovich to man its ships. Although there was a good deal of confusion because of problems with tugs and, according to the U.S. embassy, a distinct slackening of maritime activity, ships did sail.

The incoming administration was of two minds. It wanted to help the union but not have trade disrupted. It displayed enough force in the port area that violence was limited, but it did occur. In one incident, gunfire erupted between strikers and supporters of the company, leaving one of the latter dead and another wounded. This was far from the only such event. Despite intense vigilance, when the *Apipé*, which was manned by strikebreakers, was set to sail, a bomb was placed on board. An anonymous phone call warned the authorities, who then flooded the hold to prevent the explosion and thereby delayed its departure. According to Osvaldo Bayer, the man who claimed to have planted the bomb was Severino Di Giovanni, the famous Italian Anarchist, and he did so without the knowledge of the FOM.

The Yrigoyen administration became determined to reach a settlement. The parties to the dispute met regularly with the naval minister and more frequently with Minister of Interior González, and at times with Yrigoyen himself. The government backed its desire for a settlement with orders to the port authorities not to give employment papers to substitute workers, which made staffing with strikebreakers difficult. After numerous meetings and twenty days, an agreement was hammered out that allowed the union to claim a triumph. It called for reincorporation of all workers on ships flying Argentine flags and recognition of the right of association, and the company promised to respect existing work and salary conditions. The union failed to win the dismissal of strikebreakers. This led to a disagreement on whether strikers would sail on the same ship as before the stoppage, thereby expelling the strikebreakers. The government decided in the union's favor.[11] Problems continued, however, and the company did not display any more willingness to accept the union. The Uruguayans, who had struck in support of the Argentines, remained locked out, and

---

11. Consejo de Relaciones Marítimas, *Actas*, 34–48, September 28–November 16, 1928; *Bandera Proletaria*, September 15–November 3, 1928; *La Prensa*, October 1–November 1, 1928; *La Epoca*, October 1–November 1, 1928; *La Acción*, October 9, 14, 1928; *Boletín de Sevicios*, July 1929, 315–16; *El Obrero Municipal*, November 1, 1928; DNT, *Crónica Mensual*, January 1929, 2625; Rivarola, *Obreros, utopías y revoluciones*, 253; "Strike in the Mihanovich River Company" (enclosure in U.S. Diplomatic Dispatch, Buenos Aires, no. 835.5045/219, November 28, 1928); Osvaldo Bayer, *Anarchism and Violence: Severino Di Giovanni in Argentina, 1923–1931*, trans. Paul Sharkey (London: Elephant Editions, 1986), 117–21.

the FOM felt it could do nothing. González refused to see the union, though later delegations met with both him and Yrigoyen.[12]

The government could see the outcome as a triumph. The union was not unhappy. *La Prensa* editorialized that this was the way strikes should be handled, with firmness and government negotiations. It saw this as optimal, while criticizing the hands-off attitude that it saw in Rosario. The U.S. embassy reported to Washington that "the press was unanimous in approving the firm yet mediatory attitude of the Government."[13] By the end of October, the U.S. military attaché had this to say:

> The very pessimistic way in which the idea of D. Irigoyen's return to the Presidency was viewed by a large circle, seems to be changing. The following is a quote from an editorial which appeared in the "Buenos Aires Herald" in this city: "There is no denying the fact that there is a growing spirit of optimism in local business and commercial circles regarding the actuation of the Irigoyen government. This has not been caused so much by the interviews which have been accorded by the President to various industrial and financial delegations and his expressed desire to assist traders, railways and producers to extend their operations in Argentina, but by his evident refusal to follow in the path which labor agitators and others are attempting to draw him."[14]

From the government's perspective, the port strike had worked out well. A simultaneous strike wave in Rosario appeared much more ominous. Because it began before Yrigoyen assumed the presidency, he could not rationally be blamed for it. Still, the strikes disrupted Rosario's economic life for months, affecting its port and such public utilities as electrical power, telephones, streetcars, and buses. It also spread to the city of Santa Fe and the other ports of Santa Fe province, and began spilling over into the cereal belt, in both Santa Fe and Córdoba provinces.

The Rosario strike wave helped set the tone for Yrigoyen's second term, but a detailed account is unnecessary because two recent works have discussed it at some length.[15] It is necessary, however, to give an overview in

---

12. Consejo de Relaciones Marítimas, *Actas*, 48–49, November 16, 17, 1928; *Bandera Proletaria*, November 24, 1928.

13. *La Prensa*, October 30, 1928; "Strike in the Mihanovich River Company," 5.

14. U.S. Military Intelligence Report, Buenos Aires, no. 3905, October 31, 1928, 4.

15. Roberto P. Korzeniewicz, "The Labor Politics of Radicalism: The Santa Fe Crisis of 1928," *Hispanic America Historical Review* 73, no. 1 (February 1993): 1–32; Matthew B. Karush,

order to see the scope of the challenge to the desire for an orderly society. The wave of strikes started in May 1928 and only began to die out in mid-1929. Moreover, the strike wave had ties to politics and the Radical Party, which made it more troubling to those who saw it as a harbinger of the future.

The labor unrest began right before Miguel Gómez Cello assumed office as governor of Santa Fe. Gómez Cello was a Personalist Radical and had defeated a candidate of the governing Anti-Personalists. He appointed Ricardo Caballero, a mercurial Radical politician who specialized in appeals to the working class and had been an Anarchist in his youth, to be chief of police of Rosario. The police chief was the governor's key political operative in the city, and Caballero's role underlines the importance of the police in Radical politics. It also reiterates the role that police play in labor agitation. When police hold back and permit workers to use intimidation based on their numbers, the balance of power swings in their favor.

In 1927 approximately 50 percent of the dockworkers had been provided by the Asociación del Trabajo, but the union had begun to rebuild. In May 1928 it struck for an increase of one peso per day and the withdrawal from the port of the inspectors of the AT. The national authorities (still Anti-Personalists) controlled the port through the port prefecture, which kept a tight lid on the situation.

On May 8, however, a strikebreaker by the name of Juan Romero got down from a streetcar to enter the port. A group of female strike supporters approached Romero and attempted to hand him propaganda. Romero pulled a revolver and mortally wounded nineteen-year-old Luisa Lallana. Romero was arrested, as was Tiberio Podestá, the head of the company union. The latter was charged with inciting Romero to shoot but was later cleared. Thousands attended the funeral for Lallana, and her death generated a twenty-four-hour general strike in the city. This was just the first death and the first general strike of the many that shut down Rosario in 1928 and 1929.

The port remained in the hands of the national authorities, but on May 10 Caballero became police chief and outside the gates of the port, the strikers and their supporters had almost a free hand. Caballero intended to reap working-class political support in return for his tolerant attitude. Moreover, he made clear that there were other reasons as well. He claimed

---

"Workers or Citizens," 268–85. The following argument on Rosario in 1928 is informed by these two works.

that those who worked for the AT and distributed jobs in the port also functioned as political bosses for the ruling conservative (Anti-Personalist) interests. A union victory would cost them their source of patronage.

The port strike spread to other ports in Santa Fe province and also briefly to Bahía Blanca, in southern Buenos Aires Province. During its course, a forty-eight-hour solidarity strike shut down Rosario. Even the labor press noted that the suburbs seemed to lack any police protection. Considerable violence and looting occurred. The Anarchists even tried to shut down Buenos Aires with a sympathy strike but were largely unsuccessful. The port strike was settled on May 22 with a victory for the workers.[16]

Once the barriers went down, wave after wave of major strikes punctured whatever tranquility existed in Rosario. With stoppages of telephone and trolley service the fabric of urban life was threatened. Seemingly unending sabotage and violence accompanied the strikes.[17] Caballero did mediate some strikes, but the hands-off attitude of the police, the sense of exaltation that permeated the Rosario working class, and the possibility of real gains drove the strikers. The laissez-faire attitude of the police was not the product of the paranoia of employers or the establishment press; in fact, it was something that even the Syndicalists acknowledged.[18]

Confusion reigned in Santa Fe politics. The governor closed the legislature with the hope that the national government would intervene and call new elections. The excuse was that the majority had been fraudulently elected. The provincial Radical Party split over Caballero and went into the municipal elections in Rosario divided. Despite charges that it used the police to gain votes, Caballero's group lost to the more orthodox Radical faction. It did fare well, however, in working-class neighborhoods.[19]

Alvear had refrained from intervening in Santa Fe, restrained by the overwhelming electoral victory of the Personalists in Santa Fe and the na-

---

16. *Boletín de Servicios*, July 20, 1927, 278, 317, May 20, 1928, 217, June 5, 1928, 244–47, November 5, 1928, 483; Ricardo Caballero, *Discursos parlamentarios y documentos políticas del doctor Ricardo Caballero*, compiled by Roberto A. Ortelli (Buenos Aires: Sociedad de Publicaciones El Inca, 1929), 503; *La Prensa*, May 1928, esp. May 5, 6; *La Epoca*, May 1928; *Bandera Proletaria*, May 12–June 9, 1928; *El Obrero Municipal*, May, June 1, 1928; Cámara de Diputados, *Diario de sesiones*, 11, July 12, 1928, 214–37.

17. For the scope of the disruption, see either *La Vanguardia* or *La Prensa* for July 1928.

18. *Bandera Proletaria*, May 26, 1928. See *La Internacional*, January 12, 1929; *La Acción*, July 26, 1928; *Libertad*, June 25, 1928; *La Prensa*, July 9, 1928.

19. *La Prensa*, June 11, 27, November 2–17, 1928; *Libertad*, June 21, 1928; *La Acción*, November 16, 1928; *Bandera Proletaria*, August 4, 11, 1928; Karush, "Workers or Citizens," 280–83.

tion as a whole. Strikes in rural areas pushed Yrigoyen to become involved. These were partially inspired by Rosario's wave of unrest and, according to Eduardo Sartelli, by the lower wages produced by the increasing use of trucks and harvesters. The strikes began in mid-1928 and by December had spread widely, affecting carters, stevedores, and others. The demands focused on union recognition, closed shops, and higher wages. As always in this type of conflict, considerable violence erupted.

Farmers and agricultural interests asked the national government for help. After sending an agent of the DNT to investigate, on December 2 Yrigoyen ordered troops to Santa Fe. Despite pretending to be neutral, the troops favored the farmers over the workers, as union protests demonstrated. The rural unrest petered out and the harvest was finished, largely unhampered. This did not satisfy those who had been calling for action. An editorial in *La Prensa* on December 4 argued that maintaining order was the duty of the provincial government and not the national government.[20]

Nine days after troops entered the province, Caballero submitted his resignation, undoubtedly fearing that he would be fired by a governor who worried that Yrigoyen would take over the province.[21] In 1929 strike activity continued at an extremely high rate in Rosario. Despite the hopes that had greeted Yrigoyen's election among major sectors of the labor movement and the popular classes, less than two months after he assumed office he had sent troops to dampen down labor unrest.

The Administration's Retreat

The administration's ability to make grand gestures became very limited. In early May 1929 *Crítica* commented on the poor price of wheat. Employment in the capital had been volatile since mid-1928 but began declining in mid-1929. This reflected the falling prices for exports and the flow of capital toward New York. Tax receipts of the central government

20. See, for example, *Bandera Proletaria*, June 24, 30, July 14, 21, August 4, 11, September 1, October 27, December 1–29, 1928; *Boletín de Servicios*, December 5, 1928, 529–34; December 20, 1928, 557–59; *La Prensa*, November 22–December 10, 1928; *La Epoca*, November 24–December 16, 1928. Eduardo Sartelli, "Rehacer todo lo destiudo: Los conflictos obrero-rurales en la década 1927–1937," in *Conflictos obrero-rurales pampeanos (1900–1937)*, ed. Waldo Ansaldi (Buenos Aires: Centro Editor de América Latina, 1993), 3:241–91.

21. Caballero, *Discursos parlamentarios*, 499–521.

declined markedly in 1930, though this did not have, as yet, an impact on spending.²²

The administration's relations with the Unión Ferroviaria were rocky. It appears that Yrigoyen found the strength of the UF disturbing because of the prominent positions held by Socialists and the close ties many leaders had forged with the Alvear administration. Also, according to Paul Goodwin, Yrigoyen desired good relations with the rail companies. A key player in developing that relationship was the principal lawyer for the Central Argentino, Altanasio Iturbe, who had been a Radical from the earliest days and had served as Yrigoyen's private secretary. Yrigoyen wanted good relations with British capital, in part because he feared Yankee capital. British Ambassador Malcolm Robertson reported that Yrigoyen told him, "I know I am speaking in the name of my country as well as in my own when I say we have confidence in British capital and British railways which we know." Yrigoyen even blocked a rollback of freight costs that the Alvear administration had called for.²³

The Personalists developed a complex relationship with the railroaders. The UF's rivals met regularly with Yrigoyen and other major officials. These parallel unions had significant support in some provinces. Communists and Syndicalists, however, began to withdraw their backing, particularly the latter, after the effort began in 1929 to merge Syndicalist and Socialist-dominated union confederations.²⁴

The administration remained willing to intervene in local conflicts on the side of the UF. In early 1929 the Pacífico railroad laid off 160 workers from its shops in Junín and Mendoza, which employed 3,200, claiming lack of work. The UF charged that the dismissals occurred in order to permit the hiring of twenty-five foreigners and the outsourcing of work. Contracts called for as much work as possible to be done in the shops, and the union was making a nationalistic appeal. The workers struck the shops for eight days, backed by large-scale popular agitation in Junín. Government officials, including Yrigoyen, had been meeting with the parties, but firmer

22. *Crítica*, May 7, 1929; DNT, *Crónica Mensual*, July 1929, 2839, October/December 1930, 3342–43; *La Epoca*, July 2, 1930; Di Tella and Zymelman, *Las etapas del desarrollo*, 380–81; Comité Nacional de Geografía, *Anuario*, 396.

23. Goodwin, *Los ferrocarriles británicos*, 270–76, esp. 273; Graciela I. Giordano de Rocca, "El conflicto ferroviario de 1929/1930: Empresas y trabajadores," *Todo es Historia*, May–June 1982, 60; Wright, *British-Owned Railways*, 134, 130–35.

24. *El Obrero Ferroviario*, December 16, 1928; *Crítica*, January 23, 25, 1929; *La Epoca*, January 20, 1929; *La Prensa*, February 4, 1929; *Bandera Proletaria*, January 12, June 22, August 10, December 21, 1929, March 8, 22, 1930; Marotta, *El movimiento sindical argentino*, 3:287–99.

intervention happened after March 7, 1929. Workers halted all Pacífico traffic near Buenos Aires for fifteen minutes during the morning rush hour and threatened to begin a work-to-regulation. The highest reaches of the government applied pressure on the company, including the minister of public works and Yrigoyen, with the president coming down strongly in favor of rehiring the workers. The Pacífico agreed to take back the workers and pay salaries for the strike days. Studies were to be made of other pending matters.[25] The UF continued to meet with key leaders, including the president, and get cooperation on small, but important items.[26]

Larger issues were more problematic. For some time, the UF had pressed for a number of improvements, including a minimum salary of 150 pesos a month, a contract for administrative employees, and paid holidays for those workers who did not yet receive them. In November 1929 the union held a series of short but expanding strikes, provoking intervention by Yrigoyen and González. The protest was called off, and negotiations with the companies continued. According to internal railroad company papers, the government was not very sympathetic to the workers. The government did make sure that several job categories began to receive paid vacations in December. No further progress had occurred when in February 1930 railroaders belonging to a recently reconstituted Federación de Sindicatos Ferroviarios, a parallel union with ties to the Communists, began to work-to-regulation. Although not a very large organization, it had strong support among signalmen, who slowed traffic on the Central Argentino. The slowdown threatened to spread to other lines. After negotiating the return of all the strikers, the movement ended, but the threat hung in the air.

On March 11, 1930, the UF announced that on the following day rail traffic would stop between three and four in the afternoon. Work-to-regulation began the next day, which as always slowed traffic. *La Prensa* blamed the government for failing to take stronger measures to resolve problems before the strike began. As frequently happened during work-to-regulation on commuter lines, passengers rioted. At the Villa Luro station on the Ferrocarril Oeste, a train was sacked and ten cars burned. Elsewhere lesser levels of violence occurred. The companies blamed the railroaders for the violence, but it appears likely that the passengers were responsible. It re-

25. See especially *El Obrero Ferroviario*, March 16, 1929; *Crítica*, March 2, 1929; *La Prensa*, March 3-9, 1929; *La Epoca*, March 7, 1929; Fernández, *La Unión Ferroviaria*, 234-36. The latter uses the date 1928, but it is clearly 1929.
26. See *El Obrero Ferroviario*, January 16, July 1, 1929, July 16, 1930.

mains possible that they were egged on by the workers. A solution was difficult because the union was under great pressure from the rank and file. The companies claimed that because their economic position was deteriorating, they had too many employees. After both parties met with Yrigoyen and various cabinet members, on March 20 a solution was announced. Service was to be regularized within forty-eight hours and all contracts without fixed expiration dates were to be revised. Under the director of railroads, a joint commission met, but no agreements could be reached, leaving the workers in the same position as before. No major improvement in conditions occurred until after 1943.[27]

The Rosario trolley strikes in 1929 illustrate the willingness of the government to mediate labor unrest outside recognized channels and the limited possibility of political gains through such activity. The trolley workers' union had been formed in 1928 and had struck twice during that year. A third strike began on the morning of December 31 when at 9:30 the union issued an order to return the trolleys to the station. This unexpected stoppage occurred because the company had hired men to be trained as drivers, without consulting the union, as the contract required. A driver had refused to train one of the new hires and was fired. According to a report in *Crítica*, workers claimed that the company director had pressured them to vote for the Anti-Personalist presidential candidate Leopoldo Melo, and the director was retaliating because they had voted for Yrigoyen. True or not, the company could not immediately restore service because it lacked workers. When it appeared to be successfully moving in that direction, on January 5 switches were destroyed and several trolleys were attacked with pistol shots, rocks, and bricks. Windows were broken and several employees wounded. The company pulled the trolleys off the streets, which placed great pressure on the government, because there were not enough buses to carry commuters and there were threats of a bus strike.

The interim police chief, who had replaced Caballero, spoke to both sides and promised to try to protect the streetcars, but service remained suspended. Negotiations took place, but according to the union, the com-

27. *La Prensa*, November 5–December 8, 1929, February 5–13, March 12–22, 1930; *La Epoca*, December 11, 17, 19, 1929; *Bandera Proletaria*, December 21, 1929, March 8, 1930; *Review of the River Plate*, February 7, 1930, 5–9, March 14, 1930, 11, March 21, 1930, 5–7; *El Obrero Ferroviario*, January 1, June 1/16, November 16, December 1/16, 1929, March 16/April 1, 1930; Comisión especial de representantes de empresas y obreros ferroviarios, *Revisión de escalafones*; Goodwin, *Los ferrocarriles británicos*, 276–83; Rögind, *Historia del Ferrocarril Sud*, 263–65; Partido Socialista, *Anuario socialista 1931* (Buenos Aires: La Vanguardia, 1930), 134–35; Giordano de Rocca, "El conflicto ferroviario," 59–71; Horowitz, *Argentine Unions*.

pany insisted on firing some workers and lowering the salary of others. The national government's position was murky. The commander of the troops sent to Santa Fe waited for orders while sabotage continued. When a worker delegation went to the capital to present its position to the president, they failed to arrange a meeting but did see Minister of Interior González. The stumbling block was the company's insistence that it keep the two hundred workers that it had hired to break the strike. Conflicts existed within the union about whether it should negotiate through the national government. On January 15 Yrigoyen offered to arbitrate and made a finding that favored the union, calling for the rehiring of all strikers and general improvements in conditions. Trolley service was slowly restored.[28]

The problems did not end. Friction developed between former strikebreakers and union men, which turned to violence. Both parties met with Yrigoyen and agreed to accept a government representative to investigate the problem. Yrigoyen's choice of Manuel Claps, the director general of the State Railroads and personal confidant, ignored bureaucratic niceties. In a federal system, the president had no legal right to intervene in a conflict in the city of Rosario nor did Claps's job have anything to do with trolleys. This was not the sort of thing that bothered Yrigoyen, although it certainly did *La Prensa*. Clashes between the two groups of workers continued, despite each group working on a different shift. The president and his representatives continued to mediate, but union members grew increasingly unhappy.

In July, in the midst of another Rosario dock strike, the union adopted a pure Anarcho-Syndicalist position by rejecting further involvement of the national government. It preferred to deal directly with the employer and handed a petition for betterments to the company. The company refused to consider it and the union struck. The company, while claiming to have enough workers to put the cars in service, waited for permission from the government. The impact of having no streetcars was compounded by a general strike intended to back the dockworkers. Almost all transportation, both public and private, ceased, creating food shortages. The national government dispatched the minister of public works to Rosario. He and others helped shape a settlement to the port strike, which included a government promise of freedom of work, which in this case meant that the AT lost its special role in the port.

28. *Crítica*, January 9–19, 1929; *La Prensa*, January 1–19, 1929; *Bandera Proletaria*, January 5, 12, 1929; *La Epoca*, January 10, 15, 1929.

With the end of the general strike, the trolley company and the police promised to restart service and the city began fining the company for every trolley that did not circulate. On August 3 the company put a quarter of its cars on the streets, and the number increased in subsequent days. The trams, however, only circulated with a fireman armed with a rifle on the front platform on urban trips and an additional armed fireman on the rear platform on suburban ones. The cars could only run during the day and violence was constant. Understandably, the public feared riding the trolleys. Little hope of a settlement existed, because the workers refused to accept mediation from either local or national authorities, preferring to deal directly with the company. The latter seemed determined to break the union but was willing to accept arbitration by Yrigoyen.

With no progress being made, the Rosario unions turned to their traditional weapon, a general strike, which they called for August 21. Unions and workers did not respond with their normal vigor. After a year of constant turmoil, workers appeared tired. The authorities acted with more determination than usual, putting all their forces into the streets. By August 23 most workers had returned to their jobs. The trolley strike continued, but trams began to circulate within the city without armed guards and even made runs at night. With the approval of the provincial authorities, the company announced that it would take back strikers who returned to work, but it only took back a portion. By the end of the first week of September, service on the trolley lines had returned to normal, although guards remained necessary at night. The strikers still continued their efforts but to no avail. A combination of the ideological views of the workers, the tiredness of the working class, and the increased determination of the authorities doomed the union, despite obtaining the intervention of Yrigoyen.[29] The violence and turmoil that marked Rosario in 1928 and 1929 fed the fears of key elements in Buenos Aires that the upheavals of 1917–21 were bound to return.

Even unions that had connections to the government could not depend on continuous help. The telephone workers' union of the capital demonstrates this. It had grown in scope since its founding. Affiliated unions

29. *La Prensa*, January 22–February 7, July 5–September 15, 1929; *Crítica*, January 23, February 15, April 4, 1929; *La Epoca*, January 22, 25, April 4–7, May 21, 27, June 26, July 28, August 1, 1929; *Bandera Proletaria*, July 27–October 12, 1929; *La Chispa* (Rosario), September 14–October 1, 1929; U.S. Military Intelligence Report, Buenos Aires, no. 4021, July 31, 1929, no. 4029, August 31, 1929. In August 1930 a series of bombings against streetcars was carried out, in part, by former workers of the company. *La Prensa*, August 8, 14, 1930.

existed in the interior—though some were weak—in Córdoba, Bahía Blanca, La Plata, Rosario, Tucumán, and Santiago del Estero. Problems began when telephone workers formed a union in the city of Santa Fe in May 1930. A strike started in mid-July, but the union refused to accept an offer of mediation from the provincial department of labor. Nor would it meet with the employer without the presence of a delegate from the union in Buenos Aires, which the company would not permit. Later union publications would argue that both tactics were serious mistakes. Sabotage became the weapon of choice. Other telephone strikes had also used sabotage but had combined direct action with access to the government. There seemed no way to end the strike favorably. The telephone union in the capital called a twenty-four-hour strike on August 28 for all its affiliated organizations, with the hope of pressuring the company in Santa Fe and of settling its own complaints about changes in the work rules that it considered dangerous. Despite union representatives having personally assured Minister of Interior González that they had no intention of helping any political movement against the government and were willing to accept any reasonable offer from the company, the government did not respond neutrally. The police came out in force for the strike, and the reporting of it in *La Prensa* appears more favorable than in *La Epoca*. The strike had a limited impact because union activists tended to be men who worked in installation and repair and therefore had little short-term ability to cut communications. Female operators supported the union in much fewer numbers. The September coup ended the effort to save the strike, and many activists in Santa Fe lost their jobs.[30]

The government efforts to stay close to the FOM continued. The port remained plagued, however, by the competition between the FOM and the UOMar. As important, friction over discipline and other issues upset the relationship between officers and the subordinate ranks. The largest waterfront employer, Mihanovich, was determined to have company-dominated unions. Finally, as the Depression progressed, the government could ill afford to have the port of Buenos Aires tied up.

In February 1929 a short strike by stevedores seconded by other port workers produced a promise from the chief of police that the agents of the AT would be excluded from the port. For the first time since 1921, the

---

30. FOET, *Luchas y conquistas*, 49–50, 63–71; *Federación*, August–November/December 1930; Luis Gay, author interview, December 10, 1975; *La Epoca*, August 21–29, 1930; *La Prensa*, July 27, August 28–30, 1930; U.S. Diplomatic Dispatch, Buenos Aires, no. 835.504/67, September 26, 1930.

AT would not control a segment of port hiring. From the government's perspective, those doing the hiring would not be unfavorable to the Radicals. The AT had been accused of supporting Yrigoyen's political opponents.

Almost simultaneously, the FOM reiterated a series of demands to the shippers. The Council of Relations met regularly with Yrigoyen and Elipidio González, as did the shippers. According to *Crítica*, Yrigoyen expressed amazement at the low salaries that some job categories received. Ultimately both parties consented to have Yrigoyen mediate a settlement. In May an agreement considerably raised salaries for almost all subordinate job categories. Two important shipping magnates, including Alberto Dodero, the head of Mihanovich, wrote to Yrigoyen to express their appreciation for "his valuable intervention."

The FOM continued to agitate about a series of different issues, including the eight-hour day, and the waterfront remained plagued by conflicts over the manning of ships. The FOM met with the port authorities, González, and occasionally the president, but nothing of value was achieved. Part of the problem may have been, as claimed by the Communist Party paper, that on one occasion Yrigoyen did not want to meet with the FOM because he was too old. Moreover, Syndicalist and Anarchist stevedores began to openly fight for control of the port, including through the use of violence. Ideological conflict wracked the FOM. The different sections of the union could not agree on whether a new union confederation should be created. Cooperation between officers and the subordinate ranks deteriorated. The FOM still retained ties to the government, as can be seen when Francisco García died in March 1930. González and the police chief of Buenos Aires attended his wake, a surprising gesture in an environment in which open relationships between the government and unions remained unusual. Without the presence of García any hope of keeping the union together proved impossible. Conflicts between officers and subordinates worsened, as did those among the different crafts on the ships. The Council of Relations practically stopped meeting after February 1930.[31]

31. Ministerio del Interior, *Memoria 1928–29*, 142; Confraternidad Ferroviaria, *Memoria y balance, 1 de abril 1927–31 mayo de 1929* (Buenos Aires, 1929), 100; see especially *Bandera Proletaria*, December 22, 1928, February 2, 23, April 20, 27, May 4, July 20, November 23, 30, December 14, 21, 1929, January 1, 11, 18, February 22, March 22, April 12, 1930; *Crítica*, February 19–21, March 1–3, May 4, 1929; *La Internacional*, January 12, March 9, September 21, 1929; Concejo de Relaciones Marítimos, *Actas*, 55, 58, 64, 66–69, 71–79, March 22, 1929–April 9, 1930; *La Vanguardia*, May 2/3, 23, 1930; *La Prensa*, January 6, February 6, 21–22, 1929; *La Nación*, April 16–20, May 1–8, 1929; *La Epoca*, May 4, 15, 1929; *Boletín de*

When the DNT tried to sum up union activity in Buenos Aires at the end of 1929, it saw a movement that was incoherent and unable to make significant gains because of rivalries and its forms of organization. Although far from an unbiased source—the DNT clearly favored the type of organization created by the railroaders—its summary was not far off the mark.[32] The return of Yrigoyen had little positive impact on the labor movement.

The Coup

The overthrow of Yrigoyen presents two distinct challenges for the historian. The first is the most obvious and the one that most historians have dealt with: why the political and military elite resorted to force and ousted Yrigoyen. This will be discussed in a brief manner below. More in line with the thrust of this book and equally important is why the coup was so popular among large sectors of the population. What had so dramatically changed from the Personalists' overwhelming victory in the capital in the congressional elections of 1928, when they captured 46 percent of the vote, to their humiliating second-place finish in March 1930, just nosing out the Socialists with 28 percent of the vote?[33]

Although support for the regime existed until the end, what drove many followers of the Radicals to apathy or outright opposition? Of particular importance to the popular classes was Yrigoyen's unwillingness or inability to fulfill the high expectations that existed upon his return to office. The failure of most unions to make major advances created a sense of frustration. Heightened ideological feelings plus the pressures created by the Depression led to violence, and not always between workers and employers.

The role of violence can be seen during a furniture strike called in June 1930 by a Communist-led organization with the hope of gaining union recognition and a wage increase. The Communists had just separated from a Syndicalist-controlled union, and tremendous bitterness existed. The Communist Party had recently entered a period of extreme aggressiveness with employers, the government, and other ideological tendencies—

Servicios, May 20, 1929, 218–21, July 20, 1929, 315–16; DNT, *Crónica Mensual*, November/December 1929, 2990.

32. DNT, *Crónica Mensual*, November/December 1929, 2989–92.
33. Walter, *The Socialist Party*, 215, 222.

even those on the Left. A strike in the furniture industry was bound to create sectarian struggles, but ethnic tensions worsened the situation. Factories making inexpensive furniture tended to be owned by and employ eastern European Jews. Many of the Jewish-worker activists were Communists, and their ethnicity and positions within the industry were resented by the more skilled workers. The latter built more expensive furniture, tended to be Spaniards or Italians, and favored the Syndicalists. Seven of the ten union members suspended for supporting the Communist position had eastern European names.

A key tactic of the strike, which seemed to lack widespread support, was the use of violence to shut factories down. For example, on June 4 a group of people, including several women, lured police away from a factory. Then a larger group invaded the plant in order to prevent work from continuing and did considerable damage. According to *La Prensa*, this was the dominant tactic. On June 10 the four hundred furniture workers confined in the Villa Devoto prison went on a hunger strike. Not surprisingly, a few days later the Communists allowed work to begin in the few factories where owners had made concessions. The strike ended in failure.[34]

As always in the Radical era, the Buenos Aires waterfront became a crucial arena for confrontation. More threatening than the problems of the onboard personnel, from the government's perspective and from those who wanted order, were the frequent gun battles in 1930 between groups of dockside workers. Bystanders did not always escape. In a shootout in February 1930, three were hit, including a high official of the Sud railroad. Exchanges of gunfire also took place in the streets of La Boca.

Severe friction between Syndicalists and Anarchists in the port area dates to the early 1920s, if not before, but only after the Yrigoyen government had excluded the AT from hiring in the port did a breaking point come. A desire to protect sympathizers from the shrinking quantities of work combined with ideological rivalry to produce violence. In November 1929 with the help of the FOM, the USA, and the Syndicalists in general, the stevedores' union, Diques and Dársenas, was reconstituted with the

---

34. *La Prensa* and *La Vanguardia*, June 5–19, 1930; *Bandera Proletaria*, January 11, 18, 1930; Edgardo Bilsky, "Ethnicité et classe ouvrière: Les travailleurs juifs à Buenos Aires (1900–1930)," *Le mouvement social* 159 (April–June 1992): 51; *El Obrero Ferroviario*, July 1, September 1, 1930; *Acción Obrera*, February–June/July 1930; DNT, *Crónica Mensual*, June 1930, 3174; *La Internacional*, July 7, 1926, January 12, February 2, 1929; *El Trabajador Latino Americano*, August–September 1930, supplement "El movimiento huelguístico latino americano," 10–11; Confederación Sindical Latino-Americana, *Bajo la bandera de la CSLA*, 256; Partido Comunista de la Argentina, *Esbozo*, 70n112.

idea of confronting the Anarchist-controlled Boca y Barracas union, which had its base in the southern port area. Within a month Boca y Barracas demanded that all stevedores carry its card. Both the Syndicalists and the Socialists charged that Boca y Barracas worked with the thugs that had run the port for the AT. The Communists made similar charges but reversed the accusation.

Both unions tried to expand their influence by allying with related occupations—carters and teamsters—and calling boycotts. Violence became frequent. By April the unions had agreed to divide jobs equally, but as this often did not work, gunplay continued. For example, the Italian ship *Attivitá* had for several days been unloaded by men belonging to Boca y Barracas. When men from the other union approached the foreman to demand that the agreement be fulfilled, he claimed to have no knowledge of it. Harsh words were exchanged. A shot rang out and then a generalized shower of bullets. By the time the police arrived, most of the participants had fled, but two men had been killed and five injured. One of the dead men, Wenceslao Balbín, was the pro-secretary of Boca y Barracas. The Syndicalists charged that Balbín had been assassinated by one of his own men. In another incident the pro-secretary of Diques y Dársenas was killed. The quarrel between ideologies spread to the port of Rosario. Violence began to occur onboard ships. Although the government had wanted to rid the port of patronal control for its political benefit, the disturbances threatened trade and also the general peace.[35]

Bread makers also faced a wave of violence. According to the organization of the owners of the bakeries, some four hundred violent incidents had occurred in Greater Buenos Aires in the last years. Seven bosses and eight workers had been killed, and material damage was high. Bakery owners placed some of the blame on provincial caudillos, who supposedly made sure that those arrested were let go.[36] In the usually peaceful city of Córdoba, a trolley strike deteriorated into violence and bombings, and provoked a partially successful forty-eight-hour general strike, despite efforts by the authorities and the provincial senate to mediate. The trolley

---

35. *Bandera Proletaria,* November 23, 30, December 14, 1929–February 8, 22, March 22, 29, April 12, 19, May 17–June 7, July 26, August 2, 9, 30, 1930; *La Prensa,* February 6, August 2, 6, 17, 26, 1930; *La Nación,* March 16, 19, April 6–14, 1930; *Crítica,* April 7, 12, 1930; *Acción Obrera,* April 1930; *Diques y Dársenas,* July 1, 1930; *La Vanguardia,* May 23, 1930; Laureano Riera Díaz, *Memorias de un luchador social* (Buenos Aires: Edición Argentina, 1981), 2:12–13.

36. See, for examples, *La Prensa,* July 17–23, 1930.

workers ultimately lost the strike.[37] The violence made many nervous and reminded them of Yrigoyen's first presidency.

In an attempt to restore his shrinking political base, in April 1930 Yrigoyen freed Simón Radowitzky and sent him into exile. An Anarchist, Radowitzky had been imprisoned since 1909 for assassinating the police chief of Buenos Aires in retaliation for a May Day demonstration massacre. Radowitzky had been the center of a long, if not terribly effective, campaign to free him. Yrigoyen's action parallels the gesture made by Alvear in freeing Mañasco. Yrigoyen hoped to firm up support among the popular classes, but such a gesture would only confirm negative opinions among others. It was unlikely to have a major impact. The mass-circulating newspaper *Crítica* supported the freeing but remained stridently opposed to the president.[38]

High expectations of a major shift in favor of the working class had not been fulfilled and the situation appeared to be deteriorating. The Depression played a large role in shaking confidence in the political system, causing hardship and helping to undermine elements of clientelism. Certainly, the government's inability to help fulfill the expectations of the working class was at least partially due to the Depression. Still, as Peter Smith pointed out over a quarter century ago, the hardest impacts of the Depression were felt only after the planning for the coup had been long underway. Therefore, while a necessary condition, the Depression alone cannot have caused the coup.[39]

Yrigoyen always had ignored the bureaucracy, preferring to hold power close to himself. He had felt the need to become involved in all issues. This became increasingly difficult in his second term as his personal strength lessened. Whether he was ill or senile, as some of the opposition charged, he clearly lacked his previous vigor. This created problems with decision making because there was little government apparatus to fill the gap. The collapse of the legislative bodies in 1930 compounded the situation. The Chamber of Deputies never got beyond discussing credentials, while the Senate met only once. The Buenos Aires city council tied itself in knots over the staffing of committees.[40] The Radical Party began splintering.

---

37. *La Prensa*, June 5–July 4, 1930; *Bandera Proletaria*, June 21–August 16, 1930.
38. See, for examples, *La Internacional*, November 26, 1927, March 24, 1928; *Libertad*, March 20–22, 1928; *Boletín de Servicios*, April 5, 1928, 145, May 20, 1929, 217; *Bandera Proletaria*, December 1, 1928, April 19, 1930; *Crítica*, May 20, 1929, March 29–April 15, 1930; Saítta, *Recuerdos de tinta*, 239–43.
39. Smith, "The Breakdown of Democracy in Argentina," esp. 5–8.
40. *La Acción*, January 23, 24, March 25, 1928; Cámara de Diputados, *Diario de sesiones*,

Traditional elites felt uncomfortable. The government had a middle-class air about it because many of the more elite Radicals were Anti-Personalists. There was fear of labor unrest. The Personalists used the power of the national government to upset local political arrangements. The Radicals claimed that such interventions permitted free and fair elections, while their opposition believed that they represented the raw use of power. Elements of truth existed in both contentions. The fourteen provinces experienced government intervention eighty-two times between 1860 and 1911, thirty-four times during the period of Radical hegemony, twenty times during Yrigoyen's first term, and four more during his abbreviated second presidency.[41] Particularly worrisome was the violence that accompanied politics and interventions in San Juan and Mendoza, especially the assassination of Carlos Lencinas of Mendoza. The populist Radical dissident Lencinas, whose credentials had recently been rejected by the Senate, was supported by the Anti-Personalists and loathed by the Personalists. The intervention in these provinces would inevitably lead to a Personalist majority in the Senate, giving them control of all government branches for the first time.[42]

Creation of the so-called Klan Radical further exacerbated tensions. A group of bullyboys that was used to intimidate the opposition, the Klan had connections to some of the neighborhood Radical bosses in Buenos Aires. The opposition did not shy away from similar tactics.[43] The sense of unease was made worse in the minds of some of the traditional elites by their perception that the Radical government did not comprehend democracy. In 1927 an article in *La Nación* referred to Yrigoyenism as a type of Bolshevism combined with idolatry of its chief. *Crítica* called the government "worse than dictatorships" and a "tyranny without violence," implying that Yrigoyen was able to hold the Argentine population in thrall

---

1 (1930); Concejo de Deliberantes, *Actas*, April 2–19, 1930, 15–141; Cámara de Senadores, *Diario de sesiones*, April 30, 1930, 1–2.

41. Anne L. Potter, "The Failure of Democracy in Argentina 1916–1930: An Institutional Perspective," *Journal of Latin American Studies* 13, no. 1 (1981): 101.

42. See, for example, Rodríguez, *Lencinas y Cantoni*; Lacoste, *La Unión Cívica Radical en Mendoza*, 38–116; *La Prensa*, November 11, 1929, February 14, 1930; *La Epoca*, May 4, 1929; David Rock, "Argentina from the First World War to the Revolution of 1930," in *The Cambridge History of Latin America*, ed. Leslie Bethell, (Cambridge: Cambridge University Press, 1986), 5:449.

43. See, for example, Rock, *Politics in Argentina*, 249–50; Bard, *Estampas de una vida*, 163–64; Luciano de Privitellio, "Sociedad urbana y actores políticos en Buenos Aires: El 'partido' independiente en 1931," *Boletín del Instituto de Historia Argentina y Americana "Dr. E. Ravignani,"* 3rd ser., 9, no. 1 (primer semestre de 1994): 83.

without violence. After the coup, Alvear was quoted as saying, "It had to be thus. Yrigoyen with an absolute ignorance of all methods of democratic government seemed to take pleasure in harming the institutions."[44] The idea of liberal democracy had also come to be questioned by many.[45]

The drop in revenue caused by the Depression helped to loosen the loyalty of government employees by delaying the payment of salaries. This argument needs to be made carefully; frequently, even prior to the Depression, government workers received their wages late, primarily due to inefficiency. In 1930, however, in many cases the lateness had become serious enough to shatter any ties of loyalty. Municipal workers in Santiago del Estero formed a union and struck when owed two months of salary. The municipal authorities claimed that they simply lacked funds. In La Rioja the police struck because they were owed five months or more of their modest salaries of sixty pesos per month. They were jailed. Workers in the municipal slaughterhouse in Córdoba walked out due to delayed payments. Teachers and municipal workers in the city of Buenos Aires received their pay late, as did state workers in general.[46] If loyalty existed because of obtaining a job, this could be broken by not being paid for that job. Breaking that loyalty had a potential cost because a change in government might mean a loss of the job, but anger, fear, and hope of change might have outweighed other factors.

The working of the political system had collapsed in the midst of a burgeoning economic crisis. Political elites looked to the military for a way out and the military, motivated by the same goals and upset by what they saw as favoritism in promotions, joined the plots.[47] Despite an uninspiring term from almost all angles, certain unions openly backed the government until the bitter end. The day before the coup, representatives of La Fraternidad, the UF, and the maritime workers (undoubtedly the FOM, but no union name was mentioned) met with Minister of Interior González and offered their support, surmising correctly that the alternatives were worse. According to the Anarchist intellectual Diego Abad de Santillán, after the coup representatives of different anarchist groupings, the USA, the state

---

44. Sidicaro, *La política mirada desde arriba*, 99; *Crítica*, March 20, 21, 1929; *La Razón*, September 8, 1930, as cited in Cattaruza, *Marcelo T. de Alvear*, 48.

45. Halperín Donghi, *Vida y muerte*.

46. *La Prensa*, February 23, 24, August 25, 1929, February 25, April 19, 21, 29, June 6, 11,12, 21 July 30, September 7, 1930; *Crítica*, February 23, 1929; *La Nación*, April 3, 4, 1930; *La Epoca*, August 28, 29, 1930.

47. See Potash, *The Army and Politics in Argentina*, 29–54.

workers, and the FOM, among others, planned resistance but were foiled by the actions of the police.[48]

The government fell easily on September 6, 1930, to a military force primarily composed of army cadets. There was little violence and the cadets were greeted by enthusiastic crowds. An era had ended.

Conclusion

In the less than two years of his second term, Yrigoyen managed to dissipate much of the enthusiasm that had surrounded his election. He should not bear responsibility for the economic downturn, and the worst was yet to come. Still, like any politician's popularity, Yrigoyen's suffered because of a bad economy. Moreover, he had done little to consolidate his hold over the popular classes. In part the economic conditions hindered him, as did his seeming eagerness to cultivate British interests. His own lack of energy contributed. The state of the union movement made deepening the relationship difficult. Efforts to recreate an alliance with workers on the waterfront foundered in part because of their own divisions. With whom could Yrigoyen make an alliance? Would it even be stable?

The violence was unsettling. In 1919 and 1921 it had created political problems, and the situation was even more unstable in 1929 and 1930. Violence, especially the sectarian violence that at times involved innocent bystanders, could not have been popular with the overwhelming majority of the people. It produced little or nothing for the practitioners. Even the strike wave in Rosario wore out the participants. By the time the economic and political elite decided to encourage a coup, much of the popular support for Yrigoyen had evaporated. Ample proof can be found in the limited negative response to the coup, an uprising that was in fact little more than an armed demonstration. Support had indeed faded fast.

---

48. *La Epoca*, September 5, 1930; Diego Abad de Santillán, "El movimiento obrero argentino ante el golpe de estado del 6 de setiembre de 1930," *Revista de Historia* 3 (primer trimestre de 1958): 129–30.

Conclusion

Argentina's first experience with full democracy opened on a hopeful note. Yrigoyen entered the Casa Rosada as president with tremendous advantages. He had won significant electoral support and the Radicals had an important voice in congress, even if they did not control the legislative body. The country was wealthy and largely literate, and its divisions seemed manageable. A new era of fair elections had begun and voter support had become critical for the first time. New styles of politics and gaining popular support developed, but the Radicals and Yrigoyen adapted older traditions as well. The employment of the police chiefs of Buenos Aires to negotiate with unions is a perfect example.

The way that Yrigoyen and the Radicals sought support profoundly alienated certain sectors of the population. It is important to keep in mind, however, that Yrigoyen won the 1928 presidential elections by a landslide. The malaise that developed in the next two years was partially conjunctural, but the failure of the Radical Party to sustain democracy had long-lasting impacts. Until the 1980s national leaders were rarely chosen by fair and open elections, and military coups became increasingly frequent.

Yet the Radical Party cast a long shadow. The politics of the next era, 1930–43, revolved around the Neoconservatives trying to maintain themselves in power by excluding the Radicals. For most of the period, the government had a facade of democracy, but the Radicals were not permitted to win elections. Juan Perón, the dominant figure from 1945 to 1955, always claimed to be revitalizing Radical traditions. The Radicals clearly stood for something worthwhile politically.

Why did the Radicals have such a large impact? The appeal of the Radicals to the population is not obvious today. They do not seem to offer a sharp break with the past, but the break was far greater than it first appears. The Radicals assumed much of the credit for bringing fair voting to Argentina. They created an image of a party that symbolized moral integrity and portrayed others as corrupt. The Radicals also stood for nationalism. Yrigoyen helped produce an image of himself as a caring and almost saintly figure. He truly cared about the average person. The strategy labeled *obrerismo* did have an impact. It conveyed a message that the party and Yrigoyen cared about the popular classes. Alvear tried to use this strategy but with much less success. Unions, or rather some unions, were used as bridges to the working class. Unions had influence far beyond their small number of members, as their ability to summon larger numbers to join strikes indicates. Unions also provided legitimacy to connections with the government in an ideological world in which this was still viewed with suspicion. This strategy was complicated by the Radicals' reluctance to move beyond personal contacts and embed the relationship in a bureaucracy or laws. The relationship of Alvear and Ortiz with the railroaders stands as a major exception. The nature of the popular classes worked against the creation of formal relationships as well because both Anarchists and Syndicalists rejected them and the large number of noncitizens limited working-class political importance. Still, compared with past attitudes, the Radicals' relationship with labor was a major improvement. It allowed many in the working class to feel that they were part of the larger society. The Radical Party became the party of inclusion.

The use of patronage and clientelism does not and cannot explain Radical popularity. Both wings, Personalist and Anti-Personalist, used it freely, but only the former won significant support. Patronage allowed the Radicals to create elaborate party structures and involve a large part of the population in campaigns.

The Radicals' popularity also had a downside. By 1930 many found the Radicals to be threatening. They had upset the delicate balance of Argentine society. Politics had become less of an elite preserve.[1] The Radicals had made attempts to incorporate the working classes into the larger political and social world. Nonbelievers found the Radicals' style, especially that of the Personalists, off-putting. The Radicals' rhetoric, which defined themselves as patriotic and others as unworthy or worse, contributed to the mood of the country. No such thing as a legitimate opposition existed; there could be no loyal opposition. As the Radical control of congress expanded, along with their dominance of the provinces, non-Radical political elites felt that they had no place within the system.

A characteristic of Argentine politics has been the paramount role of a leader within a party or movement. This did not start with the Radicals and Yrigoyen. At the turn of the twentieth century, men like Julio Roca and Bartlomé Mitre dominated politics as larger-than-life figures. This became

---

[1]. Smith, *Argentina and the Failure of Democracy*, esp. 94–95.

more pronounced, however, under Yrigoyen. He dominated the Radical Party and the political scene almost completely. As we have seen, there grew up what could almost be called a cult of personality. In Buenos Aires, party followers knelt on the Avenida de Mayo before Yrigoyen as he greeted them from a balcony. Portraits of Yrigoyen were placed in post offices, which went very much against Argentine traditions, and were only removed after protests from the press.[2] This kind of adoration of a leader repelled many, even inside the Radical Party.

The major split inside the party in the 1920s cannot be explained by labeling the Anti-Personalists more conservative. Many of them were, but far from all. The Cantoni or Anastasi cannot be labeled conservative. The only uniting factor was resentment of Yrigoyen's dominance of the party. By 1930 a significant segment of the population disliked what they saw as his overwhelming political influence.

Personalism was also a management style. Both Alvear and Yrigoyen depended to a large extent on personal contacts, though the former less than the latter. We have examined this in regard to unions. The position of unions was never defined by law, nor did they ever have formal relationships with the Radical Party. Everything depended on personal connections. This made a union's relationship with the state totally dependent on personal whim. The shifting fortunes of the port unions under Alvear demonstrate labor's vulnerability. The personal approach also meant that no bureaucracy existed to handle the growing number of labor laws and problems. When Yrigoyen became less vigorous, there was no governmental apparatus to replace his personal role. Things just stagnated. The DNT's role expanded, but not its size. The legal system did not change enough to fit the growing needs of a more industrialized and urban society.[3] With the exception of the UF and La Fraternidad, and to a lesser extent the municipal workers' organization, the position of unions was always built on shifting sand.

The Radicals' attitude fit nicely with the ideologies of much of the labor movement, which rejected all involvement with bourgeois politics but frequently was more than happy to use connections with the government to negotiate with employers. This meant that there was little reason to change the nature of the relationship and formalize it. Some commentators have

    2. Padoan, *Jesús, el templo*, 40; Archivo General de la Nación, Fondo Documental, Ministerio del Interior, Serie Comisión investigadora de la presidencia de H. Irigoyen, document 14, 269–76.
    3. See Schjolden, "Suing for Justice."

seen institutional weakness as a key source of Argentina's chronic political turmoil.[4]

The labor movement's skepticism about the role of the state, with the partial exception of the Socialists, meant that it became extremely difficult to enact legislation that would attach the working class more firmly to the sociopolitical structure. Although pension plans continued to be created for key industries, a wider plan, law 11.289, which would have included an extensive number of workers, became a political liability instead of an asset. It united employers and unions in agitation to block its implementation. The success of the opposition prevented any future legislation from having a chance of enactment. Argentina was left without an all-encompassing pension system even under Perón.

The pressure to incorporate the working class was limited by the massive number of foreigners in key urban areas, especially Buenos Aires. If Argentine laws and customs had encouraged the nationalization of immigrants, workers would have been an even more attractive target for the Radicals. Given their political drive, the Radicals would have been more diligent in their attempts to incorporate workers into the larger society.

Contemporary observers found troubling the use of large-scale patronage, and some historians have argued that the Radicals built their popularity on it. Radical popularity, however, did not depend on patronage. The number of government employees did expand greatly during the Radical era, but to a significant degree this reflected both the growing needs of the society and the expanding role of the government. Nevertheless, personal and political connections remained critical for securing jobs. Government employment became more attractive because working conditions and salaries improved dramatically. Large numbers of Radicals filled government offices. Both branches of the party used clientelism and patronage, but the Anti-Personalists never succeeded in creating a truly wide base. Other parties shared in the spoils. People appreciated the jobs, the toys, and the medical care, but it did not seem to translate into fervent support. There were too many alternative sources of help in a complex society like Buenos Aires. The love for Yrigoyen came from other sources.

Nevertheless, patronage helped the Radicals build and operate a series of political machines. Clients provided many of the foot soldiers for the electoral campaigns. The tremendous turnouts for internal party elections

---

4. Steven Levitsky and María Victoria Murillo, eds., *Argentine Democracy: The Politics of Institutional Weakness* (University Park: Pennsylvania State University Press, 2005).

can be partially explained by it as well. Politics remained to a large extent a game of giving out jobs and handouts. Government employees consumed a growing portion of budgets, allowing less of a share for infrastructure and other permanent endowments. The existence of a patronage system is not surprising, nor in itself necessarily very deleterious. It was common enough around the Atlantic world. Neither the Radicals nor their immediate successors, however, made any serious attempts to reform government employment and create a reasonably efficient bureaucracy, making government policies increasingly difficult to fully implement.

During the early years of his first term, Yrigoyen aided unions in an attempt to win support among the working class. The way he did so, through the support of certain strikes, won him both friends and enemies. The tactic might have been more effective at some other period. He tried it as the world witnessed an international strike wave created by the dislocation of war, pent-up demands, inflation, the Russian Revolution, and ensuing upheavals elsewhere. Change seemed to be in the air, which produced both hope and fear. In Argentina, the strike wave and the accompanying violence were intense. Yrigoyen did win fervent support. Not surprisingly, however, there was an intense adverse reaction from other sectors of the society. The Liga Patriótica and the AT were a direct result, and so were the Tragic Week of January 1919 and the slaughters in Patagonia. By mid-1921 Yrigoyen felt compelled to abandon his strategy because the political costs had become too high. Although Yrigoyen remained interested in developing a relationship with labor, with the collapse of union pressure in the second half of 1921 this became less important. He did begin to explore new types of relationships with the railroad unions.

Alvear, or perhaps Ortiz, also developed a strategy for attracting support through the labor movement. This came out of a pragmatic desire for votes, which became increasingly necessary once the split in the Radical Party occurred if the Anti-Personalists were not going to become irrelevant. What the administration wanted can be seen in its dealings with La Confraternidad. It desired unions that were strong enough to keep order and willing to work with the government to improve the conditions of their members. The administration aided the rail unions in achieving this goal, and the UF, in particular, became the model union for the next several decades.[5] The Alvear administration proved unable or unwilling to extend

---

5. Horowitz, *Argentine Unions*.

this tactic very far. It failed in its attempt to help create a similar organization onboard ships. The failure occurred because of its inability to adopt a unified strategy, but also because the workers could not agree on what type of union they desired. The administration's attempts to create unions among government employees had little impact.

Yrigoyen's return to the presidential palace in 1928 produced high expectations for a change in the nature of labor relations. Some welcomed the idea, while others feared it. Little came from the endeavor to recreate Yrigoyen's initial strategy. Government interest had waned, driven by a desire to firm up relations with the British and the restraints brought about by the onset of economic problems. The fractured labor movement, with its inclination for infighting, also contributed. Still, the threat of a return to the "chaos" of the first term hung in the air and fed the fears of Yrigoyen's opponents.

Long-Range Impacts

In many ways the political styles of the succeeding eras can be seen as having been derived from the Radical Party. This is particularly true of the Neoconservative era after the return of elections, 1932–43. The dominant politicians were Radicals, even if they were of the Anti-Personalist variety. They had learned much of their style during the earlier period. It is only enough to name the two elected presidents to give an idea of the impact of the Radical era. Agustín Justo and Roberto M. Ortiz had served in Alvear's cabinet as minister of war and minister of public works, respectively. The key opposition party, the Radicals, was headed by Alvear, who had returned to the original party with the blessing of Yrigoyen.

Other key politicians had also gotten their start with the Radical Party, and the lessons that they had learned were not forgotten. We can see these lessons in the government's approach to labor. Although not particularly interested in labor, the Anti-Personalists of the 1930s had learned that it was frequently more efficacious to make concessions when challenged by nonhostile unions. In 1932 the government forced the telephone company to settle a strike on terms not unfavorable to the workers, despite the strikers consistent use of sabotage, in part because the government wanted to send a message to the unions that it would not always be hostile.[6] Ortiz's

---

6. For the Neoconservative labor strategies, see Horowitz, *Argentine Unions*, esp. 129–33.

attempt to influence the direction of the nation's strongest labor organization, the UF, and, upon failing to do so, to create a parallel organization was made possible by his role under Alvear in helping the UF make major gains. Even the Conservatives had learned that labor support could be important. In the 1931 elections, the Conservatives in the Province of Buenos Aires placed on their list of candidates for the Chamber of Deputies two members of the UF. One of these, Bernardo Becerra, had had a distinguished union career. Both were elected, but Becerra died before taking office.[7] This experiment was never repeated, presumably because the Conservatives felt that they could maintain control of the province through fraud and that popular support was unnecessary.

The political legacy of the Radicals did not cease with the 1943 coup that ended the Neoconservative era. Juan Perón always claimed that he had picked up the fallen banner of Yrigoyen that the Radicals had abandoned. Although this could be considered empty political rhetoric, there is a great deal of truth to the claim. Many of his tactics mirrored those of the Radicals. The Radicals had grasped the importance of the working class and the potential role of unions. The latter could act as a bridge to the workers. Aiding unions could win popular support and ties to unions could legitimize that popularity. The UF continued to be the model union and, at least in the early stages, a key focus of Perón. Perón pushed these tactics much further than had Yrigoyen. The scenario for Perón was very different because he had to win popularity without the aid of an organized political party. In addition, the country had changed. By 1943 the urban working class had potentially become much more important politically. Industrialization was at a more advanced stage than it had been in the 1920s. There had been a large inflow of workers from rural areas to Buenos Aires, and a smaller percentage of workers were foreign-born because immigration essentially had stopped with the onset of the Depression. Perón also believed in something that the Radicals had not—the efficacy of embedding labor in state structures. The bureaucracies that the Radicals failed to expand became larger. Only with Perón was the working class fully incorporated into the society. The nature of that incorporation has shaped the labor movement and much of the political system to the present day.[8]

---

7. Ibid., 139; Alberto Ferrari Etcheberry, "Sindicalistas en la bancada conservadora," *Todo es Historia*, September 1993, 74–83.

8. See, for example, Horowitz, *Argentine Unions;* Juan Carlos Torre, ed., *Los años peronistas (1943–1955)*, vol. 8 of *Nueva Historia Argentina* (Buenos Aires: Editorial Sudamericana, 2002); Collier and Collier, *Shaping the Political Arena*.

The employment by the Perón regime of a combination of personal and state charity to aid the poor bears some resemblance to the tactics of Yrigoyen and the Radicals, though on a much larger scale. Yrigoyen's use of personal charity and his attempt to appear saintly was a clear antecedent of the role that Evita Perón played through her foundation. She personally dispensed aid to the poor, but most of the funding came from government sources. Evita was portrayed as self-sacrificing, kissing lepers and the like, and deeply attached to the poor, but, unlike Yrigoyen, she was never one to be abstemious.[9] The scale was much larger under the Peróns, but there are clear continuities.

The Radical style of rhetoric, which denied that opponents had any legitimacy, continued after the September 1930 coup. This rhetoric very much characterized almost all governments and political movements until the 1980s. Politics in the 1930s revolved around the exclusion of the Radicals. The Peronists in the 1940s and 1950s did not permit the opposition a full voice, although the Peronists had firm control of all government branches. After the overthrow of Perón, the victors refused to allow the Peronists a role in the electoral system. In the 1970s the attitude of nontolerance turned ever more brutal and deadly, and Argentines killed each other in great numbers. The Radicals of the 1916-30 era cannot be blamed for others extending their rhetoric and making it harsher and deadly. There had been plenty of opportunities to shape new forms of rhetoric and allow for a legitimating of the opposition, but it did not happen. What is worse is that rhetoric turned into reality.

A single leader dominating political parties did not end with Yrigoyen. In both Radical and Peronist parties, leaders solidified their power and hung onto it for many years. There were periods of disputed leadership, but someone always consolidated authority. In the Radical Party dominance passed from Yrigoyen to Alvear to Ricardo Balbín to Raúl Alfonsín, and in the Peronist Party power went from Perón to Carlos Menem; as of 2007 Néstor Kirchner is consolidating his control.

The legacy of the first experiment in democracy was very large. It set many of the styles of Argentine politics for several generations. The manner in which the Radicals mobilized political support was to be a model. The coup of September 1930 began a cycle of military takeovers with ever-shorter periods of civilian rule in between. The violence associated with military governments increased over time. The opportunity for democracy

---

9. Navarro, *Evita*, 225-54; Plotkin, *Mañana es San Perón*, 215-55.

to become fully established again came only in the 1980s. Although the Radicals helped establish much of the political style of Argentina, they cannot be held responsible for what was to come. Whatever their errors, Argentina was a functioning democracy between 1916 and 1930 and a society with a great deal of hope and promise. It is this disconnect that helps make Argentina's collapse so tragic and underlines the difficulty in sustaining democracy.

History is not the sweater in the old Italian saying, which if you start buttoning it up wrong will come out wrong on the top. There are always opportunities to change directions. The 1930 coup only became inevitable in the immediately preceding weeks. Still, the political traditions begun under the Radicals cast a long shadow.

Bibliography

Archival Sources

Archivo General de la Nación. Fondo Documental. Ministerio del Interior.
———. Legajo N. 1962. Tambor IIII. "Obra del gobierno Radical" Film.
———. Ministerio del Interior. Serie Comisión Investigadora de la presidencia de H. Irigoyen.
Cámara de Diputados. *Diario de sesiones.*
Cámara de Senadores. *Diario de sesiones.*
Clipping books of Marcelo T. de Alvear.
Concejo Deliberante de la Municipalidad de Buenos Aires. *Actas.*
Consejo de Relaciones Marítimas. *Actas.*
Copiadores de Cartas de USA.
Fundación Simón Rodríguez. Francisco Pérez Leirós collection.
Library of the Instituto Ravignani. Colección Emilio Ravignani.
Policía Federal Argentina. Archivo General.
Unión Ferroviaria. *Libros de actas de la Comisión Directiva.*
U.S. Diplomatic Dispatches. Buenos Aires.
U.S. *Military Intelligence Reports: Argentina, 1918–1941.* Frederick, Md.: University Publications of America, 1984.

Articles, Books, Documents, and Papers

Abad de Santillán, Diego. *Gran enciclopedia argentina.* 8 vols. Buenos Aires: Ediar, 1956.
———. "El movimiento obrero argentino ante el golpe de estado del 6 de setiembre de 1930." *Revista de Historia* 3 (primer trimestre de 1958): 123–32.
Adelman, Jeremy. "El Partido Socialista Argentino." In *El progreso, la modernización y su límites (1880–1916)*, vol. 5 of *Nueva Historia Argentina*, ed. Mirta Zaida Lobato, 261–90. Buenos Aires: Editorial Sudamericana, 2000.
———. "State and Labour in Argentina: The Port Workers of Buenos Aires, 1910–21." *Journal of Latin American Studies* 25, no. 1 (February 1993): 73–102.
Alari, Julio G. de. *Almafuerte: Su vida y su obra.* Buenos Aires: Editorial "Agora," 1965.
Alén Lascano, Luis C. *La Argentina ilusionada, 1922–1930.* Buenos Aires: La Bastilla, 1975.
———. "El principismo argentino ante la primera guerra mundial." *Res Gesta* (Rosario) 37 (1998–99): 5–21.

———. *Yrigoyenismo y antipersonalismo*. Buenos Aires: Centro Editor de América Latina, 1986.
Alexander, Robert J. *Communism in Latin America*. New Brunswick, N.J.: Rutgers University Press, 1960.
Allswang, John M. *Bosses, Machines, and Urban Voters*. Rev. ed. Baltimore: Johns Hopkins University Press, 1986.
Allum, P. A. *Politics and Society in Postwar Naples*. Cambridge: Cambridge University Press, 1973.
Almafuerte. *Obras completas*. Buenos Aires: Ediciones Antonio Zamora, 1954.
Almanaque del Trabajo para el año 1929. Buenos Aires: Partido Socialista Independiente, 1928.
Alonso, Paula. *Between Revolution and the Ballot Box: The Origins of the Argentine Radical Party in the 1890s*. Cambridge: Cambridge University Press, 2000.
———."La Unión Cívica Radical: Fundación, oposición y triunfo (1890–1916)." In *El progreso, la modernización y sus límites (1880–1916)*, vol. 5 of *Nueva Historia Argentina*, ed. Mirta Zaida Lobato, 209–59. Buenos Aires: Editorial Sudamericana, 2000.
American Society of Newspaper Editors. *International Year Book, 1929*. New York: Editor and Publisher, 1929.
Amin, Shahid. "Gandhi as Mahatma: Gorakhpur District, Eastern UP, 1921–2." In *Selected Subaltern Studies*, ed. Ranajit Guha and Gayatri Chakravorty Spivak, 288–342. New York: Oxford University Press, 1988.
Anales de legislación argentina. Vols. 2–5. Buenos Aires: La Ley, 1942–54.
Ansaldi, Waldo, ed. *Conflictos obrero-rurales pampeanos (1900–1937)*. 3 vols. Buenos Aires: Centro Editor de América Latina, 1993.
———. "La trunca transición del régimen oligárquico al régimen democrático." In *Democracia, conflicto social y renovación de ideas (1916–1930)*, vol. 6 of *Nueva Historia Argentina*, ed. Ricardo Falcón, 15–57. Buenos Aires: Editorial Sudamericana, 2000.
Auyero, Javier. *Poor People's Politics: Peronist Survival Networks and the Legacy of Evita*. Durham, N.C.: Duke University Press, 2001.
Auza, Néstor Tomás. "La legislación laboral y la complejidad del mundo del trabajo: El Departamento Nacional del Trabajo, 1912–1925." *Revista de Historia del Derecho* 17 (1989): 59–104.
Baer, James A. "Buenos Aires: Housing Reform and the Decline of the Liberal State in Argentina." In *Cities of Hope: People, Protests, and Progress in Urbanizing Latin America, 1870–1930*, ed. Ronn Pineo and James A. Baer, 129–52. Boulder, Colo.: Westview, 1998.
———. "Urbanization and Mobilization: Housing and Class Identity in Argentina, 1870–1925." Paper delivered at Latin American Studies Association Congress, 1992.
Barbero, María Inés, and Susana Felder. "Los obreros italianos de la Pirelli Argentina (1920–1930)." In *Asociacionismo, trabajo e identidad étnica: Los italianos en América Latina en una perspectiva comparada*, ed. Fernando J. Devoto and Eduardo J. Míguez, 189–203. Buenos Aires: CEMLA-CSER-IEHS, 1992.
Barbero, María Inés, and Fernando Rocchi. "Industry." In *A New Economic History of Argentina*, ed. Gerardo Della Paolera and Alan M. Taylor, 261–94. Cambridge: Cambridge University Press, 2003.
Bard, Leopoldo. *Estampas de una vida: La fe puesto en un ideal "llegar a ser algo."* Buenos Aires: Talleres Gráficos J. Perrotti, 1957.

Barrancos, Dora. *Anarquismo, educación y costumbres en la Argentina de principios de siglo.* Buenos Aires: Editorial Contrapunto, 1990.
———. *La escena iluminada.* Buenos Aires: Editorial Plus Ultra, 1996.
———. "Vita materiale e battaglia ideologica nel quartiere della Boca (1880–1930)." In *Identità degli italiani in Argentina,* ed. Gianfausto Rosoli, 167–204. Rome: Edizioni Studium, 1993.
Bayer, Osvaldo. *Anarchism and Violence: Severino Di Giovanni in Argentina, 1923–1931.* Trans. Paul Sharkey. London: Elephant Editions, 1986.
———. *Los vengadores de la Patagonia trágica.* 4 vols. Vols. 1–3, Buenos Aires: Galerna, 1972–74; vol. 4, Wuppertal: Peter Horner Verlag, 1978.
Bergquist, Charles. *Labor in Latin America.* Stanford, Calif.: Stanford University Press, 1986.
Bermeo, Nancy. *Ordinary People in Extraordinary Times: The Citizenry and the Breakdown of Democracy.* Princeton, N.J.: Princeton University Press, 2003.
Bernal, Eduardo Rubén. "Pedro Bidegain, un hombre de Boedo." *Desmemoria* 13–14 (1997): 82–101.
Bertolo, Maricel. *Una propuesta gremial alternativa: El sindicalismo revolucionario.* Buenos Aires: Centro Editor de América Latina, 1993.
Bertoni, Lilia Ana. *Patriotas, cosmopolitas y nacionalistas: La construcción de la nacionalidad argentina a fines del siglo xix.* Buenos Aires: Fondo de Cultura Económico, 2001.
Biddle, Nicholas. "Oil and Democracy in Argentina, 1916–1930." Ph.D. diss., Duke University, 1991.
Bidegain, Pedro. *Mi radicalismo.* Buenos Aires, 1929.
Bielsa, Rafael. *El cacique en la función pública: Patología política criolla.* Buenos Aires: Imprenta Nacional de Lajouane y Cía, 1928.
Bilsky, Edgardo. "Ethnicité et classe ouvrière: Les travilleurs juifs à Buenos Aires (1900–1930)." *Le mouvement social* 159 (April–June 1992): 319–56.
———. *La semana trágica.* Buenos Aires: Centro Editor de América Latina, 1984.
Bonaudo, Mirta. "Society and Politics: From Social Mobilization to Civic Participation (Santa Fe, 1890–1909)." In *Region and Nation: Politics, Economy, and Society in Twentieth-Century Argentina,* ed. James P. Brennan and Ofelia Pianetto, 1–47. New York: St. Martin's Press, 2000.
Borda, Angel. *Perfil de un libertario.* Buenos Aires: Editorial Reconstruir, 1987.
Botana, Natalio R. *El orden conservador: La política argentina entre 1880 y 1916.* Buenos Aires: Editorial Sudamericana, 1977.
Botana, Natalio R., and Ezequiel Gallo. *De la República posible a la República verdadera (1880–1916).* Buenos Aires: Ariel, 1997.
Bra, Gerardo. *La organización negra: La increíble historia de la Zwi Migdal.* Buenos Aires: Corregidor, 1999.
Bravo, María Celia. "Cuestión regional: Azúcar y crisis canera en Tucumán durante la primera presidencia de Yrigoyen." *Ruralia* 4 (October 1993): 45–60.
Bravo, Mario. *Capítulos de legislación obrera.* Buenos Aires: Imprenta A. García y Cía, 1927.
Bridges, Amy. *A City in the Republic: Antebellum New York and the Origins of Machine Politics.* Cambridge: Cambridge University Press, 1984.
Brown, Jonathan C. *A Brief History of Argentina.* New York: Checkmark, 2004.
Bryce, James. *South America: Observations and Impressions.* New York: Macmillan, 1912.

Bucich Escobar, Ismael. *Buenos Aires ciudad*. Buenos Aires: Editorial Tor, 1936.
Bunge, A. E. "Personal de los servicios públicos desde 1903 hasta 1923." Dirección General de Estadística de la Nación. Informe no. 3, serie A, no. 1, August 10, 1923.
Bunge, Alejandro. *Una nueva Argentina*. Buenos Aires: Editorial Guillermo Kraft, 1940.
Burke, Peter. *The Fabrication of Louis XIV*. New Haven, Conn.: Yale University Press, 1992.
Buyán, Marcelino. *Una avanzada obrera*. Buenos Aires: La Vanguardia, 1933.
Caballero, Ricardo. *Discursos parlamentarios y documentos políticas del doctor Ricardo Caballero*. Comp. Roberto A. Ortelli. Buenos Aires: Sociedad de Publicaciones El Inca, 1929.
Cabona, Andrés. "Un homenaje y una reivindicación." In *Vida, obra y trascendencia de Sebastián Marotta*, 139–62. Buenos Aires: Editorial Palomino, 1971.
Caja Nacional de Jubilaciones y Pensiones Civiles. *Informe y balance técnico-actuarial al 30 de junio de 1935*. Buenos Aires: Guillermo Kraft, 1937.
———. *Memoria correspondiente al año 1927*. Buenos Aires: Talleres Gráficos de L. C. López y Cía, 1928.
Camarero, Hernán. *A la conquista de la clase obrera: Los comunistas y el mundo del trabajo en la Argentina, 1920–1935*. Buenos Aires: Siglo XXI/Editora Iberoamericana, 2007.
———. "Los clubes deportivos comunistas." *Todo es Historia*, November 2004, 16–25.
———. "Socialismo y movimiento sindical: Una articulación débil: La COA y sus relaciones con el PS durante la década de 1920." In *El Partido Socialista en Argentina*, ed. Hernán Camarero and Carlos Miguel Herrera, 185–217. Buenos Aires: Prometeo Libros, 2005.
Campo, Hugo del. *Sindicalismo y peronismo: Los comienzos de un vínculo perdurable*. Buenos Aires: CLASCO, 1983.
Campos, Martín. "El cierre de la Caja de Conversión en 1929: Una decisión de política económica." *Desarrollo Económico* 176 (January–March 2005): 537–66.
Canton, Darío. *Elecciones y partidos políticos en la Argentina*. Buenos Aires: Siglo XXI, 1973.
———. *Materiales para el estudio de la sociología política en la Argentina*. 2 vols. Buenos Aires: Editorial del Instituto, 1968.
Canton, Darío, and Jorge Raúl Jorrat. *Elecciones en la ciudad 1892–2001*. 2 vols. Buenos Aires: Instituto Histórico de la Ciudad de Buenos Aires, 2001, 2005.
Capdevila, Arturo. "Primera presidencia de Yrigoyen." In *Historia argentina contemporánea*, by Academia Nacional de la Historia, 1:sección 2, 247–69. Buenos Aires: El Ateneo, 1965.
Cárdenas, Felipe. "Ese enigmático conductor." In *Los radicales (I)*, ed. Félix Luna, 87–99. Buenos Aires: Todo es Historia, 1976.
Casaretto, Martín S. *Historia del movimiento obrero argentino*. 2 vols. Buenos Aires: José Vescovo, 1946, 1947.
Caterina, Luis María. *La Liga Patriótica Argentina: Un grupo de presión frente a las convulsiones sociales de la década de '20*. Buenos Aires: Corregidor, 1995.
Cattaruza, Alejandro. *Marcelo T. de Alvear: El compromiso y la distancia*. Buenos Aires: Fondo de Cultura Económica, 1997.

Centro de Estudios. Unión para la Nueva Mayoría. "Composición de la Cámara de Diputados, 1916–1930." *Cuaderno* 21 (October 1991).
Chaquesien, Donato. *Los partidos porteños en la vía pública.* Buenos Aires: Talleres Gráficos Araujo, 1919.
Chiroleu, Adriana R. "La Reforma Universitaria." In *Democracia, conflicto social y renovación de ideas (1916–1930)*, vol. 6 of *Nueva Historia Argentina*, ed. Ricardo Falcón, 357–89. Buenos Aires: Editorial Sudamericana, 2000.
Chiti, Juan B., and Francisco Agnelli. *Cincuentenario de "La Fraternidad."* Buenos Aires: Revshino Hnos., 1937.
Cicciari, María Rosa, and Mariano Prado. "Un proceso de cambio institucional: La reforma electoral de 1912." *Cuadernos del CISH* 6 (segundo semestre de 1999): 95–145.
Clark, Colin. *The Conditions of Economic Progress.* London: Macmillan, 1940.
Collier, Ruth Berins, and David Collier. *Shaping the Political Arena: Critical Junctures, the Labor Movement, and Regime Dynamics in Latin America.* Princeton, N.J.: Princeton University Press, 1991.
Collier, Simon, and William F. Sater. *A History of Chile, 1808–1994.* Cambridge: Cambridge University Press, 1996.
Columba, Ramón. *El congreso que yo he visto.* 3 vols. Buenos Aires: Editorial Columba, 1988.
Comisión especial de representantes de empresas y obreros ferroviarios. *Revisión de escalafones, convenios y reglamentos.* Buenos Aires: Guillermo Kraft, 1930.
Comisión Nacional del Censo. *Tercer censo nacional, levantado el 1º de junio de 1914.* 10 vols. Buenos Aires: Talleres Gráfico de L. J. Rosso, 1916–19.
Comité Nacional de Geografía. *Anuario geográfico argentino 1941.* Buenos Aires: Comité Nacional de Geografía, 1941.
Confederación Sindical Latino-Americana. *Bajo la bandera de la CSLA.* Montevideo: Imprenta La Linotipo, 1929.
Confraternidad Ferroviaria. *Memoria y balance, 1 de abril 1927–31 mayo de 1929.* Buenos Aires, 1929.
Conniff, Michael L. *Urban Politics in Brazil: The Rise of Populism, 1925–1945.* Pittsburgh: University of Pittsburgh Press, 1981.
Corbière, Emilio J. *Orígenes del comunismo argentino.* Buenos Aires: Centro Editor de América Latina, 1984.
Cordero, Héctor Adolfo. *El profeta del hombre: Pasión de Almafuerte.* Buenos Aires: Julio E. Rossi e Hijos, 1958.
Cornblit, Oscar. "Inmigrantes y empresarios en la política argentina." In *Los fragmentos del poder*, ed. Torcuato S. Di Tella and Tulio Halperín Donghi, 389–437. Buenos Aires: Editorial Jorge Alvarez, 1969.
Cornelius, Wayne A., Jr. "Contemporary Mexico: A Structural Analysis of Urban Caciquismo." In *The Caciques*, ed. Robert Kerr, 135–50. Albuquerque: University of New Mexico Press, 1973.
Cortés Conde, Roberto, *La economía argentina en el largo plazo.* Buenos Aires: Editorial Sudamericana/Universidad San Andrés, 1997.
———. *El progreso argentino, 1880–1914.* Buenos Aires: Editorial Sudamericana, 1979.
Cuadrado Hernández, G. "La rebelión de los braceros." *Todo es Historia*, October 1982, 78–96.
De la Fuente, Ariel. *Children of Facundo: Caudillo and Gaucho Insurgency During*

the *Argentine State-Formation (La Rioja, 1853–1870)*. Durham, N.C.: Duke University Press, 2000.

Della Paolera, Gerardo, and Alan M. Taylor, eds. *A New Economic History of Argentina*. Cambridge: Cambridge University Press, 2003.

Departamento de Hacienda. *Memoria correspondiente al año 1919*. Buenos Aires: Talleres Gráficos Argentinos, 1920.

———. *Memoria correspondiente al año 1926*. Buenos Aires: Talleres Gráficos de G. Pesce, 1927.

DeShazo, Peter. *Urban Workers and Labor Unions in Chile, 1902–1927*. Madison: University of Wisconsin Press, 1983.

Deutsch, Sandra McGee. *Counterrevolution in Argentina, 1900–1932: The Argentine Patriotic League*. Lincoln: University of Nebraska Press, 1986.

Devoto, Fernando. *Historia de la inmigración en la Argentina*. Buenos Aires: Editorial Sudamericana, 2003.

Díaz Alejandro, Carlos F. *Essays on the Economic History of the Argentine Republic*. New Haven, Conn.: Yale University Press, 1970.

Díaz Araujo, Enrique. *1930 conspiración y revolución*. 3 vols. Mendoza: Universidad Nacional de Cuyo, Facultad de Filosofía y Letras, 1998.

Dickmann, Enrique. *Recuerdos de un militante socialista*. Buenos Aires: La Vanguardia, 1949.

Dirección General de Correos y Telégrafos. *Censo general del personal*. Buenos Aires: Casa OUCINDE, 1930.

———. *Memoria 1934*. Buenos Aires: Talleres Gráficos de Correos y Telégrafos, 1935.

Dirección General de Finanzas. *El ajuste de los resultados financieros de los ejercicios de 1928 a 1936*. Buenos Aires: Gerónimo J. Pesce y Cía, 1938.

Di Stefano, Roberto, and Loris Zanatta. *Historia de la iglesia argentina: Desde la conquista hasta fines del siglo XX*. Buenos Aires: Grijalbo Mondadori, 2000.

Di Tella, Guido, and Manuel Zymelman. *Las etapas del desarrollo económico argentino*. Buenos Aires: EUDEBA, 1967.

Di Tella, Torcuato. "Perón and the Unions: In Search of the Roots." Unpublished paper, 2001.

DNT. División de Estadística. *Estadística de las huelgas*. Buenos Aires, 1940.

Documentos de Hipólito Yrigoyen: Apostolado cívico, obra de gobierno, defensa ante la corte. Buenos Aires: Talleres Gráficos de la Dirección General de Institutos Penales de la Nación, 1949.

Donoso, Ricardo. *Alessandri, agitador y demoledor: Cincuenta años de historia política de Chile*. 2 vols. Mexico: Fondo de Cultura Económica, 1952, 1954.

Dorfman, Adolfo. *Historia de la industria argentina*. Buenos Aires: Solar/Hachette, 1970.

"Dossier: La cirsis de 1890. Políttica, sociedad y literatura." *Entrepasados* 12, no. 24–25 (2003): 19–14.

Drake, Paul W. *Socialism and Populism in Chile, 1932–52*. Urbana: University of Illinois Press, 1978.

Eisenstadt, S. N., and L. Roniger. *Patrons, Clients, and Friends: Interpersonal Structure of Trust in Society*. Cambridge: Cambridge University Press, 1984.

Etchepareborda, Roberto. *Biografía, Yrigoyen*. 2 vols. Buenos Aires: Centro Editor de América Latina, 1983.

———. "La segunda presidencia de Hipólito Yrigoyen y la crisis de 1930." In

Historia argentina contemporánea, by Academia Nacional de la Historia, 1:sección 2, 347–75. Buenos Aires: El Ateneo, 1963.
Falcón, Ricardo. *Los orígenes del movimiento obrero (1857–1899)*. Buenos Aires: Centro Editor de América Latina, 1984.
———. "La relación estado-sindicatos en la política laboral del primer gobierno de Hipólito Yrigoyen." *Estudios Sociales* 4, no. 10 (primer semestre de 1996): 75–85.
Favaro, Orietta. "Estado y empresas públicas, el caso YPF, 1922–1955." *Estudios Sociales* 9, no. 16 (primer semestre de 1999): 57–75.
Federación Obreros y Empleados Telefónicos. *Luchas y conquistas: Las organizaciones telefónicas en el país*. Buenos Aires, 1944.
Fernández, Alfredo. *El movimiento obrero en la Argentina*. 8 vols. Buenos Aires: Plus Ultra, 1935–37.
Fernández, Manuel F. *La Unión Ferroviaria a través del tiempo: Veinticinco años al servicio de un ideal*. Buenos Aires: Unión Ferroviaria, 1948.
Fernández Irusta, Pablo. "El Partido Conservador de la Provincia de Buenos Aires y el proceso de democratización bonaerense, 1908–1918." *Estudios Sociales* 31 (segundo semestre de 2006): 95–136.
Ferns, H. S. *The Argentine Republic, 1516–1971*. New York: Barnes and Noble, 1973.
Ferrari, Marcela P. "Los que eligen: Colegios electorales y electores en tiempos de la 'República Verdadera,' 1916, 1922, 1928." *Estudios Sociales* 24 (primer semestre de 2003): 31–59.
———. "El voto del silencio: Algunas consideraciones sobre el abstencionismo en la provincia de Buenos Aires, 1913–1931." *Cuadernos del CLAEH* (Montevideo) 83–84, no. 1–2 (1999): 175–97.
Ferrari Etcheberry, Alberto. "Sindicalistas en la bancada conservadora." *Todo es Historia*, September 1993, 74–83.
Ferreras, Norberto. "Evolución de los principales consumos obreros en Buenos Aires (1880–1920)." *Ciclos* 11, no. 22 (segundo semestre de 2001): 157–80.
Folino, Norberto. *Barceló, Ruggierito y el populismo oligárquico*. Buenos Aires: Ediciones de la Flor, 1983.
Fraser, Steve. *Labor Will Rule: Sidney Hillman and the Rise of American Labor*. New York: Free Press, 1991.
Frydenberg, Julio, and Miguel Ruffo. *La semana rojo de 1909*. Buenos Aires: Centro Editor de América Latina, 1992.
Gallo, Ezequiel. "Argentina: Society and Politics, 1880–1916." In *The Cambridge History of Latin America*, ed. Leslie Bethell, 5:359–91. Cambridge: Cambridge University Press, 1986.
———. *La pampa gringa: La colonización agrícola en Santa Fe (1870–1895)*. Buenos Aires: Editorial Sudamericana, 1983.
Gálvez, Manuel. *Vida de Hipólito Yrigoyen: El hombre de misterio*. 2nd ed. Buenos Aires: Guillermo Kraft, 1939.
García Costa, Víctor. *Alfredo Palacios: Entre el clavel y la espada*. Buenos Aires: Planeta, 1997.
García Pulido, José. *El gran Chaco y su imperio Las Palmas*. 2nd ed. Resistencia: Casa García, 1977.
Garguin, Ernesto. "Mediaciones corporativas entre estado y sindicatos, Argentina (1916–1930)." Paper delivered at Latin American Studies Association Congress, 1998.

Gellner, Ernest. "Patrons and Clients." In *Patrons and Clients in Mediterranean Societies*, ed. Ernest Gellner and John Waterburg, 1–6. London: Duckworth, 1977.
Gerchunoff, Pablo, and Lucas Llach. *El ciclo de la ilusión y el desencanto*. Buenos Aires: Ariel, 1998.
Germani, Gino. *Estructura social de la Argentina*. Buenos Aires: Editorial Raigal, 1955.
———. *Política y sociedad en una época de transición*. 5th ed. Buenos Aires: Editorial Paidós, 1974.
Giacobone, Carlos, and Edit Rosalía Gallo. *Radicalismo bonaerense, 1891–1931: La ingeniería política de Hipólito Yrigoyen*. Buenos Aires: Corregidor, 1999.
Giordano de Rocca, Graciela I. "El conflicto ferroviario de 1929/1930: Empresas y trabajadores." *Todo es Historia*, May–June 1982, 59–71.
Giusti, Roberto F. *Visto y vivido: Anécdotas, semblanzas, confesiones y batalles*. Buenos Aires: Editorial Losada, 1965.
Godio, Julio. *Historia del movimiento obrero argentino: Inmigrantes asalariados y lucha de clases, 1880–1910*. Buenos Aires: Editorial Contemporánea, 1973.
———. *El movimiento obrero argentino (1910–1930)*. Buenos Aires: Legasa, 1988.
———. *La semana trágica de enero de 1919*. Buenos Aires: Hyspamérica, 1985.
Goldberg, Heidi. "Railroad Unionization in Argentina, 1912–1929: The Limitations of Working Class Alliance." Ph.D. diss., Yale University, 1979.
Goñi Demarchi, Carlos A., José Nicolás Scala, and Germán W. Berraondo. *Yrigoyen y la gran guerra*. Buenos Aires: Ediciones Ciudad Argentina, 1998.
González, Ricardo. "Lo propio y lo ajeno: Actividades culturales y fomentismo en una asociación vecinal, Barrio Nazca (1925–1930)." In *Mundo urbano y cultura popular*, ed. Diego Armus, 93–128. Buenos Aires: Editorial Sudamericana, 1990.
González Bollo, Hernán. "Ciencias sociales y sociografía estatal: Tras el estudio de la familia porteña, 1889–1932." *Estudios Sociales* 9, no. 16 (primer semestre de 1999): 19–39.
Goodwin, Paul B. *Los ferrocarriles británicos y la UCR, 1916–1930*. Trans. Celso Rodríguez. Buenos Aires: Ediciones La Bastilla, 1974.
Gordillo, Mónica. *El movimiento obrero ferroviario desde el interior del país (1916–1922)*. Buenos Aires: Centro Editor de América Latina, 1988.
Gorelik, Adrián. *La grilla y el parque: Espacio público y cultura urbana en Buenos Aires, 1887–1936*. Bernal, Argentina: Universidad Nacional de Quilmes, 1998.
Gori, Gastón. *La Forestal: La tragedia del quebracho colorado*. Buenos Aires: Editoriales Platina/Stilcograf, 1965.
Graham, Richard. *Patronage and Politics in Nineteenth-Century Brazil*. Stanford, Calif.: Stanford University Press, 1990.
Graziano, Luigi. *A Conceptual Framework for the Study of Clientelism*. Western Societies Program. Occasional Paper no. 2. Ithaca, N.Y.: Center for International Studies, Cornell University, 1975.
———. "Patron-Client Relationships in Southern Italy." *European Journal of Political Research* 1, no. 1 (March 1973): 3–34.
Grunfeld, José. *Memorias de un anarquista*. Buenos Aires: Nuevohacer, 2000.
Guido, Horacio J. "Los cismas radicales." *Todo es Historia*, July 1981, 38–54.
Gutiérrez, Leandro. "Condiciones de la vida material de los sectores populares en

Buenos Aires, 1880–1914." *Siglo* XIX (Monterrey, Mexico) 3, no. 6 (July–December 1988): 41–75.
Gutiérrez, Leandro, and Luis Alberto Romero. "Ciudadanía política y ciudadanía social: Los sectores populares en Buenos Aires, 1912–1955." *Indice* 5, no. 2 (April 1992): 75–101.
———. *Sectores populares, cultura política: Buenos Aires en la entreguerra*. Buenos Aires: Editorial Sudamericana, 1995.
Gutiérrez, Leandro, and Juan Suriano. "Workers' Housing and Living Conditions in Buenos Aires, 1880–1930." In *Essays in Argentine Labuor History*, ed. Jeremy Adelman, 35–51. London: Macmillan, 1992.
Guy, Donna. *Sex and Danger in Buenos Aires: Prostitution, Family, and Nation in Argentina*. Lincoln: University of Nebraska Press, 1991.
Halperín Donghi, Tulio. *Historia contemporánea de América Latina*. 13th ed. Madrid: Alianza Editorial, 1990.
———. *Historia de la Universidad de Buenos Aires*. Buenos Aires: EUDEBA, 1962.
———. *Vida y muerte de la República verdadera (1910–1930)*. Buenos Aires: Ariel, 2000.
H. Cámara de Diputados de la Nación. *Nomina de Diputados de la Nación por distrito electora: Periodo 1854–1991*. Buenos Aires: Secretaría Parlamentaria, Dirección de Archivo, Publicaciones y Museo, 1991.
Healey, Mark. *In the Spirit of Batlle: The Shaping of the Political Arena and the Great Uruguayan Exception*. Working Paper 21. Durham, N.C.: Duke–University of North Carolina Program in Latin American Studies, 1996.
Herrero, Antonio. *Hipólito Yrigoyen: Maestro de la democracia*. La Plata: Talleres Gráficos Olivieri y Domínguez, 1927.
"Hipólito Yrigoyen en al intimidad: Entrevistado por Luis Pozzo Ardizzi." *El Hogar*, June 13, 1930, in *Grandes entrevistas de la historia argentina, 1879–1988*, ed. Sylvia Saítta and Luis Alberto Romero, 98–102. Buenos Aires: Aguilar, 1998.
Hora, Roy. *The Landowners of the Argentine Pampas*. Oxford: Oxford University Press, 2001.
Horowitz, Joel. "Argentina's Failed General Strike of 1921: A Critical Moment in the Radicals' Relations with Unions." *Hispanic American Historical Review* 75, no. 1 (1995): 57–79.
———. *Argentine Unions and the Rise of Perón*. Berkeley: Institute of International Studies, University of California, Berkeley, 1990.
———. "Bosses and Clients: Municipal Employment in the Buenos Aires of the Radicals, 1916–1930." *Journal of Latin American Studies* 31 (1999): 617–44.
———. "Occupational Community and the Creation of a Self-Styled Elite: Railroad Workers in Argentina." *The Americas* 42, no. 1 (July 1985): 55–81.
Inda, Enrique S. "La vivienda obrera en la formación del Gran Buenos Aires (1890–1940)." *Todo es Historia*, February 1992, 71–88.
Iñigo Carrera, Héctor. *La experiencia radical, 1916–1922*. 2 vols. Buenos Aires: Ediciones La Bastilla, 1980.
Isuani, Ernesto A. *Los orígenes conflictivos de la seguridad social argentina*. Buenos Aires: Centro Editor de América Latina, 1985.
James, Daniel. *Doña María's Story: Life, History, Memory, and Political Identity*. Durham, N.C.: Duke University Press, 2000.
———. *Resistance and Integration: Peronism and the Argentine Working Class, 1946–1976*. Cambridge: Cambridge University Press, 1988.

Jankowski, Paul. *Communism and Collaboration: Simon Sabiani and Politics in Marseille, 1919–1944*. New Haven, Conn.: Yale University Press, 1989.
Jáuregui, Aníbal. "El despegue de los industriales argentinos." In *Argentina en la paz de dos guerras, 1914–1945*, ed. Waldo Ansaldi et al. Buenos Aires: Editorial Biblos, 1993.
Johns, Michael, and Fernando Rocchi. "The Industrial Capital and Urban Geography of a Primate City: Buenos Aires at the Turn of the Century." Paper delivered at the American Historical Association Convention, 1991.
Jones, Gareth Stedman. "Rethinking Chartism." In *Languages of Class: Studies in English Working-Class History, 1832–1982*, 90–178. Cambridge: Cambridge University Press, 1983.
Karush, Matthew B. *Workers or Citizens: Democracy and Identity in Rosario, Argentina (1912–1930)*. Albuquerque: University of New Mexico Press, 2002.
———. "Workers or Citizens: The Construction of Political Identities in Democratic Argentina, Rosario, 1912–1930." Ph.D. diss., University of Chicago, 1997.
Katz, Ricardo Santiago. *Almafuerte: Un maestro y periodista combativo*. La Plata: El Autor, 2005.
Kindgard, Adriana M. "Procesos sociopolíticos nacionales y conflictividad regional: Una mirada alternativa a las formas de acción colectiva en Jujuy en la transición al peronismo." *Entrepasados* 11, no. 22 (principios de 2002): 67–87.
Klein, Teodoro. *Una historia de luchas: La Asociación Argentina de Actores*. Buenos Aires: Ediciones Asociación Argentina de Actores, 1988.
Knight, Alan. "Is Political Culture Good to Think?" In *Political Cultures in the Andes, 1750–1950*, ed. Nils Jacobsen and Cristóbal Aljovín de Losada, 25–57. Durham, N.C.: Duke University Press, 2005.
Korn, Francis. *Buenos Aires: Los huéspedes del 20*. Buenos Aires: Editorial Sudamericana, 1974.
Korzeniewicz, Roberto P. "The Labor Politics of Radicalism: The Santa Fe Crisis of 1928." *Hispanic America Historical Review* 73, no. 1 (February 1993): 1–32.
Krause, Karl Christian Friedrich. *Ideal de la humanidad para la vida*. Commentaries and introduction by Julián del Río. 2nd ed. Madrid: F. Martínez García, 1871.
Lacoste, Pablo. "Radicalismo, lencinismo y bloquismo en Mendoza y San Juan." In *Populismo en San Juan y Mendoza*, ed. Pablo Lacoste, 9–40. Buenos Aires: Centro Editor de América Latina, 1994.
———. *La Unión Cívica Radical en Mendoza y en la Argentina (1890–1946)*. Mendoza: Ediciones Culturales de Mendoza, 1994.
Laforcade, Geoffroy de. "Ideas, Action, and Experience in the Labor Process: Argentine Seamen and Revolutionary Syndicalism." Paper delivered at the Tenth Annual Latin American Labor History Conference, 1993.
———. "Port Cities, Trade Unions, and the Merchant Marine." Paper delivered at Latin American Studies Association Congress, 1994.
Larroca, Jorge, and Armando Vidal. *Rieles de lucha: Centenario de La Fraternidad*. Buenos Aires: La Fraternidad, 1987.
Lépori Pithod, María Estela de, ed. *Selección de informes franceses sobre Argentina, 1897–1930*. Mendoza: Universidad Nacional de Cuyo, Facultad de Filosofía y Letras, 1998.
Levitsky, Steven. *Transforming Labor-Based Parties in Latin America: Argentine Peronism in Comparative Perspective*. Cambridge: Cambridge University Press, 2003.

Levitsky, Steven, and María Victoria Murillo, eds. *Argentine Democracy: The Politics of Institutional Weakness*. University Park: Pennsylvania State University Press, 2005.

Lewis, Colin. "Economic Restructuring and Labour Scarcity: Labour in the 1920s." In *Essays in Argentine Labour History, 1870–1930*, ed. Jeremy Adelman, 177–98. London: Macmillan, 1992.

———. "Social Insurance: Ideology and Policy in the Argentine, 1920–66." In *Welfare, Poverty, and Development in Latin America*, ed. Christopher Abel and Colin Lewis, 175–200. London: Macmillan, 1993.

Lipset, Seymour Martin. "Some Social Requisites of Democracy: Economic Development and Political Legitimacy." *American Political Science Review* 53, no. 1 (March 1959): 69–105.

Llairó, María Monserrat, and Raimundo Siepe. *Argentina en Europa: Yrigoyen y la Sociedad de las Naciones (1918–1920)*. Buenos Aires: Ediciones Macchi, 1997.

Lobato, Mirta Zaida. "La ingeniería, la industria y la organización en la Argentina de las primeras décadas del siglo xx." Paper delivered at the Latin American Studies Association Congress, 1995.

———. *La vida en las fábricas: Trabajo, protesta, y política en una comunidad obrera, Berisso (1904–1970)*. Buenos Aires: Prometeo Libros/Entrepasados, 2001.

———. "Una visión del mundo del trabajo: Obreros inmigrantes en la industria frigorífica 1900–1930." In *Asociacionismo, trabajo e identidad étnica: Los italianos en América Latina en una perspectiva comparada*, ed. Fernando J. Devoto and Eduardo J. Míguez, 205–29. Buenos Aires: CEMLA-CSER-IEHS, 1992.

Lobato, Mirta Zaida, and Juan Suriano. *Atlas histórico de la Argentina, Nueva Historia Argentina*. Buenos Aires: Editorial Sudamericana, 2000.

López, Alfredo. *¿Qué pasa en la Confederación General del Trabajo?* Buenos Aires, 1943.

López D'Alesandro, Fernando. *Historia de la izquierda uruguaya*. 2 vols. Montevideo: Ediciones del Nuevo Mundo, Vintén Editor, 1988.

López Morillas, Juan. *El krausismo español: Perfil de una aventura intelectual*. Mexico: Fondo de Cultura Económica, 1956.

Lozza, Arturo Marcos. *Tiempo de las huelgas*. Buenos Aires: Editorial Anteo, 1985.

Luna, Félix. *Alvear*. Buenos Aires: Libros Argentinos, 1958.

———. *Historia integral de la Argentina: Los años de prosperidad*. Vol. 8. Buenos Aires: Planeta, 1997.

———. *Ortiz: Reportaje a la Argentina opulenta*. Buenos Aires: Sudamericana, 1978.

———. "Los radicales en el gobierno." In *Nueva historia de la nación argentina*, by Academia Nacional de la Historia, 7:235–64. Buenos Aires: Planeta, 2001.

———. *Yrigoyen*. Buenos Aires: Hyspamérica, 1986.

Maier, Charles S. *Recasting Bourgeois Europe*. Princeton, N.J.: Princeton University Press, 1975.

Marinelli, Fortunato. *Por el derecho obrero: Resumen histórico de la gran huelga marítima (febrero 12 de 1920–marzo 10 de 1921)*. Buenos Aires, 1921.

Marotta, Sebastián. *El movimiento sindical argentino*. 3 vols. Vols. 1–2, Buenos Aires: Ediciones "Lacio," 1960–61; vol. 3, Editorial Palomino, 1970.

Marrone, Roberto. *Apuntes para la historia de un gremio (empleados de comercio de Rosario)*. Rosario: Tipografía Llordén SRL, 1974.

McDonald, Austin F. *Government of the Argentine Republic*. New York: Thomas Y. Crowell, 1942.

Mercado Luna, Ricardo. *Los rostros de la ciudad golpeada*. La Rioja: Editorial Canguro, 1995.
Ministerio del Interior. *Memoria del Ministerio del Interior presentada al Honorable Congreso de la Nación, 1921/22–1928/29*. Buenos Aires, 1922–29.
———. Subsecretaría de Informaciones. *Las fuerzas armadas restituyen el imperio de la soberanía popular*. 2 vols. Buenos Aires: Imprenta de la Cámara de Diputados, 1946.
Ministerio de Obras Públicas. Caja Nacional de Pensiones de Empleados Ferroviarios. *Memoria correspondiente al año 1941*. Buenos Aires, 1942.
———. Dirección General de Ferrocarriles. *Estadística de los ferrocarriles en explotación, 1916–41*. Buenos Aires: Talleres Gráficos del Ministerio de Obras Públicas, 1924–43.
Molina, Raúl A. "Presidencia de Marcelo T. de Alvear." In *Historia argentina contemporánea*, by Academia Nacional de la Historia, 1:sección 2, 271–345. Buenos Aires: El Ateneo, 1965.
Monsalvo, Luis. *Testigo de la primera hora del peronismo*. Buenos Aires: Editorial Pleamar, 1974.
Montequín, Adriana. "Sector público y sistema tributario argentino, 1914–1932." *Ciclos* 5, no. 9 (segundo semestre de 1995): 133–65.
Mouzelis, Nicos. "On the Concept of Populism: Populist and Clientelist Modes of Incorporation in Semi Peripheral Politics." *Politics and Society* 14 (1985): 329–48.
Moya, José C. *Cousins and Strangers: Spanish Immigrants in Buenos Aires, 1850–1930*. Berkeley and Los Angeles: University of California Press, 1998.
Mullaney, Michael F. "The Argentine Socialist Party, 1890–1930: Early Development and Internal Schisms." Ph.D. diss., University of Essex, 1983.
Mulleady, Ricardo T. *Breve historia de la telefonía argentina (1886–1956)*. Buenos Aires: Guillermo Kraft, 1956.
Municipalidad de Buenos Aires. *Presupuesto general de gastos y cálculo de recursos para el ejercio, 1920–1930*. Buenos Aires, 1920–30.
Municipalidad de Buenos Aires. Departamento Ejecutivo. *Memoria del Departamento Ejecutivo de la Municipalidad de la Ciudad de Buenos Aires, Año 1935*. Buenos Aires: Guillermo Kraft, 1936.
Municipalidad de la Capital. *Anuario estadístico de la Ciudad de Buenos Aires 1910 y 1911; 1914; 1915–23*. Buenos Aires: [Publisher varies], 1913–25.
Municipalidad de la Ciudad de Buenos Aires. *Censo de personal administrativo y obreros de la Municipalidad de la Ciudad de Buenos Aires*. Buenos Aires, 1928.
Mustapic, Ana María. "Conflictos institucionales durante el primer gobierno radical: 1916–1922." *Desarrollo Económico* 93 (April–June 1984): 85–108.
———. "El Partido Conservador de la Provincia de Buenos Aires ante la intervención federal y competencia democrática: 1917–1928." Documento de Trabajo 95. Instituto Torcuato Di Tella, Centro de Investigaciones Sociales, 1987.
Nahum, Benjamín. *La época batllista: 1905–1930*. Montevideo: Ediciones de la Banda, 1975.
Nario, Hugo. *Los picapedreros*. Tandil: Ediciones del Manantial, 1997.
Navarro, Marysa. *Evita*. Buenos Aires: Corregidor, 1981.
Oddone, Jacinto. *Gremialismo proletario argentino*. 2nd ed. Buenos Aires: Ediciones Líbera, 1975.
Oddone, Juan A. "The Formation of Modern Uruguay, c. 1870–1930." In *The Cam-*

bridge History of Latin America, ed. Leslie Bethell, 5:453–74. Cambridge: Cambridge University Press, 1986.
Ospital, María Silvia. Estado e inmigración en la década del veinte: La política inmigratoria de los gobiernos radicales. Buenos Aires: Centro Editor de América Latina, 1988.
———. Inmigración y nacionalismo: La Liga Patriótica y la Asociación del Trabajo (1910–1930). Buenos Aires: Centro Editor de América Latina, 1994.
Otero, Héctor Horacio. "La reorganización administrativa durante el segundo gobierno radical (1922–1928): El caso del Ministerio de Agricultura." Tesis de Licenciatura, Universidad de Buenos Aires, 1996.
Oved, Iaacov. El anarquismo y el movimiento obrero en Argentina. Mexico: Siglo XXI, 1978.
———. "El trasfondo histórico de la ley 4.144 de residencia." Desarrollo Económico 61 (April–June 1976): 123–50.
Padoan, Marcelo. Jesús, el templo y los viles mercaderes: Un examen de la discursividad yrigoyenista. Bernal, Argentina: Universidad Nacional de Quilmes, 2002.
Palacio, Juan Manuel. "La antesala de lo peor: La economía argentina entre 1914 y 1930." In Democracia, conflicto social y renovación de ideas (1916–1930), vol. 6 of Nueva Historia Argentina, ed. Ricardo Falcón, 101–50. Buenos Aires: Editorial Sudamericana, 2000.
Palacios, Alfredo L. Almafuerte. La Plata: Universidad Nacional de La Plata, 1944.
———. El nuevo derecho. Buenos Aires: Claridad, 1934.
Palermo, Silvana. "Democracia, progreso y modernidad: El radicalismo y la expansión de los Ferrocarriles del Estado." Paper delivered at the Latin American Studies Association Congress, 2001.
———."Railways and the Making of Modern Argentina." Ph.D. diss., SUNY, Stony Brook, 2001.
Panettieri, José. Las primeras leyes obreras. Buenos Aires: Centro Editor de América Latina, 1984.
Panizza, Francisco. "El clientelismo en la teoría contemporánea." Cuadernos del CLAEH (Montevideo), April 1988, 63–69.
Partido Comunista de la Argentina. Esbozo de historia del Partido Comunista de la Argentina. Buenos Aires: Editorial Anteo, 1947.
Partido Socialista. Anuario socialista 1930. Buenos Aires: La Vanguardia, 1929.
———. Anuario socialista 1931. Buenos Aires: La Vanguardia, 1930.
Pasolini, Ricardo O. "Entre la evasión y el humanismo: Lecturas, lectores y cultura de los sectores populares: La Biblioteca Juan B. Justo de Tandil, 1928–1945." Anuario del IEHS 12 (1997): 373–401.
Pastoriza, Elisa, and Rodolfo Rodríguez. "El radicalismo perdedor: Las bases sociales de la UCR en el municipio de General Pueyrredón en la década de 1920." In La construcción de las democracias rioplatenses, ed. Fernando J. Devoto and Marcela P. Ferrari, 247–68. Buenos Aires: Editorial Biblos, 1994.
Persello, Ana Virginia. "Administración y política en los gobiernos radicales, 1916–1930." Cuadernos del CISH 8 (segundo semestre de 2000): 121–52.
———. El partido radical: Gobierno y oposición, 1916–1943. Buenos Aires: Siglo XXI Editores Argentina, 2004.
Peter, José. Crónicas proletarias. Buenos Aires: Editorial Esfera, 1968.
Pianetto, Ofelia. "The Labour Movement and the Historical Conjuncture: Córdoba, 1917–1921." In Essays in Argentine Labour History, 1870–1930, ed. Jeremy Adelman, 142–59. London: Macmillan, 1992.

Pintos, Francisco R. *Batlle y el proceso histórico del Uruguay*. Montevideo: Claudio García y Cía, n.d.
Plotkin, Mariano Ben. *Mañana es San Perón: Propaganda, rituales políticos y educación en el régimen peronista (1946–1955)*. Buenos Aires: Ariel Historia Argentina, 1993.
Policía de Buenos Aires. *Memoria, antecedentes y datos estadística correspondiente al año 1928*. Buenos Aires: Imprenta y encuadernación de la Policía, 1928.
Policía de la Capital Federal. *Memoria, antecedentes, datos estadísticos y crónica de actos públicos, correspondiente al año 1923*. Buenos Aires, 1924.
Porto, José H. "Caja Nacional de Jubilaciones y Pensiones Civiles: Estudio financiero." In *Investigaciones de seminario de Facultad de Ciencias Económicas de la Universidad de Buenos Aires*, 3:475–88. Buenos Aires: Talleres Gráficos A. Baiocco y Cía, 1923.
Potash, Robert A. *The Army and Politics in Argentina, 1928–1945: Yrigoyen to Perón*. Stanford, Calif.: Stanford University Press, 1969.
Potter, Anne L. "The Failure of Democracy in Argentina, 1916–1930: An Institutional Perspective." *Journal of Latin American Studies* 13, no. 1 (1981): 83–109.
De Privitellio, Luciano. "El Concejo Deliberante y el fomentismo en el municipio porteño." PEHESA, Documento de Trabajo, April 1996.
———. "Inventar el barrio: Boedo 1936–1942." *Cuadernos de Ciesal* (Rosario) 2, no. 2–3 (1994): 113–28.
———. "Sociedad urbana y actores políticos en Buenos Aires: El 'partido' independiente en 1931." *Boletín del Instituto de Historia Argentina y Americana "Dr. E. Ravignani,"* 3rd ser., 9, no. 1 (primer semestre de 1994): 75–96.
———. *Vecinos y ciudadanos: Política y sociedad en la Buenos Aires de entreguerras*. Buenos Aires: Siglo XXI Editores Argentina, 2003.
Rama, Carlos M. "Batlle y el movimiento obrero y social." In *Batlle: Su vida, su obra*, ed. Jorge Batlle, 37–59. Montevideo: Editorial "Acción," 1956.
Ramicone, Luis. *Apuntes para la historia: La organización gremial obrera en la actualidad*. Buenos Aires: Editorial Bases, 1963.
Randall, Laura. *An Economic History of Argentina in the Twentieth Century*. New York: Columbia University Press, 1978.
Rapalo, María Ester, and María Victoria Grillo. "La organización de los obreros molineros y la confrontación con la empresa Molinos Río de la Plata (1917–1918)." *Estudios Sociales* 10, no. 18 (primer semestre de 2000): 137–60.
Riera Díaz, Laureano. *Memorias de un luchador social*. 2 vols. Buenos Aires: Edición Argentina, 1979, 1981.
Rigotti, Ana María. "La ciudad y vivienda como ámbitos de la política y la práctica professional." In *Democracia, conflicto social y renovación de ideas (1916–1930)*, vol. 6 of *Nueva Historia Argentina*, ed. Ricardo Falcón, 283–322. Buenos Aires: Editorial Sudamericana, 2000.
Rivarola, Milda. *Obreros, utopías y revoluciones: Formación de las clases trabajadores en el Paraguay liberal*. Asunción: CDE, 1993.
Rocchi, Fernando. "La armonía de los opuestos: Industria, importaciones y la construcción urbana de Buenos Aires." *Entrepasados* 4, no. 7 (fines de 1994): 43–66.
———. *Chimneys in the Desert: Industrialization in Argentina During the Export Boom Years, 1870–1930*. Stanford, Calif.: Stanford University Press, 2006.
Rock, David. "Argentina from the First World War to the Revolution of 1930." In

The Cambridge History of Latin America, ed. Leslie Bethell, 5:419–52. Cambridge: Cambridge University Press, 1986.
———. "Machine Politics in Buenos Aires and the Argentine Radical Party, 1912–1930." *Journal of Latin American Studies* 4, no. 2 (November 1972): 233–56.
———. *Politics in Argentina, 1890–1930: The Rise and Fall of Radicalism*. London: Cambridge University Press, 1975.
———. *State Building and Political Movements in Argentina, 1860–1916*. Stanford, Calif.: Stanford University Press, 2002.
Rodríguez, Adolfo Enrique. *Historia de la policía federal argentina, 1916–1944*. Vol. 7. Buenos Aires: Editorial Policial, 1978.
Rodríguez, Celso. *Lencinas y Cantoni: El populismo cuyano en tiempos de Yrigoyen*. Buenos Aires: Editorial de Belgrano, 1979.
Rögind, William. *Historia del Ferrocarril Sud*. Buenos Aires: Establecimiento Gráfico Argentino, 1937.
Roig, Arturo Andrés. *Los krausistas argentinos*. Puebla, Mexico: Editorial José M. Cajica Jr., 1969.
Rosanvallon, Pierre. *Le sacre du citoyen: Histoire du suffrage universel en France*. Paris: Editions Gallimard, 1992.
Ross, Arthur M., and Paul Hartman. *Changing Patterns of Industrial Conflict*. New York: Wiley, 1960.
Royko, Mike. *Richard J. Daley of Chicago*. New York: Dutton, 1971.
Ruffini de Grané, Martha. "Un aspecto de la relación Yrigoyen-Crotto: Agro política en la provincia de Buenos Aires." In *Estudios de historia rural*, 3:33–58. Buenos Aires: Facultad de Humanidades y Ciencias de la Educación, 1993.
Sabato, Hilda. *La política en las calles: Entre el voto y la movilización: Buenos Aires, 1862–1880*. Buenos Aires: Editorial Sudamericana, 1998.
Sáenz, Mario. *El presupuesto de 1938*. Buenos Aires, 1938.
Sáenz Peña, Roque. *La reforma electoral y temas de política internacional americana*. Buenos Aires: Editorial Raigal, 1952.
Saítta, Sylvia. *Recuerdos de tinta: El diario Crítica en la década de 1920*. Buenos Aires: Editorial Sudamericana, 1998.
Salaman, Graeme. *Community and Occupation: An Exploration of Work/Leisure Relationships*. London: Cambridge University Press, 1974.
Sánchez Román, José Antonio. "Economic Elites, Regional Cleavages, and the Introduction of the Income Tax in Argentina." Unpublished paper, 2003.
Sanguinetti, Horacio. *Los socialistas independientes*. Buenos Aires: Editorial de Belgrano, 1981.
Sartelli, Eduardo. "Rehacer todo lo destruido: Los conflictos obrero-rurales en la década 1927–1937." In *Conflictos obrero-rurales pampeanos (1900–1937)*, ed. Waldo Ansaldi, 3:241–91. Buenos Aires: Centro Editor de América Latina, 1993.
Scher, Ariel, and Héctor Palomino. *Fútbol: Pasión de multitudes y de elites*. Buenos Aires: Documentos del CISEA, 1988.
Schjolden, Line. "Suing for Justice: Labor and the Courts in Argentina, 1900–1943." Ph.D. diss., University of California, Berkeley, 2002.
Schvarzer, Jorge. *Empresarios del pasado: La Unión Industrial Argentina*. Buenos Aires: CISEA/Imago Mundi, 1991.
Schwartz, Barry. "George Washington and the Whig Concept of Heroic Leadership." *American Sociological Review* 48, no. 1 (February 1983): 18–33.

Scobie, James R. "Buenos Aires as a Commercial-Bureaucratic City, 1880–1910: The Characteristics of a City's Orientation." *The American Historical Review* 77, no. 4 (October 1972): 1035–73.
Seibel, Beatriz. *Crónicas de la semana trágica*. Buenos Aires: Corregidor, 1999.
Shils, Edward. *The Constitution of Society*. Chicago: University of Chicago Press, 1982.
Shipley, Robert E. "On the Outside Looking In: A Social History of the Porteño Worker During the Golden Age of Argentine Development." Ph.D. diss., Rutgers University, 1977.
Sidicaro, Ricardo. *La política mirada desde arriba: Las ideas del diario, La Nación, 1909–1989*. Buenos Aires: Editorial Sudamericana, 1993.
Siegfried, André. *Impressions of South America*. Trans. H. H. Hemming and Doris Hemming. New York: Harcourt, Brace, 1933.
Sinclair, Upton. *The Jungle*. 1906. Reprint, New York: Bantam, 1981.
Smith, Peter H. *Argentina and the Failure of Democracy: Conflict Among Political Elites, 1904–1955*. Madison: University of Wisconsin Press, 1974.
———. "The Breakdown of Democracy in Argentina, 1916–1930." In *The Breakdown of Democratic Regimes: Latin America*, ed. Juan J. Linz and Alfred Stepan, 3–27. Baltimore: Johns Hopkins University Press, 1978.
———. *Democracy in Latin America: Political Change in Comparative Perspective*. New York: Oxford University Press, 2005.
———. *Politics and Beef in Argentina: Patterns of Conflict and Change*. New York: Columbia University Press, 1969.
Sojo, José Tomás, and Manuel V. Ordóñoz. "Historia y organización de la Federación Obrera Marítima." *Revista de la Facultad de Derecho y Ciencias Sociales* (January–March 1924): 166–200.
Solberg, Carl E. *Oil and Nation in Argentina*. Stanford, Calif.: Stanford University Press, 1979.
———. *The Prairies and the Pampas: Agrarian Policy in Canada and Argentina, 1880–1930*. Stanford, Calif.: Stanford University Press, 1987.
Stach, Francisco. "Empleados nacionales civiles en la República Argentina: Su situación social y económica." *Boletín del Museo Social Argentino* 4 (1915): 527–54.
Suriano, Juan. *Anarquistas: Cultura y política libertaria en Buenos Aires, 1890–1910*. Buenos Aires: Manantial, 2001.
———. "Estado y conflicto social: El caso de la huelga de maquinistas ferroviarios de 1912." *Boletín del Instituto de Historia Argentina y Americana "Dr. E. Ravignani,"* 3rd ser., no. 4 (segundo semestre de 1991): 91–115.
———. "Vivir y sobrevivir en la gran ciudad: Habitat popular en la Ciudad de Buenos Aires a comienzos del siglo." *Estudios Sociales* 4, no. 7 (segundo semestre de 1994): 49–68.
Tato, María Inés. *Viento de Fronda: Liberalismo, conservadurismo y democracia en la Argentina, 1911–1932*. Buenos Aires: Siglo XXI Editores Argentina, 2004.
Thompson, Ruth. "The Engineer Drivers' and Firemen's Strike of 1912." Unpublished paper.
———."The Making of the Confraternidad Ferroviaria." Unpublished paper.
———. "Trade Union Organisations: Some Forgotten Aspects." In *Essays in Argentine Labour History, 1870–1930*, ed. Jeremy Adelman, 160–76. London: Macmillan, 1992.

Torre, Juan Carlos, ed. *Los años peronistas (1943–1955)*. Vol. 8 of *Nueva Historia Argentina*. Buenos Aires: Editorial Sudamericana, 2002.
Torres, Juan Guillermo. "Labor Politics of the Radicalism in Argentina (1916–1930)." Ph.D. diss., University of California, San Diego, 1982.
Troncoso, Oscar. *Fundadores del gremialismo obrero*. 2 vols. Buenos Aires: Centro Editor de América Latina, 1983.
Tulchin, Joseph S. *Argentina and the United States: A Conflicted Relationship*. Boston: Twayne, 1990.
Unión Ferroviaria. *Memoria y balance de la Comisión Directiva, 1922/1923–1930*. Buenos Aires: [Publisher varies], 1924–31.
Vanger, Milton I. *José Batlle Ordóñez of Uruguay: The Creator of His Times, 1902–1907*. Cambridge, Mass.: Harvard University Press, 1963.
———. *The Model Country: José Batlle Ordóñez of Uruguay, 1907–1915*. Hanover, N.H.: University Press of New England, 1980.
Varone, Domingo. *La memoria obrera*. Buenos Aires: Editorial Cartago, 1989.
Vidal, Gardenia. "La modernidad y el espacio público en Argentina: Repensando la Reforma Universitaria de 1918." *Avances del CESOR* (Rosario) 5, no. 5 (2005): 109–31.
———. "Los partidos políticos y el fenómeno clientelístico luego de la Ley Sáenz Peña: La Unión Cívica Radical de la Provincia de Córdoba, 1912–1930." In *La construcción de las democracias rioplatenses: Proyectos institucionales y prácticas políticas, 1900–1930*, ed. Fernando J. Devoto and Marcela P. Ferrari, 189–217. Buenos Aires: Editorial Biblos, 1994.
———. *Radicalismo de Córdoba, 1912–1930*. Córdoba: Universidad Nacional de Córdoba, Dirección General de Publicaciones, 1995.
———. "La reforma universitaria de 1918 y su repercusión en los resultados electorales." In *La política y la gente: Estudios sobre modernidad y espacio público en Córdoba, 1880–1960*, ed. Gardenia Vidal, 115–41. Córdoba: Ferreyra Editor, 2007.
Viguera, Aníbal. "Participación electoral y practicas políticas de los sectores populares en Buenos Aires, 1912–1922." *Entrepasados* 1, no. 1 (comienzos de 1991): 5–33.
Walter, Richard J. "Elections in the City of Buenos Aires During the First Yrigoyen Administration: Social Class and Political Preferences." *Hispanic American Historical Review* 58, no. 4 (November 1978): 595–624.
———. "Municipal Politics and Government in Buenos Aires, 1918–1930." *Journal of Interamerican Studies and World Affairs* 16, no. 2 (May 1974): 173–97.
———. *Politics and Urban Growth in Buenos Aires: 1910–1942*. Cambridge: Cambridge University Press, 1993.
———. *The Province of Buenos Aires and Argentine Politics, 1912–1943*. Cambridge: Cambridge University Press, 1985.
———. *The Socialist Party of Argentina, 1890–1930*. Austin: University of Texas Press, 1977.
Weingrod, Alex. "Patrons, Patronage, and Political Parties." *Comparative Studies in Society and History* 4 (July 1968): 377–400.
White, Leonard. *Trends in Public Administration*. New York: McGraw-Hill, 1933.
Whyte, William F. *Street Corner Society: The Social Structure of an Italian Slum*. 4th ed. Chicago: University of Chicago Press, 1993.
Winkler, Max. *Investments of United States Capital in Latin America*. 2nd ed. Port Washington, N.Y.: Kennikat, 1971.

Wright, Winthrop R. *British-Owned Railways in Argentina: Their Effect on the Growth of Economic Nationalism, 1854–1948*. Austin: University of Texas Press, 1974.

Yablon, Ariel. "'Empleomanía': Prácticas políticas y denuncias en corrupción de Buenos Aires, Argentina, 1880–1910." Paper delivered at the Latin American Studies Association Congress, 2006.

———. "Patronage and Party System in Buenos Aires, 1880–1886." Paper delivered at the Conference on Latin American History, 2005.

———. "Patronazgo en la ciudad de Buenos Aires, 1880–1916." Paper delivered at the Latin American Studies Association Congress, 2003.

Yacimientos Petrolíferos Fiscales. *Desarrollo de la industria petrolífera fiscal, 1907–1932*. Buenos Aires: Jacobo Peuser, 1932.

Yankelevich, Pablo. *Miradas australes: Propaganda, cabildeo y proyección de la Revolución Mexicana en el Río de la Plata, 1910–1930*. Mexico City: Instituto Nacional de Estudios Históricos de la Revolución Mexicana, 1997.

Zanatta, Loris. *Del estado liberal, a la nación católica: Iglesia y ejército en los orígenes del peronismo, 1930–1946*. Bernal, Argentina: Universidad Nacional de Quilmes, 1996.

Zaragoza, Gonzalo. *Anarquismo argentino (1876–1902)*. Madrid: Ediciones de la Torre, 1996.

Zimmermann, Eduardo A. *Los liberales reformistas: La cuestión social en la Argentina, 1890–1916*. Buenos Aires: Sudamericana/San Andrés, 1995.

Periodicals

La Acción
Acción Obrera
Anglo-South American Bank Ltd., *Cabled Reports from Branches*
La Antorcha
La Argentina
Bandera Proletaria
Boletín de la Unión Industrial Argentina
Boletín de Servicios
Boletín de Unión del Marino
Boletín La Antorcha
Boletín Oficial del Sindicato Unión de Cocineros, Mozos y anexos de a Bordo
La Chispa (Rosario)
La Confederación
Confederación Argentina del Comercio, de la Industria y de la Producción, *Estudios de problemas nacionales*
La Confraternidad
El Constructor Naval
Crítica
DNT, *Boletín*
DNT, *Crónica Mensual*
Diques y Dársenas
La Epoca
La Internacional
Libertad

London Times
Ministerio del Interior, *Crónica Informativa*
La Nación
New York Times
Nuestra Palabra
Nueva Era (Avellaneda)
El Obrero Ferroviario
El Obrero Gráfico
El Obrero Municipal
La Organización Obrera
La Prensa
La República
Review of the River Plate
Revista Argentina de Ciencias Políticas
Revista de Ciencia Económica
Revista de Economía Argentina
Revista de Estadística Municipal
El Telégrafo
El Trabajador Latino Americano (Montevideo)
La Unión del Marino
Unión Sindical
La Vanguardia

Oral Histories

Domenech, José. Instituto Di Tella Oral History Program.
Gay, Luis. Instituto Di Tella Oral History Program.
———. Author interview. October 17, December 10, 1975.
Marotta, Sebastián. Interview by Robert J. Alexander. November 27, 1946.
Pérez Leirós, Francisco. Instituto Di Tella Oral History Program.
Rodríguez, Juan. Instituto Di Tella Oral History Program.
Rodríguez, Luis M. Instituto Di Tella Oral History Program.

Web Sites

Almagro-Historia-Apéndice: Presidentes del Club. http://cablemodem.fibertel.com.ar/almagro/historia/apenpres.html, 1/26/07.
Bush, George W. "President Bush Discusses Freedom in Iraq and Middle East: Remarks by the President at the 20th Anniversary of the National Endowment of Democracy." November 6, 2003. http://www.whitehouse.gov/news/releases/2003/11/20031106-2.html, 12/29/2005.
Mundo Azulgrana. Estadio Pedro Bidegain. http://www.gasometro.com.ar/casla/estadio.php, 21/3/2008.
LANACION.com, August 18, 2002, http://www.lanacion.com.ar/archivo/note.id = 4234908origen = acumulado&acumulaodid = , 4/4/08.

Oxford Latin America Economic History Database. http://oxlad.qeh.ox.ac.uk/results.php, 9/2/2005.
Sitio Oficial Club Almagro. Historia en tres colores. http://www.calmagro.com.ar/historia.htm, 2/2/2007.
http://www.torcuatoditella.com, 7/10/2004 [no longer available].

Index

All cities, provinces, and regions are located in Argentina unless otherwise specified.

Abad de Santillán, Diego, 42, 198
Acción, La (newspaper), 36, 60, 61, 63, 78, 107, 156, 168
Adelman, Jeremy, 117, 118
Admiral Brown Library, 168, 169
Alem, Leandro, 16
Alessandri, Arturo, 49
Alfaro, Manuel, 52
Alfonsín, Raúl, 208
Almagro (soccer club), 72
Almafuerte, 47–48
Alonso, Paula, 16, 35
Altrudi, Miguel, 171
Alvear, Marcelo T. de, 3–4, 52, 58–62, 208
  appeals to voters, 171–72, 203
  budgets of, 86, 87, 88
  image of, 8, 9, 62
  labor policies, 10, 56, 149–50, 175, 206–7
  obrerismo practices, 9, 52, 59–61, 174, 175
  patronage practices, 9, 82
  pension plan legislation support, 95–96, 100–101, 105–6, 108, 110, 113
  railroad unions' relationships with, 10, 59, 134, 150–60, 186, 202, 205–6
  shipboard unions' relationship with, 160–70, 175
  strike responses by, 184–85
  unions' relationships with, 61, 149–75
  Yrigoyen's relationship with, 29–30, 198, 206
Alvear, Regina P. de, 76, 160
Amin, Shahid, 37
Anarchists, 18, 202
  culture of, 47, 58, 70
  pension plan legislation opposition, 104, 107
  Socialists' rivalry with, 17
  strike activities, 124, 127, 128, 138, 144–45, 184, 189, 194–95
  Syndicalists' rivalry with, 109–11, 145, 194–95

  union ties, 28, 96, 192, 198
Anastasi, Leónidas, 31, 76, 203
  union ties, 60, 160, 161, 165, 167–68, 175
Anchorena, Joaquín, 59, 108
Antille, Armando, 62–63
Anti-Personalist faction of Radical Party, 30–33, 39, 197, 203, 206. *See also* Radical Party
  appeals to voters, 164, 169–70, 188
  defeats of, 44, 62–63
  image of, 58–62
  labor policies, 149, 150, 170
  lack of popularity, 65, 154, 175, 204, 205
  Mañasco pardon and, 60, 61
  patronage practices, 65, 77, 94, 172, 174, 184, 202
  pension plan legislation responses, 112, 113
  Personalist rivalry with, 38, 73, 94
  railroad unions' relationships with, 150–60
  shipboard unions' relationships with, 160–70, 180
  Socialists' rivalry with, 174
  unions' relationships with, 52, 54, 61, 100, 174–75
  Yrigoyen's relationship with, 30, 36, 45, 149
Argentina, La (newspaper), 167, 171
Armour (meatpacking company), 108–9
army. *See* military, the
Asociación del Trabajadores del Estado, 171
Asociación del Trabajo (AT), 61, 129, 205
  pension plan legislation opposition, 104–5, 107, 112
  shipboard unions and, 163, 164, 165, 184, 192
  strike responses, 129, 138, 142, 143, 183, 189, 194–95
Asociación Ferroviaria Nacional, 134, 153, 154
Asociación Trabajadores de la Comuna (ATC), 172–74

INDEX

Bahía Blanca, 121, 184, 191
bakers, strikes by, 195
Balbín, Ricardo, 208
Balbín, Wenceslao, 195
Barceló, Alberto, 173
Bard, Leopoldo, 27, 41, 163
Batlle y Ordóñez, José, 48–49
Bayer, Osvaldo, 181
Becerra, Bernardo, 151 n. 6, 207
Bergquist, Charles, 117, 118
Beschinsky, Gregorio, 92
Bidegain, Pedro, 27, 57, 73, 76
Bielsa, Rafael, 51
Biondi, Américo, 173
Biondi, Atilio, 173
Blanco Party (Uruguay), 48
Boca y Barracas (union), 195
Bolsa de Comercio, 104
Bolshevik Revolution, 28, 116, 197
bosses, political, 7, 9, 66–78, 83, 93, 173. *See also* caudillos; machines, political; patronage
Boston (Mass.), patronage in, 67
boycotts, 130, 132, 141–44, 162, 195. *See also* lockouts; strikes
Britain, 11, 122
  strike responses, 130, 131, 140–41, 143
  trade with, 21
  Yrigoyen's relationship with, 150, 178, 186, 199, 206
Briulo, Miguel, 77
budgets, government, 86, 87–93, 205
Buenos Aires (city), 3, 5, 11, 12–13, 22–23. *See also* La Boca
  budgets for, 85–86
  city council, 79–80, 196
  elections in, 32, 131, 167, 175, 177
  employment in, 21, 22, 74, 185
  immigrants in, 204
  municipal workers in, 78–86, 135, 172, 198
  nationalization of, 14–15
  patronage practices in, 65, 67–86, 90, 93, 94
  police chiefs in, 51–52, 116
  politics in, 27, 35, 37
  port of, 117–21, 170, 180–85
  Radical Party's activities in, 3, 51, 83, 85–86
  Socialists' activities in, 19, 115, 117, 167
  strikes in, 106–12, 117–21, 126–27, 137, 139–40, 142–46, 179, 190, 193–95
Buenos Aires province, 57, 83, 109, 121, 137, 153, 184

Bunge, Augusto, 98
Bunge and Born exporting company, 127
bureaucracies
  Alvear's, 59
  disunity among, 92, 118–19
  expansion of, 87, 88–92, 207
  patron's intervention with, 66, 67, 74–75, 83, 94
  Yrigoyen's rejection of, 5–6, 51, 196, 203, 205
business owners
  pension plan legislation opposition, 96, 101, 104–9, 114
  strike responses, 118, 142
Buyán, Marcelino, 153–54

Caballero, Ricardo, 183–84, 185
Campana, strikes in, 51, 108, 132, 137–38
Cantilo, José Luis, 80, 132
Cantoni family, 31, 203
Cárcano, Ramón J., 4
Carlés, Manuel, 61, 129, 179
carters' union, boycotts by, 142–43, 195
Catholic Church, 43, 46, 57–58
caudillos, 50, 68, 72–74, 172, 195
Central Argentino railroad company, 124, 177, 186–87
Central Córdoba railroad company, strikes against, 139
centralization, union, 152–53, 159, 164–65, 178
Chamber of Deputies
  Radical Party majority in, 25, 55–56, 131, 196
  weakening of, 113, 196
chauffers' union, strikes by, 132, 143–44
Chicago (Ill.), patronage in, 66, 82, 83
Chile, 48, 49
Christophersen, Pedro, 131
chusma (rabble), 27, 47
citizenship, 13–14, 46, 115–17, 204
Claps, Manuel, 189
Clark, Colin, 11
clientelism, 3, 7, 9, 27, 65–94, 196, 202, 204–5
  Radical Party practices, 126–27, 135
clubs, Radical, 76 n. 31, 161
Colmeiro, Juan, 119–20
Colorado Party (Uruguay), 48
Columba, Ramón, 39
Communists, 18–19, 60, 174. *See also* Socialists
  patronage practices, 78, 80
  pension plan legislation opposition, 103–4

in railroad unions, 152, 154, 186, 187
in shipboard unions, 161, 162, 165, 167, 175
strike activities, 144, 193–95
Syndicalists' rivalry with, 111, 193
union ties, 28–29, 84, 97
Confederación del Comercio,de la Industria y de la Producción, 104
Confederación Obrera Argentina (COA), 29
Conservatives, 25, 31, 72, 126,139,151 207
electoral reform and, 4, 27
patronage practices, 65, 67, 74, 83
constitution, 15, 29
conventillas (housing), 23
Córdoba province, 26–27,38,52,75,93,182,191,195–96, 198
Cortés Conde, Roberto, 11–12
Costa, Julio, 142
coups. *See* September 1930 coup
Crítica (newspaper), 36, 91, 185, 188, 192, 196
Crotto, José Camilo, 136

Defensa Agrícola, 91
Dellepiane, Luis F., 128
democracy
discourse of, 37, 58
establishment of, 15, 17
failure of, 1–2, 5–6, 8–9, 33, 197–98, 201
legacy of, 208–9
Departamento Nacional del Trabajo (DNT), 56–57, 203
statistics compiled by, 106, 107, 111
strike responses by, 118–21, 127, 130, 168
studies by, 23, 85, 193
Depression. *See* Great Depression
Dickmann, Adolfo, 75
Di Giovanni, Severino, 181
Diques and Dársenas (union), 194–95
dockworkers, strikes by, 118, 142–46, 183, 189, 191–92, 194–95
Dodero, Alberto, 192
Domecq García, Manuel, 61, 76, 150, 160, 163, 175
Domenech, José, 42, 76, 157
Dorfman, Adolfo, 85
Durkheim, Emile, 57

economy, 11–15, 17. *See also* Great Depression
crises in, 20–22, 145–46, 198–99
elections. *See also* Buenos Aires (city), elections in; fair voting; voters
congressional, 47, 71, 79
municipal, 79, 81, 86

INDEX   233

1916 presidential, 25, 115
1922 presidential, 30, 146
1928 congressional, 170, 174, 175, 193
1928 presidential, 33, 38, 44, 62–63, 113, 159, 168, 177, 201
return of, 206
electoral reform, 6, 16–17, 19–20, 24–25. *See also* fair voting; secret ballots
Elena, Reinaldo, 76, 168
elites, 5, 10, 116, 151
pension plan legislation opposition, 95, 112–13
political, 15, 19, 25, 32–33, 198, 199, 202
strike responses by, 124, 129, 141
traditional, 27, 31, 197
voter mobilization by, 66, 164
empleomanía, 65. *See also* patronage
employers. *See* business owners; government, national, employment in
employment. *See also* jobs; spoils system; *and specific occupational groups*
in Buenos Aires, 21, 22, 74, 78–86, 185
government, 67, 75, 78, 80–81, 87–93, 171, 174, 198, 204–5
statistics regarding, 21–22
Entre Ríos (province),118,137, 174
Epoca, La (newspaper), 36
election campaign coverage, 62, 71
on pension plan legislation, 101
on Radical Party, 45
strike coverage, 123, 124, 127, 130, 131, 132, 137, 139, 146–47
on unions, 43, 156, 170, 177, 178
on Yrigoyen, 39, 40, 42, 44, 51, 54
ethnic organizations, 70
exports, 12, 22, 118, 141, 185

fair voting, 6–7, 8, 16–17, 19–20, 68, 197, 201. *See also*
Federacíon Argentina de Telefonistas, 131–32
Federacíon de Gentes de Teatro, strike by, 139–40
Federación de Obreros Ferroviarios (FOF), 123, 125, 133
Federacíon de Sindicatos Ferroviarios, 187
Federación Gráfica Bonaerense, 110–11
Federacíon Obrera de la Industria Textil, 106
Federacíon Obrera Irigoyenista, 72
Federación Obrera Marítima (FOM), 142, 160–70, 175
Council of Relations, 180, 192
pension plan legislation responses, 103, 113, 160–65

Federación Obrera Marítima (FOM) (*continued*)
  strikes by, 118–21, 127, 132–33, 144, 145, 180–82, 191–92, 194
  Syndicalists in, 173
  Yrigoyen's relationship with, 130–31, 198, 199
Federación Obrera Regional Argentina V (FORA V), 28, 104, 173
Federación Obrera Regional Argentina IX (FORA IX), 29, 31, 78 174
  membership in, 28, 120, 129
  pension plan legislation opposition, 97,
  strikes by, 55, 120, 126–27, 129, 144–45
Federacíon Obreros y Empleados Telefónicos (FOET), 178–79
Ferrari, Marcela P., 67
Ferrer, Sebastián, 173–74
Figueroa Alcorta, José, 20
food, 7, 24, 54, 72
foreign-born population. *See* immigrants
France, 6, 29, 37, 53
Fronda, La (newspaper), 36
Frondizi, Arturo, 72
Fuente, Ariel de la, 50
furniture workers, strike by, 193–94

Gallardo, Angel, 61
Gallo, Vicente, 30, 31, 71, 76, 169
Gálvez, Manuel, 36, 39, 43
García, Francisco J., 53, 118, 120, 142, 161, 162, 165, 169, 180, 192
Garguin, Ernesto, 116
garment industry, 159 n. 38
gauchos. *See* caudillos
Gay, Luis, 178
Germani, Gino, 22
Ghandi, Mahatma, 37
Ghioldi, Orestes, 104
Giménez, Angel M., 117
Giusti, Roberto, 47
Gómez Cello, Miguel, 183
González, Elipidio
  pension legislation vote, 101
  strike responses by, 132, 144–45, 181–82, 187, 189
  unions' relationship with, 53, 54, 178, 179, 192, 198
  Yrigoyen's relationship with, 29, 39, 52
González, Joaquín V., 96
Goodwin, Paul B., 150, 186
government, municipal, 70, 86, 92, 93, 135, 136–46
government, national

budgets, 86, 87–93, 205
employment in, 67, 75, 78, 80–81, 87–93, 171, 174, 198, 204–5
expansion of, 9, 48
interventions by, 15, 197
railroad unions' relationships with, 121–25, 133–35, 150–60, 186–87
shipboard unions' relationship with, 160–70, 181–82
strike responses by, 127, 128–33, 136–46, 180–85, 187–91, 206
unions' relationship with, 7, 53, 146, 178–79, 185–93, 198–99, 207
working classes' relationship with, 113
Great Britain. *See* Britain
Great Depression, 92, 191, 193
  consequences of, 6, 10, 196, 198, 207
  onset of, 21–22, 178, 207
Grüner, Luis N., 158, 166
Grunfeld, José, 61
Gualeguaychú, 137
Gutiérrez, Leandro, 23, 70

Halperín Donghi, Tulio, 30
Heller, Abraham, 40
Hermelo, Ricardo, 160, 163, 167, 168–70, 175
Herrero, Antonio, 40, 41, 54
Hillman, Sidney, 159 n. 38
Hora, Roy, 15
housing, 23

illiteracy rates, 24
immigrants, 18–19, 194, 207
  employment of, 11–12, 81, 90, 91–92
  living conditions for, 5, 22–23, 24
  Radical Party's appeals to, 7, 50–51, 204
  sons of, 13, 14, 115
  statistics regarding, 20, 21
  World War I's effects on, 20, 26
  Yrigoyen's appeals to, 42, 46, 115
inclusion, language of, 37, 48
Independent Socialists, 18–19, 33, 97, 113, 168. *See also* Communists; Socialists
industrialists. *See* business owners
industrialization, 12, 17, 22, 207
inflation, 21, 54–55, 86
intendentes (mayors), 51, 70, 78–80
Internacional, La (newspaper), 165
Italy, immigrants from, 11, 14, 17, 194
Iturbe, Altanasio, 186

James, Daniel, 37, 47
Jews, 14, 50, 128, 194

jobs. *See also* employment; patronage; spoils system; *and specific occupational groups*
  as political rewards, 7, 9, 93, 171, 198
  providing, 65, 74–76, 77, 81, 184, 204–5
  shipboard, 168, 169
  votes traded for, 67–69, 80
Jones, Gareth Stedman, 37–38
Juárez Celman, Miguel, 15
Junta Reorganizadora, 166
Justo, Agustín P., 158, 177, 206
Justo, Juan B., 18, 133

Kirchner, Néstor, 208
Klan Radical, 197
Knight, Alan, 6
Krause, Karl Christian Friedrich, 46

La Boca, 117–18, 194. *See also* Admiral Brown Library
  elections in, 131, 160, 167, 170, 171–73, 174
labor movement, 17–19, 113, 203–4, 205. *See also* employment; jobs; strikes; unions; working classes
La Confraternidad (railroad union), 134, 151–54, 164, 166–67, 205
Laforcade, Geoffroy de, 117
La Forestal company, strikes against, 140–41
La Fraternidad, 73, 116–17, 122–25, 157, 158
  as model union, 133–34, 150–54
  political involvement of, 59, 170, 198, 203
Lallana, Luisa, death of, 183
language, image creation through, 37–38, 40–41
La Plata, strikes in, 108
La Rioja province, strikes in, 198
Las Palmas Company, 137, 141
Lauzet, Luis, 78
law 11.289. *See* pension plan legislation (law 11.289)
League of Nations, 50
Le Bretón, Tomás, 91
Leftists, 60, 61, 128
  pension plan legislation opposition, 101, 102, 104
legislation, Radical Party's use of, 55–57. *See also* Chamber of Deputies; pension plan legislation (law 11.289)
Lencinas, Carlos, 31, 197
Ley Sáenz Peña(1912), 4, 6, 20, 24–25, 35
Liga Patriótica, 61, 205
  strike-breaking activities, 129, 132, 136–37, 141, 144, 179
  union involvement, 142, 160, 161, 175
lockouts, 9, 105, 107–11, 120, 130, 141. *See also* boycotts; strikes

longshoremen's union, 142, 143. *See also* dockworkers, strikes by
López, Angel, 174
López, Luis María, 78
Los Angeles (Calif.), municipal employment, 82
Loza, Eufrasio B., 152, 153
Luna, Félix, 58, 149, 157
Luz, José R., 172–73

machines, political, 7–8, 66–78, 83, 93–94, 204–5. *See also* bosses, political; patronage
Mañasco, Eusebio, pardon of, 59–60, 61, 196
Mansilla, Bautista V., 125
Mar del Plata, strikes in, 108
Marinelli, Fortunato, 167, 171
maritime industry. *See* dockworkers, strikes by; merchant marine; port areas, strikes in; shipboard unions
Matienzo, José Nicolás, 30, 76
mayors. *See intendentes* (mayors)
meatpackers, strikes by, 127
Melo, Leopoldo, 61, 77, 128, 169, 188
men. *See* immigrants, sons of; suffrage, universal male
Mendoza province, strikes in, 107, 108, 197
Menem, Carlos, 208
merchant marine, 72, 161, 169
middle classes, 5, 10, 116
  in Buenos Aires, 22–23
  political activities of, 19, 27, 66, 197
  strike responses by, 129
  Yrigoyen's popularity among, 52
Mihanovich lines (shipping company), 170, 191, 192
  strikes against, 119–20, 132–33, 168–69, 180–81
Milesi, Pedro, 174
military, the, 129, 199, 208
millers, strikes by, 127
Ministry of Agriculture, 91–92, 92
Mitre, Bartlomé, 202
mobilization. *See* popular classes, mobilization of; voters, mobilization of
Molina, Victor A., 107
Molinari, Diego, 76–77
Montoneras, 63 n. 86
Monteverde, Luis, 74
Monzón, Manuel, 174
Moreno, Julio, 52, 119
Múgica, Adolfo, 76

236 INDEX

municipal workers, 81–82
  in Buenos Aires, 78–86
  strikes by, 135, 138–39, 198
  unions of, 125–26, 171–74, 175, 203, 206
Mustapic, Ana María, 5
mutual aid societies, 70

Nación, La (newspaper), 53, 65, 66, 92, 197
nationalism, 7, 8, 41–42, 50–51, 131
nationalizations, 14, 32, 72, 204
naturalization. See citizenship
Neoconservatives, 201, 206, 207
newspapers, 23, 36. See also individual newspaper titles
New York City, municipal employment statistics, 82, 83
Noel, Carlos, 61

obrerismo, 7, 159
  Alvear's use of, 9, 52, 59–61, 174, 175
  failure of, 177–99
  limitations of, 115–47
  pension plan legislation and, 101
  Radical Party's use of, 3, 9
  Yrigoyen's use of, 52–58, 115–47, 202
occupational communities, 122
Oeste railroad company, 73,187
officialization, 130, 143
organizations, 70, 76 n. 31. See also soccer clubs
Ortiz, Roberto M., 54, 205, 206
  railroad unions and, 150, 153–58, 171, 202, 206–7
Ortiz de Zárate, Miguel, 72
Otero, Héctor Horacio, 91

Pacífico railroad company, 186–87
Padoan, Marcelo, 41
Palacios, Alfredo, 46–47
Palacios, Pedro B. See Almafuerte
Palermo, Silvana, 89
Palmeiro, José, 170
pampas region, 12, 141
pan radical, 7, 54, 72
Paraguay,132, 180
Partido Autonomista Nacional (PAN), 15, 16
Partido Socialista Argentina, 46–47
party bosses. See bosses, political
Patagonia region, massacres in, 50, 140–41, 205
paternalism, 7, 52, 105
patriotism, 42, 45, 51, 129, 144. See also Liga Patriótica
patronage, 65–94. See also bosses, political; machines, political; spoils system

Alvear's use of, 9, 82
Anti-Personalists' use of, 65, 77, 94, 172, 174, 184, 202
Personalists' use of, 65, 94, 202
presidential appointments, 69, 70
Radical Party's use of, 3, 6–9, 65, 80, 82–84, 91–94, 126–27, 135, 178, 204–5
  in United States, 66, 67, 69, 79, 82, 83
  in Uruguay, 48
  for women, 14, 90
  Yrigoyen's use of, 4, 9, 70, 89, 91–92
Pellegrini, Carlos, 4
Penelón, José, 76, 84
pension funds
  government employees, 88, 92–93
  railroad workers, 56, 57, 98, 154
  shipboard workers, 160–62, 166
pension plan legislation (law 11.289), 9, 95–114, 204. See also under individual political parties and unions
  Alvear's support for, 95–96, 149, 175
  history of, 96–100
  Radical Party's support for, 95–96, 101–2, 113
  reactions to, 101–14, 173
  Yrigoyen's support for, 56, 95, 97–99
Pérez Leirós, Francisco, 74–75
Perón, Eva, 2, 42, 58, 208
Perón, Juan
  image of, 42, 58
  pension plan under, 95, 101n15, 204
  police use, 51 n. 54
  Radical Party's influences on, 2, 7, 201
  tactics of, 36–37, 115, 207–8
Persello, Ana Virginia, 87
personalism. See also Yrigoyen, Hipólito, image of
  Alvear's avoidance of, 59
  Radical Party's use of, 8, 96, 113
  Yrigoyen's use of, 5, 10, 36, 38, 51–52, 196, 202–3, 208
Personalist faction of Radical Party, 30–33, 63, 149, 197. See also Radical Party
  Anti-Personalist rivalry with, 38, 73, 94
  election victories, 30–32, 62, 174–75, 177, 184, 193
  patronage practices, 65, 94, 202
  pension plan legislation support, 112, 113
  railroad unions' relationship with, 186
  shipboard union's relationship with, 167–69, 180
personería jurídica (legal status), 152–53
Peter, José, 61
Podestá, Tiberio, 183

police
    Peron's use of, 51 n. 54
    Radicals' use of, 8, 169, 183, 184
    in September 1930 coup, 199
    strike responses, 128–29, 141, 144–45, 183, 184, 188–89, 191–92
    strikes by, 198
    Yrigoyen's use of, 51–52, 116, 120, 201
politics, 13–20, 24–33. *See also individual political parties*
    Argentine system, 35, 69, 96, 202–3, 204, 208–9
    employment tied to, 92
    modern, 27–28, 48
    municipal, 78–86
    strikes related to, 138, 183
Popovich, Juan, 168, 171
popular classes
    Alvear's appeals to, 59–62, 196
    living conditions for, 22–23
    mobilization of, 6–7, 15, 16, 28, 35–37, 69, 83, 95
    Radicals' appeals to, 3, 26, 114
    Socialists' appeals to, 19
    unions' appeals to, 114
    Yrigoyen's appeals to, 52–58, 115, 196, 202
port areas, strikes in, 117–21, 180–85, 191–92, 194. *See also* Buenos Aires (city); Rosario
post offices, patronage jobs in, 90, 92
Prensa, La (newspaper), 36
    on patronage, 65–66, 76, 79, 89, 93
    on pension plan legislation, 100, 107, 109
    strike coverage, 61, 140, 144, 180, 182, 185, 187, 189, 194
printers, strikes by, 78, 106, 110, 139
Progressive Democratic Party, 98, 138
propaganda, 71, 173
    for pension plan legislation, 97, 106
    union-related, 118, 120, 167
    Yrigoyen's use of, 37, 38, 42
Protesta, La (newspaper), 145
Protti, Alejandro, 173
provinces, 14, 15. *See also individual provinces*
public works, lack of investment in, 86, 93, 205

Quintana, Manuel, death of, 19

Radical Party. *See also* Anti-Personalist faction of Radical Party; Personalist faction of Radical Party
    appeals to voters, 2–5, 25–26, 66–78
    budget deficits under, 92–93
    in Buenos Aires, 3, 51, 83, 85–86
    class relationships, 6–7, 14, 52–59, 197
    clubs, 76 n. 31, 161
    economy and, 20–22
    failings of, 5–6
    history of, 15–20, 44–45, 47
    image of, 36–38, 44–45, 201–2, 208
    legacy of, 201–9
    municipal workers' relationship with, 135
    overthrow of, 33, 193–99
    patronage practices, 3, 6–9, 65, 80, 82–84, 91–94, 126–27, 135, 178, 204–5
    pension plan legislation support, 95–99, 100, 101–2, 111–12, 113
    political machine of, 70–72
    popularity of, 3, 23, 35–37, 49–58, 63, 94, 138, 146–47, 204
    railroad unions' relationships with, 159
    shipboard unions' relationships with, 168, 180
    Socialists' rivalry with, 26, 116, 117, 126, 131
    split in, 30–33, 38, 45, 100, 124, 164, 184, 196, 203, 205
    strike responses, 128–31, 136–46, 183
    tactics, 24–29, 35–36, 50–51, 62–63, 113–14
    unions' relationship with, 7, 59, 113, 117–21, 124, 125–28, 202, 203
Radowitzky, Simón, pardon of, 196
railroad companies
    patronage jobs, 76, 89
    pension plans, 56, 57, 98
    Yrigoyen's relationship with, 186–87
railroad unions, 170, 174, 175. *See also individual railroad unions*
    Alvear's relationship with, 10, 59, 134, 150–60, 186, 202, 205–6
    reorganization of, 133–35, 151–52, 166–67, 193
    strikes by, 54, 78, 109, 121–25, 133, 139, 186–88
    Yrigoyen's relationship with, 116–17, 122–25, 133–35, 145–47, 150, 154, 156–57, 177, 186–87, 193
Ravignani, Emilio, 76
Raynoli, Francisco, 74
refinery workers, strikes by, 51, 108, 132
República, La (newspaper), 143
Review of the River Plate (magazine), 100, 141, 146
revolt of 1890, 15–16, 29
Revolutionary Syndicalism, 18. *See also* Syndicalists
Rita, Maximo. *See* Luz, José R.

Robertson, Malcolm, 186
Roca, Julio, 14–15, 202
Rocchi, Fernando, 12
Rock, David, 2–3, 68, 86, 100, 130
Rodríguez, Luis M., 155, 157
Rodríguez Saá, Adolfo, 2
Roldán, María, 47
Romero, Juan, 183
Romero, Luis Alberto, 23, 70
Rosanova, Francisco, 78, 125
Rosanvallon, Pierre, 6, 37
Rosario
   shipboard unions in, 170
   strikes in, 106–110, 124, 138–39, 182–85, 188–90, 195, 199
Rosas, Juan Manuel de, 14, 63
rural areas, 12, 140–41, 185
rural-urban migration, 207

Sabato, Hilda, 5, 35
Sabiani, Simon, 66
Sacco, Nicola, execution of, 60, 61
Sáenz Peña, Roque, 4, 20, 65–66
salaries. *See* wages
sanitation workers, strikes by, 126, 138
San Juan province, government intervention in, 197
San Lorenzo de Almagro (soccer club), 73
San Martín, José de, 2
Santa Fe province
   popular mobilization in, 16, 25
   strikes in, 140, 182–84, 191
Santiago del Estero province, strikes in, 198
Sanz del Río, Julián, 46
Sarobe, José, 77
Sartelli, Eduardo, 185
Schlesinger, Fernando, 138
Schwartz, Barry, 57
Scobie, James R., 12
secret ballots, 20, 68. *See also* fair voting
Senate, 25, 30, 32–33, 99, 101, 196–97. *See also* Chamber of Deputies
September 1930 coup, 33, 191, 193–99
   causes of, 6, 10, 25, 62
   legacy of, 208–9
   unions' opposition to, 53, 199
Shils, Edward, 39
shipboard unions, 110, 169, 173, 198, 206. *See also individual shipboard unions*
   Alvear's relationship with, 160–70, 175
   officialization of, 130, 143
   pension funds for, 166
   strikes by, 117–21, 124, 130–33, 142–46, 168–70

Smith, Peter H., 1–2, 27, 196
soccer clubs, 5, 23, 70, 72–73
Socialists, 18–19, 32, 47, 52, 204. *See also* Communists, Independent Socialists
   Anarchists' rivalry with, 17
   Anti-Personalist rivalry with, 174
   in Buenos Aires, 19, 115, 117, 167
   culture of, 58, 70
   in municipal workers' union, 172
   patronage practices, 78, 80, 91
   pension plan legislation responses, 96, 98–99, 101–2, 104, 113
   Radical Party's rivalry with, 26, 116, 117, 126, 131
   in railroad unions, 123, 150–51, 186
   in shipboard unions, 161, 166, 168–69, 170
   strike activities, 195
   Syndicalists' rivalry with, 116
   union ties, 29, 74–75, 83–84, 97, 126, 131, 172, 178, 186
social welfare legislation. *See* pension plan legislation (law 11.289); welfare system
Sociedad de Resistencia Obreros del Puerto de la Capital, 142
Sociedad Rural, 53, 142
socioeconomic factors, 11–14. *See also* economy
Soria, Arsenio, 75–76
Spain, immigrants from, 14, 50–51, 126, 128, 194
Sparnochia, Augusto, 171
spoils system, 27, 65, 79, 81. *See also* patronage
state. *See* government, national
state railroads, 54, 76, 87, 89, 123–24, 146, 153, 189
stevedores. *See* dock workers, strikes by
strikes, 83–84, 96–97, 98, 179. *See also* violence, strike-related; *and under individual unions and occupational groups*
   breaking, 129, 132, 136–37, 141, 143–44, 179, 181, 183, 189
   general, 18, 61, 124, 126–27, 137–39, 145–46, 189–90, 195–96
   government responses to, 127, 128–33, 136–46, 180–82
   1921, 136–46
   against pension plan legislation, 102, 105, 106–11, 162–65
   politics related to, 138, 183
   in rural areas, 140–41, 185
   Yrigoyen's support for, 53, 116, 119–20, 205

Sud railroad company, 194
suffrage, universal male, 3, 5, 15, 20, 37, 45, 90. *See also* elections
Syndicalists, 18, 175, 202
  Anarchists' rivalry with, 109–11, 145, 194–95
  Communists' rivalry with, 111, 193
  jobs for, 171, 172–74
  pension plan legislation opposition, 102, 103, 110
  in railroad unions, 123, 150–51, 152, 154, 186
  in shipboard unions, 161, 162, 165, 166, 192
  Socialists' rivalry with, 116
  strike activities, 184, 189, 194–95
  union ties, 28–29, 31, 96, 120, 151, 152, 172–73, 178, 193
  Yrigoyen's relationship with, 115–17, 119
Swift (meatpacking company), 108–109

Tadich, Vicente, 161
Tafí Viejo, 76, 124
Tamborini, José, 59, 71, 165, 175
teachers, 90, 140, 198
telegraph offices, patronage jobs in, 90, 92
telephone workers
  strike by, 131–32, 184, 190–91, 206
  union of, 178–79
theater workers, strikes by, 139–40
Torello, Pablo, 57, 123, 124, 134, 154
Tragic Week (January 1919), 28, 50, 65, 128–33, 205
  aftermath of, 116, 129–33, 135, 146
Tramonti, Antonio, 150–51
trolley workers, strikes by, 109, 145–46, 184, 188–90, 195–96
Trucco, Rómulo, 72
Tucumán province, strikes in, 106, 108, 109, 124

Unión Cívica Radical (UCR). *See* Radical Party
Unión del Marino, La (newpaper), 161
Unión Ferroviaria (UF), 10, 150–60, 164, 175, 178, 186–87, 198, 203, 205
  as model union, 205, 207
Unión Industrial Argentina (UIA), pension plan legislation opposition, 104, 105, 108, 109, 110
Unión Obrera Local (UOL), 173
  pension plan legislation opposition, 103, 106, 111
Unión Obrera Marítima (UOMAR), 166–70, 191

Unión Obrera Municipal (UOM), 80–84, 86, 126
  government and, 135, 146
  pension plan legislation opposition, 102
  Socialists in, 74, 75, 172
unions, 17–18, 51, 70, 77–78, 100. *See also* boycotts; strikes; *and individual unions*
  Alvear's relationship with, 54, 59, 61, 149–75
  Anarchists' ties to, 28, 96, 192, 198
  Anti-Personalists' ties to, 52, 54, 61, 100, 174–75
  as bridges to working class, 9, 159, 202, 205, 207
  centralization of, 152–53, 159, 164–65, 178
  creation of, 170, 171–75, 206
  government's relationship with, 7, 9–10, 53, 146, 178–79, 185–93, 198–99, 207
  pension plan legislation opposition, 96–99, 101–11, 113–14
  Radical Party's relationship with, 7, 59, 113, 117–21, 124, 125–28, 202, 203
  Syndicalists' ties to, 28–29, 31, 96, 120, 172–73, 178, 193
  Yrigoyen's relationship with, 3, 53–54, 115–21, 145–47, 178–79, 185–93, 192, 202, 205
Unión Sindical Argentina (USA), 28–29, 60, 151, 152, 174, 194, 198
  pension plan legislation opposition, 102–3, 105, 106, 107, 109, 111, 113
United States, 6, 22, 143
  patronage practices, 66, 67, 79, 82, 83, 679
  strike responses, 140, 182
  trade with, 21
universities, reforms in, 26–27
Urquiza, Justo José de, 137
Uruguay, 48, 180, 181

Vanguardia, La (newspaper), 75, 108
Vanzetti, Bartolomeo, execution of, 60, 61
Vasena metallurgy company, 128
Vidal, Gardenia, 27, 93
Viguera, Aníbal, 71
violence. *See also* Liga Patriótica; Patagonia region, massacres in; Tragic Week (January 1919)
  labor-related, 18, 19
  political, 197, 208
  on railroad lines, 134
  sectarian, 194, 199
  street, 32

violence (*continued*)
  strike-related, 119, 120, 124, 143, 156, 181, 184, 187–90, 192–96
voters. *See also* elections; electoral reform; fair voting; suffrage, universal male
  appeals to, 2–5, 7, 25–26, 60, 66–78, 149, 171–72, 203, 205
  delivering, 67–72, 80, 83, 93, 101
  mobilization of, 28, 66, 168–71, 201

wages, 11–12
  for government jobs, 84–86, 92–93, 198
  railroad workers', 154–56
  shipboard workers', 192
Washington, George, 57
waterfront. *See* dockworkers, strikes by; port areas, strikes in
wealth, 11–12
Weber, Max, 39
welfare system, 48, 56, 95–114. *See also* pension plan legislation (law 11.289)
West Indian Oil Company, strike against, 51, 132
Whyte, William Foote, 67
women, 14, 90
working classes, 9. *See also* pension plan legislation (law 11.289)
  Alvear's relationship with, 149–50, 175
  appeals to, 13–14, 175, 183, 196
  government's relationship with, 113
  living conditions for, 7, 22–24
  mobilization of, 66, 204–5, 207
  Radical's appeals to, 124, 146–47
  Syndicalists' influence among, 18
  unions as bridges to, 9, 159, 202, 205, 207
  Yrigoyen's popularity among, 42, 46, 52–58
work-to-regulation, 134, 155–56, 157, 187–88
World War I, effects on Argentina, 5, 20–21, 26, 28, 50, 54–55, 86, 88

Yablon, Ariel, 65
YPF (state petroleum company),87, 88
Yrigoyen, Hipólito
  Alvear's relationship with, 29–30, 198, 206
  budgets of, 86, 87, 88, 92–93
  class relationships, 52–58
  first presidential term, 25, 87, 88, 196
  image of, 3, 8, 36–49, 57–58, 201, 208
  labor polices of, 10, 81–82, 129–33, 180, 206
  legacy of, 2, 201–9
  obrerismo used by, 52–58, 115–47, 202
  opposition to, 19, 30–31, 36, 43, 62–63, 193, 196
  overthrow of, 6, 10, 25, 33, 53, 62, 191, 193–99, 208–9
  patronage practices, 9, 70, 89, 91–92
  pension plan legislation support, 97–99, 112
  police experience of, 8, 52
  popularity of, 3–5, 7–8, 9, 35–36, 49–58, 63, 65, 93–94, 115–17, 146–47, 157, 174, 180, 199, 204
  Radical Party involvement, 16–17, 28
  railroad unions' relationship with, 116–17, 122–25, 133–35, 145–47, 150, 154, 156–57, 177, 186–87, 193
  reelection of, 38, 45, 62–63, 159, 170, 201, 206
  second presidential term, 32, 45, 88, 89, 92, 177–99
  strike responses, 3, 116–17, 119–20, 122–27, 131, 136–47, 177, 181–82, 185, 189–90, 205
  unions' relationship with, 3, 53–54, 115–21, 126, 145–47, 178–79, 185–93, 199, 202, 205
  university reform by, 26–27

Zapico, Avelino, pardon for, 123
Zimmermann, Eduardo A., 95

www.ingramcontent.com/pod-product-compliance
Lightning Source LLC
Chambersburg PA
CBHW031548300426
44111CB00006BA/225